T0269732

Short Walks
to
Curious Places

Bloomsbury Publishing Plc
50 Bedford Square, London, WC1B 3DP, UK
29 Earlsfort Terrace, Dublin 2, Ireland

BLOOMSBURY, CONWAY and the Conway logo
are trademarks of Bloomsbury Publishing Plc

First published in Great Britain 2024

A catalogue record for this book is available from
the British Library
Library of Congress Cataloguing-in-Publication
data has been applied for

ISBN: 978-1-8448-6637-3; ePub: 978-1-8448-
6639-7; ePDF: 978-1-8448-6640-3

2 4 6 8 10 9 7 5 3 1

Typeset in Interstate by Nick Avery Design
Printed and bound in UAE by Oriental Press

To find out more about our authors and books
visit www.bloomsbury.com and sign up for our
newsletters

Short Walks
to
Curious Places

Fifty Walks Exploring Britain's Ancient Sites, Myths and Legends

Roly Smith

CONWAY

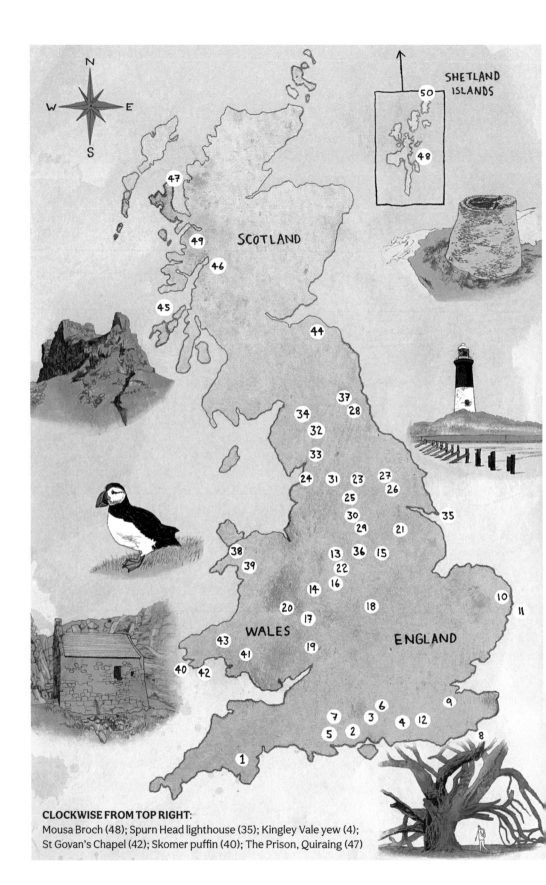

CLOCKWISE FROM TOP RIGHT:
Mousa Broch (48); Spurn Head lighthouse (35); Kingley Vale yew (4);
St Govan's Chapel (42); Skomer puffin (40); The Prison, Quiraing (47)

Contents

The Walks

South & West of England

Midlands

North of England

Wales

Scotland

A puffin on Skomer

Foreword
A twenty-first-century Hoskins

I'm jealous, really. Not only has Roly Smith written a book I wish I'd written, but he has travelled the entire British Isles seeking out beautiful, story-laden walks, which he presents to us marvellously curated, described and illustrated.

Up hill, down dale, on rocky coasts, remote moors and flat spits; in castles, woods, valleys and caves he finds and brings to us intriguing characters, fascinating geological and historical insights, nature in abundance and above all stories that swirl and settle in your heart.

My personal 'bible' is WG Hoskins' *The Making of the English Landscape*. In it Hoskins wrote, 'the English landscape is the richest historical document we possess'. And indeed it is, not least as recounted here. The stories Roly tells are compelling. Some connections are well known, such as the great battle of Glencoe and Kinder Scout's mass trespass, Elgar's love of the Malvern Hills, the Brontës' Haworth moors and Arthur Wainwright's beautifully hand-illustrated walking guides to the Lake District. Others are legends, which he revives with skill and intrigue, such as the Lambton Worm, the Lady of the Lake and the ghosts of Chanctonbury Ring.

But many of the stories written here are new to me, and may also be to you, so you are in for a treat. They also, rather poignantly, serve to remind us not how much we know but how much we have, collectively, forgotten. Thank goodness for the Roly Smiths of this world, who dig out the stories (I like to call them the spirits of a place), dust them off and re-tell them beautifully, bringing everything to life.

Roly is of course a walker as much as a storyteller, and if you want a good walk here is a treasure trove of opportunities. You can almost feel him panting as he surfaces onto the crest of High Cup Nick, or Skye's Quiraing, by contrast with his gentler exploration of Wistman's Wood, Bradgate Park or Wharram Percy. There are walks of all lengths and complexities, all in their own way enticing. The routes are all clearly described, along with useful wayfinding hints. So compelling are they that I had my OS app constantly by my side as, with Roly, I travelled round the country, zooming from Derbyshire to Carmarthenshire, and Suffolk to Scotland, tracing the routes with my forefinger, wishing it were my feet.

At one level Roly has, indeed, stolen a march and picked the best walks and stories this country has to offer. But of course in truth he hasn't. In my experience you can find a story literally everywhere in these islands, stories that are often layered over centuries, and which can all be read from the landscape we see today, if you know what to look for.

This is in fact a sort of twenty-first-century Hoskins. No longer is landscape history an armchair occupation but an active one, and this book stimulates the bug for exploration that I believe everyone has somewhere within them. And if you don't see me for a while, it's because I'm out there myself, walking one of Roly's routes, absorbed in the history and drinking in the stories that shape the place, and thanking Roly for the introduction.

Dame Fiona Reynolds DBE

**Non-Executive Chair, National Audit Office
and former Director-General of the National Trust**

Introduction
'Curiouser and curiouser'

'Curiouser and curiouser!' cried Alice (she was so much surprised, that for the moment she quite forgot how to speak good English).

Lewis Carroll, *Alice's Adventures in Wonderland* **(1865)**

John Tenniel illustration from *Alice's Adventures in Wonderland*

In Charles Lutwidge Dodgson's famous children's fantasy, he found that he had to invent an entirely new word to describe how Alice felt as she explored a land which became increasingly strange every time she discovered something new.

Precisely the same word (incidentally, that arbiter of 'good English', the *Oxford English Dictionary*, still doesn't accept it as a word, citing it only as a phrase) could just as easily be ascribed to my explorations of Britain on foot over the past 60 years, some of which are described in this book. These islands are every bit as curious as Alice's Wonderland and are home to an unparalleled wealth of geological, geographical and extraordinary natural features in addition to possessing an amazing continuity of history, myths and legends. In fact, it's a Wonderland that I suspect even Carroll's day-dreaming Alice would find 'curiouser and curiouser'.

One of the few benefits of the Covid-19 pandemic lockdowns was the huge increase in people out walking, enjoying the fresh air and our incomparable British countryside. Vast numbers of people realised the benefits, both physical and mental, of a good walk, and discovering the wonders of natural and human history that are literally on their doorsteps, only a step or two away.

A walk in the countryside, for walkers of all abilities, is made immeasurably more satisfying and enjoyable if it takes you to an interesting or curious place, through countryside with a story to tell, or which is linked to a natural feature or a historical, mythical or legendary event. The British countryside is rich in these kinds of landscapes – perhaps as rich any country in the world – and it is blessed with a network of footpaths and unrestricted open country which can lead you to them.

Before the pandemic, going for a walk in the countryside was already the number one outdoor pursuit in Britain and there is a plethora of books on guided walks. These include Wainwright-type directional guides and locally published leaflets, magazine and newspaper features, or online walking websites, which aim to satisfy this demand. Step-by-step walking guidebooks can frankly be pretty boring to read – after all, there are only a few ways in which the writer can say 'turn left at the next stile' or 'follow the path across the next two fields'. I suppose they have to be if they are to be truly practical to use on the ground. But let me give you a warning right from the start: if you are looking for that kind of guide, this book is not for you. The fact is that most walkers are now competent to find their own way using local signposting, the appropriate Ordnance Survey map, app or Google Maps.

The raison d'être of this book is to take the reader to 50 of the more curious and mysterious places in England, Scotland and Wales. You will find that directional details are minimal and that none of the walks are excessively long, all being between 2 and 10 miles (3.2 and 16km) in length and easily attainable by a reasonably fit family.

To explain, I'm a journalist by training so I was imbued from an early age by a series of hard-nosed news editors with the mantra of the great Irish American editor and publisher Sam McClure (1857–1949): 'The story is the thing'. So it's the story – and in many cases, the multiple stories – behind the walk, which usually provide the reason for it, and are paramount in this book. It will take the reader to some fascinating and intriguing places in the British countryside. And that applies equally to whether you actually do the walks yourself, when planning your next outing, or you just vicariously enjoy them while sitting at home.

The walks start at the very dawn of time with our visits to the seductively rolling Malvern Hills in Worcestershire and Bradgate Park just outside Leicester, where the exposed Precambrian rocks are some of the oldest you'll find anywhere on planet Earth. These special landscapes inspired

The Covid lockdowns tempted many people out into the countryside

people as diverse as that supremely English composer Edward Elgar, and the tragic 'Queen for Nine Days', Lady Jane Grey. Still on a 'Deep Time' theme, we visit Siccar Point in Berwickshire, where the pioneering geologist James Hutton confounded the accepted religious theory about the age of the Earth in one stunning discovery, as he and his companions stared into what they called 'the abyss of time'.

Among the other geological oddities we'll visit are the extraordinary volcanic landscape of the Quiraing on the Trotternish peninsula of the Isle of Skye, and the natural Henry Moore-esque sculpture park of Brimham Rocks, near Ripon in Yorkshire. Much more recent are the elemental landscapes which are constantly being shaped and reshaped by the sea, such as Derek Jarman's Dungeness in Kent; Orford Ness and Dunwich in Suffolk, where the shifting shingle has blocked once-thriving medieval ports; the vast 'wet Sahara' of Morecambe Bay in Lancashire; and the constantly swinging Spurn Point – 'the tail of Yorkshire' – at the mouth of the Humber. These shape-shifting landscapes really are being created and destroyed before our very eyes, as are the spectacular landslips in places like the Quiraing and the tottering gritstone towers of Alport Castles in the shadow of Bleaklow in the Peak District.

Incidentally, I've included the three Derbyshire walks – Kinder Scout, Alport Castles and Lathkill Dale – in the North of England section

because they are indisputably and topographically part of the Pennines, although some might regard Derbyshire as a Midland county.

Some of the earliest traces of humanity and first examples of art in these islands have been found in the caves of Creswell Crags, dubbed the Sistine Chapel of the Ice Age, in the former coalfield country on the Nottinghamshire–Derbyshire border. More ancient caves where early humans made their home are found at Victoria Cave beneath Attermire Scar in the Yorkshire Dales, and at Thor's Cave, a gaping void which yawns above the peaceful Manifold Valley in the Staffordshire Peak. And we'll trace the origins of the original bluestones in Stonehenge – perhaps the best-known prehistoric monument of them all – in the rugged Preseli hills of Pembrokeshire.

A lesser known but equally fascinating prehistoric henge monument, adopted by Christianity by the erection of a church at its centre, is found at Knowlton in Dorset, while the mysterious monolithic maidens known as Long Meg and her Daughters stand in quiet communion above the River Eden, just outside the Lake District in East Cumbria.

The Iron Age hill-top towns of Tre'r Ceiri on the Llŷn peninsula of North Wales, Hambledon Hill in Wiltshire, Chanctonbury Ring in Sussex and The Wrekin in Shropshire are explored, along with the many stories and legends that are invariably associated with them. The most complete example of the Scottish equivalent of the hillfort, known as brochs, is found on the uninhabited Shetland island of Mousa, which was the scene of a Viking romance and is now home to one of the world's largest roosting sites of the elusive storm petrel. If birdwatching is your thing, then the seabird city on the cliffs of Skomer Island off the Pembrokeshire coast, or Hermaness and Muckle Flugga at the very tip of northern Britain in Shetland, are the nearest thing you'll get to an avian paradise.

The troubled past of these islands is evidenced by the last battle in the Wars of the Roses, which took place on a quiet plateau near Towton in Yorkshire. This was the site of the little-known but largest, longest and bloodiest battle ever fought on British soil, in 1461. Another site of betrayal and massacre is told in our visit to Coire Gabhail, the legendary Lost Valley of the MacDonalds above the fabled and haunted valley of Glencoe in the Scottish Highlands. The massacre of Glencoe in 1692 was severely overdramatised by Victorian novelists like Charles Dickens.

Among the many other literary connections that are made on our walks, we follow in the footsteps of poet John Keats on his riverside walk in Winchester, which is said to have inspired his famous *Ode to Autumn*. Another literary giant was the pioneering parson-naturalist the Rev Gilbert White of Selborne in Hampshire, whose meticulous record of the natural history of his parish was first published in 1789 and has never been out of print since. We'll follow the famous Zig-Zag path he and his brother constructed to the top of the lovely 'hanging' beech woods of Selborne Hanger. Charles Darwin's 'Great Idea' of the evolution of species by natural selection – outlined in another perennial best-seller, his 1859 book *On the Origin of Species* – was completed and perhaps finalised on his so-called 'Thinking Path' at his gracious home at Down in Kent, and again we will follow in the great man's footsteps.

We retrace yet another kind of 'thinking path' used by authors onto the bleak West Yorkshire moors, where the talented but troubled Brontë sisters of nearby Haworth would walk to commune with nature and come up with the melodramatic plots of their romantic novels. And I relate how I came across another publishing legend when I met up with the phenomenal best-selling fell-wanderer Alfred Wainwright at Cautley Spout in the little-visited Howgill Fells, sandwiched between the Lake District and the Yorkshire Dales. A more recent writing sensation has been the *Harry Potter* series by author JK Rowling, and we visit the scene of one of Harry's most spectacular escapades around the

Glenfinnan Viaduct at the head of Loch Shiel in the Scottish Highlands.

Many of the most curious places in Britain are associated with holy men and hermits, such as the remote, fern-draped chasm of Lud's Church in the Staffordshire Peak, where banned Lollards once worshipped; at Cuddy's Cave in Northumberland, where St Cuthbert may have sheltered and where his body was hidden after his death; at St Columba's Bay on the sacred island of Iona in the Hebrides, where the saint first landed after fleeing his home in Ireland; and at St Govan's Chapel, a former hermit's home is tucked away under the beetling limestone cliffs of the Pembrokeshire Coast.

The summit of The Wrekin

At the other extreme, the Devil figures strongly in many stories about the British landscape. Old Nick pops up regularly, for example, at the enchanted ancient woodland of Wistman's on Dartmoor; the beech-capped hillfort of Chanctonbury Ring on the Sussex Downs; and at the jagged outcrop of the Stiperstones in the Shropshire Hills, where his Satanic Majesty is supposed to appear if you sit on his 'chair' at midnight on midsummer's eve.

Some of the other legendary characters we'll meet along the way include the Saxon prince known as Wild Edric, who also haunts the Stiperstones with his Wild Hunt; the beautiful fairy Lady of the Lake at remote Llyn y Fan Fach in the wildest recesses of the Brecon Beacons (recently renamed Bannau Brycheiniog); and the fabled Green Knight of Arthurian legend, who met his beheading denouement in the secret defile of Lud's Church in the Staffordshire Moorlands.

So join me as we journey from the northernmost point of the British Isles at the remote, seabird haunted headland of Hermaness in Shetland, to the wizened oak woodland of Wistman's sheltering below the Dartmoor tors to explore some of the most curious places in Britain.

I'll conclude by returning to Alice as she ventured down the rabbit hole in her 19th-century adventures in Wonderland: 'And what is the use of a book,' thought Alice, 'without pictures or conversations?'

My earnest hope is that you'll find this book has plenty of pictures and stories that spark your imagination and maybe even start a conversation about the wonders of Britain, encouraging you to visit some of these curious places yourself.

SOUTH & WEST
of England

1	2	3
Acorn Antiques: Wistman's Wood, Dartmoor, Devon	The death of a king: Rufus Stone, New Forest, Hampshire	An ode to autumn: Keats' walk, Winchester, Hampshire
3 miles/4.8km	1.5 miles/2.4km	2 miles/3.2km

4	5	6
There'll never be another yew: Kingley Vale, West Sussex	Cromwell's 'small execution' of the Clubmen: Hambledon Hill, Wiltshire	Gilbert White's Zig-Zag path: Selbourne, Hampshire
5 miles/8km	6 miles/9.7km	3.5 miles/5.6km

7	8	9
The church in the circle: Knowlton Henge, Dorset	Jarman's garden of delights: Dungeness, Kent	Darwin's 'Thinking Path': Down House, Kent
2.5 miles/4km	3 miles/4.8km	1 mile/1.6km

10	11	12
The city that fell into the sea: Dunwich, Suffolk	Secrets of the shingle: Orford Ness, Suffolk	Ring of ritual: Chanctonbury Ring, West Sussex
2 miles/3.2km	5 miles/8km	8 miles/12.9km

1.

Acorn Antiques:
Wistman's Wood, Dartmoor, Devon

BELOW Longaford Tor
RIGHT Home of the pixies? The mossy interior of Wistman's Wood

The fairy tale, lichen-encrusted oaks of Wistman's Wood, hidden away in the desolate valley of the West Dart River in the moorland heart of Dartmoor, are a bit of a mystery.

Ecologists are still puzzled over why this wood's wizened and gnarled trees, some of which are over 300 years old, are all of the lowland, pedunculate variety, whereas all those in the well-wooded valleys on the edge of the moor are the more hardy sessile oaks, usually found in the uplands of Britain.

Another mystery is that this incredibly ancient-looking wood, which feels as though it has been here since the

beginning of time, is on the move. Not only are its trees twice the height they used to be 80 years ago, but the wood itself has doubled in size over the last 60 years and is slowly but surely creeping up the clitter-clad slopes (see page 22) of neighbouring Longaford Tor.

This part of the mystery, however, is easier to solve. As the plentiful new acorns germinate, they are sheltered by the older trees from the prevailing

westerly winds, which are therefore responsible for gradually pushing the wood uphill. So despite its venerable and unchanging appearance, Wistman's Wood is what ecologists call a 'dynamic ecosystem'.

This arboreal enigma lies near Dartmoor National Park's epicentre at Two Bridges, and for many including the author it represents the essence of Dartmoor. Dartmoor is usually heralded by guidebooks as 'the last great wilderness of Southern Britain', but its spirit is not necessarily to be found on the open, tor-topped moors, described by their most famous chronicler, Arthur Conan Doyle, as 'so vast, and so barren, and so mysterious'.

Wistman's is thought to take its name from the old West Country word 'wisht', which means sad or uncanny, so 'Wistman' may mean 'Wisht-man'. It is also said to get its name from the spectral wisht hounds, an other-worldly pack of coal-black dogs that hunt for the souls of the dead, and which make the eerie woodland their home. Early Dartmoor antiquarians were equally keen to link this ancient oakwood with the activities of Dark Age Druids, who were known to favour oak groves for their pagan ceremonies.

And as you peep into the stunted, twisted, epiphyte and moss-covered branches and trunks of Wistman's Wood, which spring straight from a chaotic boulder field of moss-covered granite, you can easily start to believe in those tatty teashop souvenirs that feature the celebrated Dartmoor pixies. If they were to exist anywhere, then surely it would be here.

But perhaps the most remarkable feature of Wistman's Wood, apart from its exposed position at 1,300 feet (400m) above the sea, is its luxurious mantle of mosses, ferns, liverworts and lichens. They drip from weirdly contorted branches like the epiphytes and bromeliads of an Amazonian rain forest, and in fact represent a habitat – temperate rainforest – which is even rarer and more threatened, and which currently covers less than one per cent of the country.

The loss of the rare and beautiful moss *Antitrichia curtipendula*, which formerly hung in liana-like fronds from the branches of many of the trees in Victorian times, is blamed on the increase in air-borne pollution, and the gradual opening-up of the wood has in turn caused a loss of humidity that has affected moisture-loving ferns and liverworts.

Wistman's Wood is now a National Nature Reserve managed by Natural England under agreement with the Duchy of Cornwall, which recently announced plans to double its size. Access is strictly by written permission only. However, a footpath runs conveniently past the wood, and you can peep into it along this easy 3 mile (4.8km) stroll from Two Bridges, which also takes in an unusual seat of 'tinpot' government.

The moss-covered boulder field inside Wistman's Wood

The Walk

Start from the quarry car park on the side of the B3357, opposite the Two Bridges Hotel. The way goes clearly north along a track towards Crockern Farm, where a stile takes you out into open country and the first sighting of Wistman's Wood, low-lying like a hedge on the slopes of the valley ahead.

The prominent rocks on the hillside to your left are Beardown Tors, parts of which make up the Merrivale Firing Range, incredibly still in use by the Army for live firing - and this in a National Park set aside for the quiet enjoyment of the public. When a red flag is seen flying from the tors, firing is taking place and walking is forbidden on these hills.

The winding artificial waterway which can just be seen contouring beneath the tors is the Devonport Leat, cut between 1793 and 1796 to take water from the West Dart River, whose natural course flows down in the valley below, to the Burrator Reservoir and thence to the fast-growing dockyard town of Devonport.

As you step out across the rock-strewn moorland heading due north towards the approaching wind-stunted 'hedge' of Wistman's Wood, you may notice some broken down walls and mounds emerging from the moorland grass. The map of Dartmoor is scattered with the words 'Settlement' and 'Hut Circle' in that Gothic lettering the Ordnance Survey reserves for ancient monuments, and these humps and bumps are all that remain of medieval and earlier villages and farms that once made Dartmoor one of the most populous places in the south-west. Indeed, it is said to contain, 'fossilised' under the moor grass, the most important and complete prehistoric landscape in north-west Europe.

Walk around the top edge of the wood, looking inside at what one author has described as 'the ultimate in arboreal deformity' and 'a phantasmagoria of greenleaf and granite'. Wistman's Wood currently covers about 8.5 acres (3ha), and its amazing survival is thought to be

Factbox

Location: Wistman's Wood is near Two Bridges in the centre of Dartmoor, off the B3357 Dartmeet-Tavistock road

Postcode: PL20 6SW

Length: About 3 miles (4.8km), should take roughly 2½ hours

Terrain: Mostly over rough moorland, so appropriate footwear and clothing should be worn

Map: OS 1:25,000 Outdoor Leisure Map No. 28, Dartmoor National Park

Refreshments: The Two Bridges Hotel, Dartmoor PL20 6SW, is in a beautiful riverside setting near the junction of the West Dart River with the Cowsic and is very popular with walkers

☎ 01822 892300
🌐 twobridges.co.uk

due to the fact that the trees have grown, and continue to grow, in the shelter of the rocky crevices of the 'clitter' (the Dartmoor name for this type of loose rocks). These create a favourable micro-climate, protecting them from winter gales and frost and, above all, from the nibbling teeth of the local sheep.

The low, rectangular-shaped mounds that can be seen on the slope above the wood are pillow mounds or buries, which were constructed in medieval times to provide the newly introduced rabbits with warrens where they could live and breed. Warreners were employed to manage the rabbits – an important food source on the moor until the mid-20th century.

When you reach the northern end of the wood, turn right and head steeply uphill to reach the rocky summit of Longaford Tor, from where a splendid view opens up to the north towards 1,978 feet (603m) Cut Hill, perhaps the most remote of the Dartmoor summits. The nearer tor is Higher White Tor, and between that and Longaford Tor are the remains of one of Dartmoor's enigmatic prehistoric stone rows. No one is quite sure what they signified, but as many lead to cairns or a tall standing stone, they probably had a ritual purpose. Down in the valley to the south-west are the remains of the Powder Mills on the Cherry Brook, where gunpowder was made in the 19th century, and beyond that Bellever Tor pokes its rocky head above the conifers of Lakehead Hill.

Take the ridge due south crossing the strange masonry-like blocks of Littaford Tors and down through gaps in the walls towards Crockern Tor, where the historic palimpsest that is the Dartmoor landscape once again comes to the surface. Crockern Tor was the meeting point of the ancient Great Stannary (or tin) Court or Parliament of the Dartmoor tin miners for over three centuries, from 1494 to 1703. This remote spot was chosen because it was about equidistant from the Stannary towns of Ashburton, Chagford, Tavistock and Plympton, which all sent representatives to the parliament. The Judge's Chair – a huge, natural armchair-shaped recess in the topmost tor of Parliament Rock – is still pointed out as chief official's seat of office.

Crockern Tor was also claimed to be the home of Old Crockern, the spiritual protector of Dartmoor, who is chillingly described in the local dialect as: 'The gurt old sperit of the moors... grey as granite, and his eyebrows hanging down over his glimmering eyes like sedge, and his eyes as deep as peat water pools'. It is now a short step due west and downhill, passing some more pillow mounds, to reach Crockern Farm again and your outward route back to Two Bridges.

ABOVE Parliament, Rock, Crockern Tor
RIGHT Old water channel, Devonport Leat

2.

The death of a king:
Rufus Stone, New Forest, Hampshire

The monument enclosing the Rufus Stone

If there's one thing that can be said with any certainty about the New Forest – that astonishing survival of 220 square miles (560 sq km) of wildwood and heathland lying between Southampton Water and Salisbury Plain – it is that it's anything but 'new'.

The New Forest was first set aside as a place meriting special protection in 1079 – over eight centuries before the first of our National Parks in the Peak District and 926 years before it became a National Park itself in 2005. But just 13 years after the Battle of Hastings, William the Conqueror (c. 1027–87) designated what he called *Nova Foresta* as a royal hunting reserve, with a strict code of laws for the protection of game.

William was said to have loved the deer he hunted there 'as if he was their father'.

In Norman times the word 'forest' did not necessarily refer to a heavily wooded area as it does today, but to land that had been confiscated by the King so that it could be used exclusively for his pastime of hunting. Local people unfortunate enough to find themselves within William's *Nova Foresta* could not protect their crops or hedges, or take timber for their houses or fires, and most cruelly, they were not allowed to take any of the abundant game to feed their often hungry families. The swingeing penalties inflicted on an offender could involve mutilation or even death.

More recent research, however, has thrown some doubt on the severity of William's high-handed clearance of the forest for his sport. Many books still claim how the homes, the churches and the villages of the forest were laid waste by the Conqueror so he could enjoy his unrestricted hunting. But the Domesday Book of 1086 records that compensation was paid – almost on modern lines – to owners whose land had been put under forest law. Furthermore, there is no evidence to suggest that Forest villages and churches were destroyed to make room for the King's royal hunting preserve. In the Domesday survey, much of the New Forest was described as 'waste' – infertile woodland and furze – 'furze' being the local name for the golden-flowered bushes of pineapple-scented gorse, which still blossoms all year round on the forest's higher and drier ground.

The miracle of the New Forest is that more than nine centuries later, modern visitors can still enjoy extensive areas of landscape and scenery that would have been familiar to William of Normandy, as he hunted the native red and recently introduced fallow deer. Much of that is due to the New Forest Verderers, the direct descendants of William the Conqueror's foresters, who were charged with administering the ancient forest laws to protect the game and its habitat.

A tranquil New Forest stream

The Court of Verderers, which consists of ten local farmers, landowners and commoners, still meets every two months in the Verderers' Hall at the Queen's House in Lyndhurst. It is probably the oldest court of law in Britain and still administers the system of commoning that governs grazing and other rights to the forest.

On William the Conqueror's death in 1087, his eldest son, Robert, inherited Normandy and his second son, William, inherited the throne of England, while his youngest, Henry, was left landless. William II (nicknamed Rufus due to his red hair and ruddy, florid complexion) was not a popular king and gained many enemies during his 13-year reign. He helped himself to church funds, disagreed with his nobles and his brothers, and generally was known to treat his subjects with contempt and disdain.

He inherited his father's passion for hunting and died in what was claimed to have been an accident in the forest near the small village of Minstead in August 1100. As William was out hunting boar and deer in the New Forest with his younger brother and some other noblemen, an arrow fired at a stag by Sir Walter Tyrrell (or Tirel), a French nobleman, deflected off an oak tree and entered the King's chest, puncturing his lungs and killing him almost instantly.

William of Malmesbury described William's untimely death in his *Chronicle of the Kings of England* (c. 1128):

On receiving the wound, the king uttered not a word; but breaking off the shaft of the arrow where it projected from his body... this accelerated his death. Walter (Tyrrell) immediately ran up, but as he found him senseless, he leapt upon his horse, and escaped with the utmost speed. Indeed, there were none to pursue him: some helped his flight; others felt sorry for him.

As the Malmesbury William recounted, Tyrrell high-tailed it back home to Normandy, fearing the retribution he could possibly face for apparently killing the King. A persistent local legend is that he stopped off at a local blacksmiths in the forest to have his horse's shoes put on backwards so that it would confuse his pursuers.

It is perhaps a measure of the ill feeling towards William that his body was left abandoned where it fell by the hunting party, until an arrow maker, Eli Parratt, later found it. A local charcoal burner named Purkis put it on his cart and took it to Winchester, where the unloved King received a very low-key burial in the cathedral. His remains still lie in one of the royal mortuary chests on the presbytery screen, beside the choir.

The Anglo-Saxon Chronicle (1089) recorded that the king was 'shot by an arrow by one of his own men', and as William of Malmesbury recorded: 'William Rufus died in 1100... aged forty years. He was a man much pitied by the clergy... (but) he had a soul which they could not save... He was loved by his soldiers but hated by the people because he caused them to be plundered'.

There have been many conspiracy theories about William's death, including the fact that William's younger brother, Henry, who certainly had the most to gain by his sibling's demise, had also been on the hunt. In what appeared to be unseemly haste, Henry sped straight to Winchester to secure the royal treasury – often the wise first act of a would-be king – then went on to London, where he was crowned as Henry I within three days of the death of his brother.

Standing just outside the village of Minstead in the heart of the forest, the Rufus Stone is a slightly incongruous iron-clad monument, said to mark the site of the oak tree that was the cause of William Rufus' untimely ending. The stone was originally erected in 1745 by Lord John Delaware, although the monument we see today was re-erected in 1841 by WM Sturges Bourne, a Warden of the Forest. Of course, the oak tree that caused the fatal ricochet is long gone, but an ancient oak close by could possibly be a descendant of the original.

The three-sided stone is inscribed:

Here stood the oak tree, on which an arrow shot by Sir Walter Tyrrell at a stag, glanced and struck King William the Second, surnamed Rufus, on the breast, of which he instantly died, on the second day of August, anno 1100.

The Walk

This memorial to William Rufus is the starting point of our walk. Conveniently located next to a car park and in a beautiful forest setting, it makes a great base for an easy stroll in what the Forestry Commission call the 'Ancient and Ornamental' woods of the New Forest.

Having inspected the stone, from the car park head into the mature trees at a right angle to the road, past the cottage access. You will come to a shallow ford in a stream, which is easily crossed. Coming to a fork in the road, take the left fork, which takes you to a clearing near Grey's Farm. From here, head left across the green and coming to a gravel path past the farm, you will reach a small cottage where you should turn left, before joining a bridleway.

As you follow this bridleway through the woods, you may be lucky enough to spot some of William the Conqueror's beloved deer or the forest's 3,000 unique New Forest ponies, which are thought to be descended from primitive native horses, similar to those found on Exmoor and Dartmoor.

When you come to another bridleway signpost and a lane, follow the lane as far as the T-junction and then turn left, keeping to the road past the Sir Walter Tyrrell Inn. You could enjoy a pint or lunch at the inn, then from there, just follow the road to return to the Rufus Stone car park.

Factbox

Location: The Rufus Stone is signposted off the A31 Southampton-Ringwood road through the New Forest. There is a free car park directly opposite the stone in a woodland clearing

Postcode: SO43 7HD

Length: About 1.5 miles (2.4km); should take less than 1 hour

Terrain: Easy walking on level forest paths

Map: OS 1:25,000 Explorer OL22, New Forest

Refreshments: The Sir Walter Tyrrell Inn, Brook, Lyndhurst SO43 7HD is a traditional British pub with a large garden and children's play area

T 02380 813170
W thesirwaltertyrrell.co.uk

New Forest ponies

3.

An ode to autumn:
Keats' walk, Winchester, Hampshire

BELOW Cheyney Court in Winchester's Cathedral Close
RIGHT Frost-covered meadows lead up to the Chapel of St Cross

John Keats' 19th-century ode is probably the best-loved and most-quoted poem about autumn in the English language. It was composed by a troubled Keats during a short stay in the Hampshire cathedral city of Winchester, just 18 months before his tragic death from tuberculosis at the age of 25 in 1821.

At the time of his visit in the late summer and early autumn of 1819, Keats was a tormented soul, plagued by his still as yet unrecognised genius, his unrequited love for partners Isabella Jones and Fanny Brawne, his increasing financial difficulties, and his advancing ill health. But his visit to Winchester seems to have been a relatively happy and peaceful period of his short and troubled life. He found the city: 'An exceedingly pleasant

town, enriched with a beautiful cathedral and surrounded by a fresh-looking country'.

Keats apparently took a regular daily walk from the Cathedral Close and through the lush water meadows of the River Itchen to the wonderful Norman Gothic buildings of the 12th-century Hospital of St Cross and Almshouse of Noble Poverty on the outskirts of the city. We know this and probably even the actual day when he

Season of mists and mellow fruitfulness,
Close bosom-friend of the maturing sun;
Conspiring with him how to load and bless
With fruit the vines that round the thatch-eves run

John Keats, 'To Autumn' (1820)

composed the poem because he gave a detailed account of his walk on Sunday 19 September 1819 to his friend, fellow poet John Hamilton Reynolds. He wrote to Reynolds: 'How beautiful the season is now – how fine the air. A temperate sharpness about it.... I never lik'd the stubbled fields as much as now – aye, better than the chilly green of spring. Somehow the stubble plain looks warm – in the same way as some pictures look warm – this struck me so much in my Sunday's walk that I composed upon it'.

The extraordinary thing is that Keats' riverside walk has hardly changed in the two centuries that have passed since he enjoyed it. The cluster of medieval buildings 'mixed up with trees' of the cathedral, its Close and St Cross are still there, and the chalky trout-filled waters of the River Itchen run just as 'most beautifully clear' as Keats remembered them. And if you are fortunate enough to have done the walk in autumn, you'll see gossamer mists still rise from the river and be witness to '... a wailful choir the small gnats (which) mourn among the river sallows, borne aloft, or sinking as the light wind lives or dies...' They provide last-minute top-up fuel for the '... gathering swallows', which 'twitter in the skies' before their epic 6,000 mile (9,656km) migration to Africa.

The Walk

Our walk starts at the magnificent and recently restored, intricately traceried 14th-century west front of the cathedral, which is famed for having the longest medieval nave in the world. To the left, outlined in the grass of the churchyard, you can make out the outline of Alfred the Great's original cathedral, tiny by comparison, constructed when Winchester was his capital.

Winchester Cathedral, with its stone forest of soaring Perpendicular arches, was started by Bishop Walkelin in 1079 and greatly enlarged two centuries later by Bishop William Wykeham. His lavishly decorated tomb lies in his eponymous chantry on the south side of the nave, and to this day, alumni of Winchester College are known as Wykehamists.

Two years before Keats' visit, the romantic novelist Jane Austen, from nearby Chawton, was buried in the north aisle. Izaak Walton, renowned author of *The Compleat Angler* (1653), also spent the last years of his life in Winchester and is buried in the Silkstede Chapel. He is commemorated by a beautiful stained-glass window in the Fisherman's Chapel in the south transept, which was donated in 1914 by the anglers of England and America. Walton undoubtedly must have cast many a line into the clear, trout-rich waters of the River Itchen.

Amazingly, we owe the cathedral's survival to the present day to a deep-sea diver called William Walker, who in the early 19th century, when the cathedral was in grave danger of sinking into its

own water table, dug out peat in the crypt and replaced it with sacks of concrete. The crypt still regularly floods, casting reflections of the image of Antony Gormley's solitary bronze life-sized statue of a reading man, which was erected there in 1986.

From the west front of the cathedral, turn right under a stone arch to walk through to the elegant Close, which

Factbox

Location: Winchester is just off the M3 London-Southampton motorway. Leave at Junction 9 or 10. The cathedral is in its Close in the centre of Winchester where there are numerous car parks

Postcode: SO23 9LS

Length: About 2 miles (3.2km), there and back

Terrain: Easy pavement and gentle riverside paths

Map: OS 1:25,000 Explorer OL32, Winchester, New Alresford & East Meon

Refreshments: Many pubs, cafés and restaurants in Winchester, including the cathedral's own Refectory, Great Minster Street, Winchester SO23 9HE

☎ 01962 857258
🌐 winchester-cathedral.org.uk/welcome/cafe/

The west front of Winchester Cathedral

was described by Keats as: 'seemingly built for the dwelling place of Deans and Prebendaries – garnished with grass and shaded with trees'. The superb range of ecclesiastical buildings of the Close include the ruined Chapter House, the 14th-century Deanery, and the Pilgrim's School, where the angelic choristers of the cathedral are taught. Leave the Close by St Swithun's Gate, next to the gabled and half-timbered Cheyney Court, which was formerly the bishop's courthouse.

St Swithun has always been associated with Winchester and was an advisor to Alfred's father Aethelwulf. He is probably most remembered today for the meteorological curse he put on England when his body was moved from outside to inside the original cathedral. Posthumously, he vowed to make it rain for 40 days and 40 nights after his unwanted reburial – a curse that even modern weather forecasters still seem obliged to mention every year on 15 July, St Swithun's Day.

As you pass under Kingsgate, one of only two surviving original gates of the medieval city, and walk along College Street, you are now firmly within the precincts of Winchester College. The college was founded by Bishop Wykeham in 1382 and is the oldest public school

in England. On your left at the end of College Street is Wolvesey Palace, the home of the current bishop and beyond that the ruins of Wolvesey Castle, where their predecessors, the medieval bishops, lived. A right turn will take you into College Walk, which leads to the path that runs left, introducing you to a lovely mile beside the willows and wildflowers that line the banks of the babbling River Itchen all the way to our destination, the Hospital of St Cross.

In the distance ahead to your right, you soon see the tree-topped chalky height of St Catherine's Hill, which exercises a benign watch over the city below and where Keats claimed: 'the air is worth sixpence a pint.' The 550 foot (168m) summit of St Catherine's Hill is encircled by the ramparts of an Iron Age hillfort, and the prominent copse of beech trees also shelters the site of the former 12th-century chapel of St Catherine. There is also a turf-cut mizmaze, probably cut in the late 17th or early 18th century. It is one of only eight in the country, but it is not really a maze in the usual sense of high hedges but more a labyrinth of cut-out turf.

The grand buildings and tower of St Cross Hospital, described by Keats as 'a very interesting old place, both for its Gothic tower and alms-square', now beckon ahead. The hospital was founded by Henry of Blois, Bishop of Winchester, grandson of William the Conqueror and younger brother of King Stephen, in 1136. The adjoining Almshouse of Noble Poverty, marked by its upright array

The crystal-clear waters of the River Itchen

of exterior chimneys, has been described as 'England's oldest and most perfect almshouse.'

Looking more like a miniature Winchester Cathedral than a chapel, the Norman/Gothic-style 12th and 13th-century chapel of St Cross commands the south-east corner of the site. Caen stone vaulted throughout, with transepts and a central tower, the two-bay chancel is typically Norman, with round-headed windows and chevron ornamentation. Medieval tiles still survive on the floor, and there are also faint traces of equally ancient wall paintings.

The hospital still provides accommodation for 25 single, widowed or divorced men over 60 years of age, who are known as the Black or Red Brothers. They either belong to the Order of the Hospital of St Cross, members of which wear black trencher hats and robes, or the Order of Noble Poverty, who wear claret hats and robes.

If you are feeling peckish when you reach St Cross, you are entitled to request the ancient tradition of the Wayfarer's Dole, which consists of a small horn cup of ale and a piece of bread. The dole was started by a Cluniac monk and can be obtained by anyone who asks for it at the Porter's Lodge. I did and was made most welcome by a genial Black Brother.

Having thoroughly explored the mellow, peaceful environs of St Cross, return to Winchester by the same route and you might be treated, as I once was, by the iridescent electric-blue flash of a kingfisher, whirring low across the crystal-clear waters of the Itchen.

4.

There'll never be another yew:
Kingley Vale,
West Sussex

BELOW A contorted Kingley yew
RIGHT Looking across flower-covered meadows towards the summit of Kingley Vale

They call them 'snotty gogs' down here in Sussex; those bright coral-red berries of the yew, which nature writer Grigson described as 'one of the most tropical of English sights' when seen against a blue sky.

The mistle thrush busily gorging himself on the gem-like berries (more correctly known as 'arils') in Kingley Vale did not appear to be unduly worried by the fact that the yew is perhaps the most poisonous of British trees. The hard nut inside that candy-coated berry and the dark, dense foliage are deadly, the main symptom being clinically described by the Ministry of Agriculture as 'sudden death'. But the thrush had no need to worry because the fatal seed passes straight through its digestive system to give birth to a new yew tree elsewhere.

Geoffrey Grigson's 'black tufted density' of Kingley Vale's secret, brooding forest of yews is said to be the largest and finest in Europe – some say the world – but despite its importance, it is quite difficult to find. And it offers a truly magical walk.

Kingley Vale, or Kingley Bottom as the locals know it, was, in 1952, the first

National Nature Reserve (NNR) to be established in Britain,, so in 2022 it celebrated its 70th birthday. But the reserve is a mere stripling compared with some of those venerable yew trees for which it is most famous. Many have probably already passed their 500th birthday and some may be as much as 1,000 years old, making them among the oldest living things in Britain.

Kingley Vale lies hidden on the southern edge of the South Downs National Park, tucked away in a chalky fold of Stoke Down and Bow Hill, near the village of West Stoke, about 5 miles (8km) north-west of Chichester. It's worth the effort

to find because the walk through these incredibly ancient trees transports you through an Arthur Rackham landscape of tortured, twisted trunks and dark, cave-like clearings, where you half expect to see a fairy or a gnome pop up at every turn. The yew is a magical tree, suspected by some, including Grigson, to be the Scandinavian 'world tree', or Yggdrasil, on which the warrior god Odin hanged himself. Another Norse warrior god, Ull, the deity of bows and (rather oddly) skiing, is also said to have lived in yew forests.

But there's little evidence to support the old folk tale about English yew wood

The Devil's Humps, Kingley Vale

being used for the longbows that proved to be the medieval weapons of mass destruction against the French in battles like Crecy and Agincourt. The English yew timber was far too knotty and brittle for these medieval equivalents of the AK-47. English bowmen preferred their staves to be made from more straight-grained yew wood, imported by royal decree along with barrels of wine from Portugal and Spain. The folk tale is also the usual reason given for the traditional yew trees that stand sentinel in so many English churchyards. In fact, according to the 17th-century botanist Robert Turner, the yew was often planted there because it 'attracts and imbibes putrefaction and gross oleaginous vapours' exhaled from the graves, but a more likely explanation is that their poisonous leaves and berries deterred hungry livestock from disturbing graveyards.

Yew wood is reputedly the hardest coniferous timber in the world, as hard as iron and usually longer lasting. Used today mainly for richly figured veneers, the wood is also renowned among carpenters for its ability to blunt band saws because of embedded stones and nails. The oldest wooden artefact ever found in Britain is a spear point made of yew discovered in the clay cliffs of Clacton-on-Sea, Essex. This precious fragment had survived for an incredible 400,000 years and is now in London's Natural History Museum.

The Walk

Our exploration of Kingley's venerable yew forest starts from the small car park at the bottom of the hill just west of the church at West Stoke. Through a gate, you follow a stony farm track due north towards the looming woodland, with the vale still tantalisingly out of sight.

Passing through some mixed woodland, you emerge again into open countryside to reach a crossroads, where an ancient bridleway crosses Stoke Down. Go straight ahead to enter the Kingley Vale NNR by a sign. There's a small octagonal wooden field museum here, where children will delight in trying out 'feely' boxes and, perhaps more predictably, in seeing prime replicas of animal droppings (not to be felt) from the reserve.

As you head north again on the way-marked nature trail, the best examples and the oldest yews are found to the right. There are about 20 of these really old, twisted and contorted veterans, each one seeming to watch the walker with their ageless gaze. Some of these rich red writhing trunks seem to take on animal forms, while others just astound with their majestic presence and sheer bulk. It's a bit like walking through the hushed nave of a natural cathedral. Nothing much grows beneath the dense shade of these monarchs of the forest, so the walking is easy and the kids will love the hide-and-seek opportunities offered by the entwining boughs.

The local legend is that the original grove of yews was planted here to commemorate a battle fought in Kingley

Vale by the men of Hampshire against marauding Vikings in AD 859. The burial mounds we will pass later on at the head of the vale were supposedly where the slain Viking kings were buried – hence the name – but they are actually much earlier, dating from the Bronze Age, some 2,500 years ago.

Factbox

Location: Kingley Vale is just west of West Stoke, on the minor road between Funtington and Mid Lavant, about 5 miles (8km) north-west of Chichester

Postcode: PO18 9BN

Length: The suggested walk is about 5 miles (8km). You should allow at least 3 hours

Terrain: Easy woodland walking followed by a stiffish climb to the top of the coombe

Map: OS 1:25,000 Explorer OL120, Chichester, South Harting and Selsey

Refreshments: There are pubs in West Lavant (A286 north of Chichester) and Funtington (on the B2146). The White Horse Inn, High Street, Chilgrove, Chichester PO18 9HX is recommended for dinner

☎ 01243 519444
🌐 butcombe.com/the-white-horse-inn-west-sussex

The memorial stone to Sir Arthur Tansley

rabbit-grazed grassland where New Forest ponies were introduced to keep the unwanted scrub at bay. Fifty species of wildflowers, including bee orchids, have been recorded per square metre on these sweet-smelling slopes. Over to the right on the steep, fenced-off section of the down, evidence has been found of Stone Age flint 'mines' where glassy-black flint nodules were excavated for manufacture into tools and weapons during the Neolithic period at the dawn of humanity. The sad skeletons of dead yews are seen here; incredibly, Canadian troops were allowed to use them for target practice during training for the Second World War D-Day landings.

As you leave the ancient grove, once thought to be the meeting place of witches and druids, the vast expanse of Kingley Vale opens up before you. To the right is what is known as the 'young' yew forest. The spreading branches of these dense trees are thought to be a mere 100 years old. The trees to the left are generally about 140 years old, naturally planted by birds like that mistle thrush we met earlier.

A young yew tree needs quite a bit of help to get started, in particular 'nurse' trees like the low-lying juniper shrub, itself quite rare in England, which Natural England is trying to encourage in the vale. It protects the young trees from grazing, conserves water in drought, and offers shade to the infant yews.

A steepish climb now begins up the chalky escarpment and the sheep and

As you approach the top of the coombe, the views to the south extend to the elegant spire of Chichester Cathedral and the snaking inlets of Chichester Harbour, with the silvery glint of the English Channel and the Isle of Wight beyond. On the brow of the hill is the simple sarsen stone taken from Fyfield Down in Wiltshire, which marks the memorial to Sir Arthur Tansley, first chairman of the Nature Conservancy. Although unfortunately he died just three years after Kingley Vale's seminal designation, Tansley loved this place, and this was his favourite viewpoint in the whole of Britain. Few would argue with his choice.

The way now swings past two of the burial mounds mentioned earlier, which are also known as the Devil's Humps. After you've admired the view, turn left and downhill, through more infant yews and the so-called 'birdless grove' to return to the field museum and the short walk back to the car park.

5.

Cromwell's 'small execution' of the Clubmen
Hambledon Hill, Wiltshire

The sun sets over Hambledon Hill

Hambledon Hill, north of Blandford Forum in Dorset, dominates the Vale of Blackmoor – Thomas Hardy's 'Vale of the Little Dairies' – like a benign and brooding giant. The sweeping, sinuous curves of the double embankments that contour around its summit make it one of the most impressive examples of a multivallate Iron Age hillfort in Britain.

There's no evidence that Hambledon was ever attacked in ancient times, but during the English Civil War it became the unlikely scene of one of the most pathetic and brutal episodes in that bitter, internecine conflict. The Clubmen were a bucolic band of local yeomen, farmers and peasants, who today would probably be branded as pacifists or conscientious objectors. Sickened by a

war in which they had no interest, but that was seriously affecting their day-to-day lives as troops from the warring armies trampled their crops, pillaged their villages and commandeered their grain, they rose up with no greater motive than the desire to protect their own hearths and homes.

They also joined together to prevent themselves being forcibly conscripted

The sweeping embankments of Hambledon's hillfort, lined by natural landslip terracettes

to fight on either the Royalist or the Parliamentarian sides, while soldiers, battle followers, looters, deserters or refugees threatened their lives. In some cases, unruly soldiers of both persuasions raped their wives and daughters. As their name suggests, they were mostly armed with whatever they could find in the farmyard: cudgels, flails, scythes or sickles fastened to long poles. A white cockade was their only uniform and they marched with banners proclaiming: 'If you offer to plunder or take our cattle, be assured we will bid you battle'.

Led by the Rev Thomas Bravel, rector of nearby Compton Abbas, they eventually mustered 5,000 hearty, red-faced men, drawn from the counties of Dorset, Wiltshire and Somerset with the rallying cry: 'For England and our homes'.

At first they petitioned the King to stop the madness of the war, but they were ignored. So they stormed the Parliamentary quarters at Sturminster Newton, but this brave action had exactly the same effect. Eventually, in the summer of 1645, they entrenched themselves on Castle Hill at Shaftesbury, only to be herded off like so many of their own downland sheep by Oliver Cromwell's well-drilled New Model Army, who took 50 of them prisoner. Enraged by this, the Clubmen, now down to only about 2,000 men, encamped within the ancient ramparts of Hambledon Hill, determined to fight to the death to gain the release of their leaders. Bravel, obviously better equipped and more determined than most of his rabble army, threatened to shoot any Clubman who surrendered.

The denouement was not long in coming. Cromwell sent 50 of his well-equipped dragoons to Hambledon, but their demand for the surrender of the hill was treated with contempt and a round of lead shot from Bravel. But the weathered Iron Age defences proved no obstacle to the charging sword-slashing dragoons, who swept through the entrance and over the ditches, overwhelming the yokels after what Cromwell described as 'a short dispute'. During an hour's fighting 60 Clubmen were killed and captured 400 captured, half of whom were wounded. Cromwell, obviously with Bravel in mind, claimed that they had been stirred up by 'malignant priests, who were principal stirrers up of the people to these tumultuous assemblies'.

The Parliamentarian leader's coldly clinical report of the event to his commander-in-chief, Sir Thomas Fairfax, states: 'They beat them from the work and did some small execution upon them; I believe killed not twelve of them but cut very many'. The luckiest of the Clubmen escaped by sliding down the steep slopes of the hill. But many were taken prisoner by the dragoons and left to stew overnight in the church at Shroton (or Iwerne) Courtney (it is one of the few villages in England with alternative names) in the shadow of Hambledon Hill.

Cromwell himself came to the church and lectured them, and his scathing account of this rather sad episode to his commander sums up his barely concealed contempt for the disillusioned Clubmen. 'We have taken about 300, many of which are poor silly creatures, whom if you please to let me send home they promise to be very dutiful for time to come and will be hanged before they come out again'. Those who swore to the Covenant were subsequently released,

the others sent to imprisonment in London.

The story was an uncanny echo of events 1,600 years earlier, when the Roman Second Augusta Legion under Vespasian (later to become Emperor) attacked the neighbouring hillfort of Hod Hill, a mile (1.6km) away to the south, on its all-conquering assault on the 20 hillforts of the local Celtic tribe known as the Durotriges in AD 43. Maiden Castle, Dorset's most mighty and famous hillfort outside Dorchester, had already fallen under the power of Vespasian's armour-clad legionaries.

Excavations in the 1950s on what was thought to be the local chieftain's hut in the south-eastern part of the Hod Hill fort made the dramatic discovery of 11 iron ballista bolts, still embedded in the chalk where they had been fired from a Roman siege engine. Since there were no other signs of battle or war cemeteries on the site, it was assumed that the Durotiges might have been so intimidated by this demonstration of state-of-the-art firepower that they simply surrendered.

However, more recent research has revealed that Hod Hill, like neighbouring Maiden Castle, was largely unoccupied by AD 43. And it's even been suggested that the ballista bolts may have been fired by legionaries doing a bit of peace-time target practice! But what is clear, as if to rub in their superiority, is the Romans built one of their standard playing card-shaped forts actually within the bounds of the Iron Age hillfort – the only instance of this happening in Britain.

The Walk

Our walk to these prehistoric strongholds begins in the village of Child Okeford, on the minor road north-east of Shillingstone. That curious village name, by the way, is thought to mean 'knight's oak ford' and the prefix probably comes from the Old English *cild* meaning a youth of noble birth. Take the A357 Steepleton Road, past Fernhaynes Copse on your left, with the encircling earthworks of Hambledon frowning down from the skyline above. A chalky farm track, signposted Hambledon Hill, leads off to the left and climbs steeply up through stately beeches to a stile, which leads out onto the open downland.

Now owned by the National Trust, Hambledon Hill is also a NNR, with flowering plants that include milkwort, salad burnet, horseshoe vetch, squinancy wort, pyramidal orchid and wild thyme, and the much rarer meadow saxifrage, early gentian and dwarf sedge. Butterflies found on the downland in summer include the dingy and grizzled skippers, and the chalkhill and Adonis blues.

The path leads steeply up to the right across the small, ridged, landslip terraces aiming for the obvious saddle between the sweeping embankments of the northern end of the hillfort to your left and the slighter earthworks of an even earlier Neolithic camp on the right. At the top of the hill, turn left and walk along the bold embankments towards the 600 foot (184m) summit of Hambledon, enjoying its superb view across the 'little dairies' of the Vale of Blackmoor, towards

ABOVE Scene of the Clubmens' comeuppance
LEFT Hambledon's impressive Iron Age fortifications

the prominent Melbury Beacon and the hilltop town of Shaftesbury to the north.

Retrace your steps south to the central col and the trig point, which marks the site of one of two original Neolithic causewayed enclosures. Continue south, dropping down to the Cross Dyke and then up on the ridge through hawthorn scrub until the path descends steeply through Hambledon Plantation to reach the Child Okeford-Steepleton road near Keeper's Lodge. Bear right to the gate on the left, which gives access to the National Trust's Hod Hill Estate.

Climb up to the north-west corner of the embankments of the hillfort, where the Roman fort was superimposed within the Iron Age earthworks. Take your time as you walk round the 54 acre (22ha) fort, noting the fine, but in the event ineffective, defensive position chosen by the Durotiges on this headland above the winding River Stour in the valley below. There are good aerial views too towards the hipped stone slate roof of the 17th-century Steepleton

House in the well-wooded valley of the River Iwerne to the north.

Now take the steep path down from the south-western corner of the fort through the undergrowth to a pleasant, tree-lined riverside track along the Stour and back out onto the Steepleton road again, west of the Keeper's Lodge. Turn left on the road, passing Hanford House School on your left, to re-enter Child Okeford.

6.

Gilbert White's Zig-Zag path: Selborne, Hampshire

BELOW Sign on the Zig-Zag path
RIGHT White's home; The Wakes, Selborne

THE ZIG-ZAG PATH WAS CUT BY GILBERT WHITE AND HIS BROTHER IN THE YEAR 1753. PLEASE HELP TO PRESERVE IT BY KEEPING TO THE PATH AND NOT CUTTING THE CORNERS OR SLIDING DOWN THE BANKS.

I watched fascinated as squadrons of swept-winged, fork-tailed swallows swooped and snapped up the clouds of flies and gnats as they rose from the flower-filled meadow known as The Park. The meadow lies just behind The Wakes, the house of the 18th-century parson-naturalist Gilbert White in Selborne, on the northern boundary of the South Downs National Park in Hampshire.

Swallows and other members of the hirundine family held an abiding fascination for White, who was described by no less an authority than the eminent naturalist and broadcaster James Fisher as 'the greatest amateur naturalist Britain has known'. Over half the letters to fellow naturalists contained in White's famous *Natural History and Antiquities of Selborne*, first published in 1789 and never out of print since, concerned swallows, swifts, and house and sand martins and the vexed question of whether they migrated or hibernated during the winter.

He concluded in his letter XVIII, to fellow naturalist and explorer Daines Barrington on 29 January 1774, that because swallows were first seen above lakes

and mill ponds, and appear to withdraw followin particularly cold spring weather, this was '... a circumstance... much more in favour of hiding than migration, since it is much more probable that a bird should retire to its hibernaculum just at hand, than return for a week or two only to warmer latitudes'.

But he never really satisfactorily resolved the thorny problem that had nagged him for so many years, because he failed to find any evidence of those suggested 'secret dormitories' or 'hibernacula' in the bottom of ponds, in bushes or in holes in the numerous rock-cut holloways that abound around Selborne.

Gilbert's suggestion of hirundine hibernation is sometimes dismissed by modern observers as evidence of his amateurishness as a mere 'parson-naturalist'. But we should never forget that his detailed and meticulous daily observations over 40 years were made long before ringing and satellite tagging proved that swallows, swifts and other members of the family do, in fact, migrate over 6,000 miles (9,656km) to South Africa annually to avoid our chilly winters.

Or that he made so many other singular contributions to British natural history, including being the first observer to distinguish between wood, willow and

View of The Wakes and Selborne from The Hanger

chiffchaff warblers; the first to identify our smallest rodent, the harvest mouse and our largest bat, the noctule; the first to understand the significance of song and territory in birds; and the first to recognise, a hundred years before Darwin (see page 58), the crucial role of earthworms in the formation of soil.

Gilbert White (1720–93) was born in Selborne in his grandfather's vicarage on Selborne's Plestor, or village green. He was seven or eight when the White family moved from the vicarage to the nearby house called The Wakes, which took its name from its previous occupants, where he lived for the remaining 65 years of his life.

White was educated at Oriel College, Oxford and gained his degree as Bachelor of Arts in 1743. In 1744 he was elected a Fellow of the college and in 1746 he became a Master of Arts. He finally entered the 'family business' of the ministry and obtained his deacon's orders in 1746. He was fully ordained in 1749, subsequently holding several curacies in Hampshire and Wiltshire, including Selborne and the nearby villages of Newton Valence and Farringdon.

White became co-curate at Selborne for the fourth time in 1784. Having studied at Oriel, he was ineligible to be considered for the permanent living of Selborne, which was in the gift of Magdalen College. But his undemanding duties as a curate evidently left him plenty of time for his studies of the local wildlife, gardening, and for his abiding and forensic interest in all aspects of natural history, which he modestly called 'a meditation on the Book of Nature'.

Selborne and the surrounding countryside became White's outdoor laboratory, where he studied subjects as diverse as weather patterns and the effect of climate on plants, animals and insects, all of which now seem highly prescient. His somewhat eccentric experiments included shouting at bees through a large trumpet in order to test their hearing and searching at night by candlelight for worms on his lawn. The age of the parson-naturalist was born.

The Walk

Our walk in the footsteps of Gilbert White begins in the village car park where you take the footpath signposted to Selborne Common. The brooding woodlands of The Hanger – derived from the Old English *hangra*, meaning a wooded slope – overshadow the village and beckon you on, and are accessed through a gate.

Ahead lies the famous Zig-Zag path, originally constructed by White's younger brother John in 1753, which will take you by a series of hairpins to the 300 foot (91m) crest of the chalk and greensand escarpment. Although somewhat overgrown at times today, there are several seats by the path where you can take a rest and admire the ever more expansive vistas across the rolling countryside to the north-east over Noar Hill and the country where poet Edward Thomas made his home before the First World War.

After a relatively stiff climb and what seems an unending series of zigs and zags, you emerge into a clearing and a convenient seat from which you can again admire the superb views across northern Hampshire. The roofs of the houses in Selborne lie just below, while to the east, spread the meadows and hanging woodlands of The Lythes in the valley of the Oakhanger Stream. The white 'golf ball' radar domes of the former RAF Oakhanger are prominent in the middle distance.

You have a choice now. For a longer circuit, go straight ahead to further explore the 260 acres (105ha) of the

Factbox

Location: Selborne is on the B3006 between Alton and Greatham. Follow the brown English Heritage signs for Gilbert White's House, The Wakes, High Street, Selborne, Hampshire GU34 3JH. There is a public car park behind The Selborne Arms

Postcode: GU34 3JR

Length: About 3.5 miles (5.6km); allow 2 hours, with a longer extension

Terrain: On field and woodland paths with one steep climb up the Zig-Zag path

Map: OS 1:25,000 Explorer OL133, Haslemere & Petersfield

Refreshments: White's Café in The Wakes serves locally produced food all day, plus coffee and home-made cakes.

T 01420 511275
W gilbertwhiteshouse.org.uk

The Selborne Arms, High Street, Selborne, Alton GU34 3JR is a fine old pub and has a pleasant beer garden at the rear

T 01420 511247
W selbornearms.co.uk

National Trust's Selborne Common, or you can take the high-level path (right), which leads you through the dappled shade of the Hanger woods. The stately beeches

The Zig-Zag path from below

here are seen at their architectural best, the grey boles soaring up into the sky like the columns of the aisle of a medieval cathedral, with the satisfying crunch of their spiky copper mast underfoot. In summer, you may spot butterflies like the silver-washed fritillary, the orange tip and, if you are really lucky, the even rarer purple emperor flitting across the sun-washed glades.

At the end of the woodland, a path leads right down onto Wood Lane and back into the village. As you reach the village outskirts near Grange Farm a footpath on the left leads to Cow Lane, one of the holloways described by White as 'one of the singularities of this place', and where he thought his beloved swallows might hibernate in its crevices.

It's a short step now along the main village street to the 12th-century parish church of St Mary's and its ancient (but now dead) yew. White's simple, lichen-encrusted gravestone simply marked

'GW 26th June, 1793', lies at the northern end of the churchyard near a seat occupied by a statue of the pioneering naturalist. White disapproved of what he called the 'improper custom' of burying the dead within the body of the church and specified in his will that he should be interred 'in as plain and private away as possible'.

However, inside the church today there is a fine memorial stained-glass window by Alexander Gascoyne and Horace Hincks in the south aisle, featuring St Francis of Assisi and a host of local birdlife mentioned in his diaries, which was erected on the bicentenary of White's birth in 1920. Another more modern stained-glass window celebrates the 200th anniversary of his death in 1993.

No trip to Selborne would be complete without a visit to White's home at The Wakes, which is now a fine museum and has been lovingly restored to look something like it was in his day. It also contains on its upper floor a museum dedicated to Lawrence 'Titus' Oates, the Antarctic explorer who, badly frost-bitten, left his tent on Scott's ill-fated 1912 Terra Nova expedition with the memorable words: 'I am just going outside and may be some time'.

That's an idea with which I am sure Gilbert White would agree, albeit for entirely different reasons. In the words of his biographer, Richard Mabey, his 'deceptively simple and unpretentious' *Natural History of Selborne*: '...has come to be regarded as one of the most perfectly realised celebrations of nature in the English language'.

7.

The church in the circle:
Knowlton Henge, Dorset

Sunset over Knowlton Church

There's definitely something spiritual in the air about the roofless ruin of Knowlton Church, which stands somewhat incongruously in the centre of a Neolithic henge monument in a quiet Dorset field a few miles north of Wimborne.

Colourful ribbons and memorabilia of loved ones are still regularly tied to the branches of the two venerable yew trees at the eastern entrance to the henge, while followers of New Age religion often congregate at the monument on the summer and winter solstices, much as they do at the most famous henge of all, on Salisbury Plain.

The distinguished Cambridge archaeologist Jacquetta Hawkes seems to have felt something threatening in the atmosphere surrounding the henge when she visited it. She wrote: 'There lingers in the air some flavour of the sinister and macabre'. An indefinable air of melancholy certainly seems to hang over the site and some believe that the spirits of those who have passed this way in the last 4,000 years still linger here. Many visitors come to Knowlton seeking a spiritual experience and as is perhaps inevitable at such an evocative place,

An aerial view of Knowlton Church enclosed by its henge

there are tales of ghostly hauntings and visits by the Devil. Groups investigating the paranormal qualities of the site have been enveloped in swirling white mists and have heard ethereal voices chattering around them, although no source for the ghostly voices has ever been traced.

Other people claim to have witnessed a phantom horse and rider galloping across the site in the dead of night, passing straight through the ruined church as though it wasn't there. On some occasions, a ghostly face has been seen peering from the top window of the ruined tower, and a weeping woman, who some accounts describe as a nun, has been seen kneeling outside the church. Even in daylight hours, when a woman and her two children were visiting the site, they were startled by a tall figure dressed in black that suddenly appeared from nowhere. It proceeded to walk right across their path and then promptly vanished. Other visitors have reported

sightings of the same figure at night and have commented on a menacing aura that seemed to emanate from it.

The builders of the original Saxon chapel at Knowlton certainly weren't taking any chances when they sited it in the middle of the pagan henge. Christianity was still a relatively recent phenomenon when the first chapel at Knowlton was built. St Augustine, founder of the English Church, had arrived in Kent in AD 597 and it is said he first found shelter beneath a yew tree. The yew, now ever associated with British churchyards, has been revered ever since. The mysterious evergreen tree symbolises eternal life, immortality and resurrection and therefore plays an important role at Easter. Yews were often planted at sacred sites because their long life (they commonly live for over 1,000 years) was suggestive of eternity, or because their toxicity saw them as trees of death. An alternative, somewhat simpler explanation is that yews were planted in burial grounds to discourage farmers from letting livestock wander and browse on their highly poisonous foliage.

The Christian church often took over existing pagan sacred sites for its churches, and this may have happened at Knowlton. But the old beliefs persisted, and the builders of the chapel may just have been hedging their bets and casting a judicious nod in the direction of the Old Religion when they chose to build it inside the henge. On the other hand, as the Romans did at many other formerly pagan sites, they may simply have been attempting to utilise or even trying to nullify the ancient power of the site.

That original chapel on the site is now long gone, but early Christian activity at Knowlton was confirmed by the discovery of an Anglo-Saxon cemetery to the east of Church Henge, in 1958. Archaeologists uncovered 16 burials in chalk-cut graves, some aligned east-west in the usual fashion for Christian graves.

The all-conquering Normans, keen to mark their newly won dominance over the Saxons and the millennia of ancient British pagan practices, built their own church on the site of the Saxon chapel in the 12th century. The roofless walls of the flint and sandstone tower, chancel and nave, neatly layered a bit like a chocolate cake, still stand as a potent symbol of the transition from pagan to Christian worship. There were later additions and alterations in the 15th and 18th centuries, but sometime in the 18th century, the roof fell in and the church was eventually abandoned to the elements.

The Church Henge is one of several prehistoric monuments, including three henges, round barrows, ring-ditches and a possible cursus (a long, narrow enclosure), which are collectively known as the Knowlton Circles by their current guardians, English Heritage. They show this to be one of the most important Neolithic and Bronze Age landscapes in the country. No one knows for sure if the Church Henge once had a stone circle in its interior, but prehistoric standing stones were often toppled, broken up, buried in the ground or used in the construction of other buildings, as happened at places like Avebury.

Church Henge, which is also known as the Central Circle, is easily the best preserved of the three henges at Knowlton and is believed to have been constructed towards the end of the Neolithic period – around 2500-2000 BC. It is an oval enclosure 350 x 300 feet (107 x 91m), orientated roughly north-east to south-west, surrounded by a 30 foot (9m) wide ditch and earthwork bank.

Among the other identified prehistoric remains on the site are four enclosures, a square enclosure known as the Old Churchyard and a number of mostly ploughed-out round barrows. The largest and most visible of these is the tree-covered Bronze Age round barrow closest to the Church Henge, which is appropriately known as the Great Barrow as it is the largest round barrow in Dorset. The barrow is 130 feet (40m) in diameter and still 20 feet (6m) high, surrounded by two concentric ditches, both of which have now been largely levelled by ploughing.

The Walk

We pass the site of the ancient village of Knowlton, located on the banks of the River Allen about 500 yards west of Knowlton Church, on our walk along Lumber Lane. Knowlton was a royal manor, recorded as Chenoltone at the time of the Domesday Book, and held a regular fair, although this later moved to the nearby village of Woodlands.

On the ground, there is little to be seen of this deserted medieval village today, but aerial photographs show the faint shadows of the layout of the former settlement. The village, together with its close neighbour Brockingham, was eventually abandoned in the 17th century, probably as a result of the fearsome Black Death. But the church in the henge at Knowlton continued to serve the parish for several centuries.

When the lane ends at a T-junction, turn left towards Gussage All Saints. As the lane rises slightly, turn off to the right through a wide metal gate to follow a broad farm track. The track continues to a crossroads where you turn left and continue on this path until it descends into the village of Gussage All Saints, next to The Drovers Inn. Turn left and walk through the village to another crossroads, which is locally named Amen Corner. From here, go straight across towards Bowerswain and follow the lane until it goes downhill. Just as the lane bears to the right over a bridge, turn left onto a track with the stream on your right.

After a short distance the wide track bears left and narrows between hedgerows. Keep on this path until it widens out again at a T-junction, where you turn left. Passing some cottages on the left, carry on until you reach the lane, where you turn right to return to Knowlton Church and circle.

Today, Knowlton Church and its surrounding earthworks are protected and maintained by English Heritage and it remains an inspirational and popular site for New Age hippies, seekers of the paranormal, and curious history buffs.

Factbox

Location: From Wimborne, drive about 6 miles (9.7km) on the B3078 towards Cranborne. Knowlton Church is signposted on the left. There is limited parking in the lay-by at the site entrance on Lumber Lane

Postcode: BH21 5AE

Length: 2.5 miles (4km)

Terrain: Green lanes, tracks and quiet lanes

Map: OS 1:25,000 Explorer OL118, Shaftesbury & Cranborne Chase

Refreshments: The Drovers Inn, Gussage All Saints, Wimborne BH21 5ET, is a typical family run village pub, which serves wholesome food

☎ 01258 840550
🌐 thedroversinn.info

8.

Jarman's garden of delights: Dungeness, Kent

Derek Jarman's beloved Prospect Cottage

Dungeness is a liminal, constantly shape-shifting, other-worldly kind of place, quite unlike anywhere else in the British Isles. It can sometimes appear bleak and desolate, even forbidding to some people. But its attraction as a wild, untamed landscape makes it irresistible to wilderness lovers, like the filmmaker Derek Jarman, on the otherwise polite and gentile south coast of England.

Shaped like a prehistoric arrowhead made of the flint of which it is formed, the 4 mile (6.4km)-long shingle headland points directly from the Kentish shore towards Boulogne, across the grey waters of the English Channel. The name Dungeness derives from the Old Norse *nes*, meaning 'headland', the prefix probably coming from the nearby Denge Marsh.

Dungeness is formed almost entirely of flint shingle and is the largest cuspate (pointed) flint foreland in Europe and, with Cape Kennedy in Florida, one of the largest in the world. The succession of shingle ridges that have formed the peninsula are the result of thousands of years of longshore drift. This is caused by waves constantly striking the beach at an oblique angle and rolling along it,

The disused High Light Tower lighthouse

types of plants – a third of all found in Britain – and it is also one of the best places in the British Isles to see birdlife and invertebrates such as moths, bees, beetles and spiders.

Clinging on to life in this hostile landscape are wind-shaped stunted bushes of white-flowered blackthorn, pineapple-scented gorse and golden-flowered broom, along with tough, salt-tolerant plants like the glaucous blue-green-leaved sea kale, and a rainbow-hued host of lichens and mosses. The flooded gravel pits on the RSPB reserve of Denge Beach contain both brackish and fresh water, and also provide an important refuge for many migratory and coastal birds, and every year thousands of birdwatchers visit the peninsula and its bird observatory.

Dungeness is recognised as being of international conservation importance for its geomorphology, plant, insect and birdlife. This is confirmed through its array of official designations as a National Nature Reserve (NNR), a Special Protection Area (SPA), a Special Area of Conservation (SAC) and as part of the Dungeness, Romney Marsh and Rye Bay Site of Special Scientific Interest (SSSI).

But the first-time visitor may wonder how these exclusive conservation designations ever came about, because the southern tip of the headland consists of a ramshackle collection of black tar-walled fishermen's huts, old railway carriages, abandoned boats and rusting fishing tackle. And to cap it all, the headland is overshadowed by the two massive Lego blocks of the Dungeness nuclear power stations.

shifting the shingle as they go. Some of the corrugated ridges that form such a prominent feature on the headland may be 6,000 years old, and the best-preserved sequence has been dated to the 8th century. The exposed shingle covers about 5,330 acres (2,157ha), but there are also buried shingle banks, which underlie a further 2,840 acres (1,149ha). The entire area of the ness covers some 12 square miles (31 sq km).

By any definition, Dungeness is a peculiar place and could hardly be more different from the nearby lush green pastures of Denge Marsh and the rolling contours of the Kentish Downs and Weald inland. It is also one of the driest and sunniest parts of the UK and was once even described as Britain's only desert. Nevertheless, it is a haven for a remarkable variety of wildlife. There are over 600 different

The Walk

We start our exploration of Dungeness at the old High Light Tower lighthouse, opened in March 1904 - no longer in use but open as a visitor attraction. It stands 150 feet (46m) high and is 36 feet (11m) in diameter. There are 169 steps to the top viewing platform, which gives stunning vistas across the shifting shingle beach to the Straits of Dover, with the green expanse of Romney Marsh to the north.

There have been five successive lighthouses at Dungeness over the past four centuries. The first were built in the 17th century and this one is the fourth. The black and white striped lighthouse to the east, which opened in 1961, is the fifth and the only one that is currently operational.

From the High Light lighthouse, walk left along the tarmac road, past the Britannia Inn. Just before you reach the new lighthouse, take the wooden boardwalk, which leads out onto the beach. This is the best place to get an impression of the waves, which have created the constantly moving shingle of the spit and gradually increased the size of the headland, taking the sea further away from the lighthouses, which is the reason why several have had to be built.

Retrace your steps to the road and walk along past the collection of wooden shacks, lean-tos, one-storey bungalows and abandoned railway carriages, many of which have been turned into homes. At the second track on the right, turn off the road and walk towards a white house with a scattering of outbuildings.

Factbox

Location: Dungeness is on the minor road from the B2075 in Lydd, Kent. There is a car park next to Dungeness railway station. Alternatively, you could reach it via the narrow-gauge Romney, Hythe and Dymchurch Railway

Postcode: TN29 9ND

Length: About 3 miles (4.8km)

Terrain: Walking on shingle is tough and quite tiring, so be prepared

Map: OS 1:25,000 Explorer OL125, Romney Marsh, Rye & Winchelsea

Refreshments: Try the fish and chips as recommended by Jarman at The Pilot Inn, Battery Road, Lydd-on-Sea, Romney Marsh TN29 9NJ

☎ 01797 320314
🌐 thepilotdungeness.co.uk

The Britannia Inn, Dungeness Road, Dungeness, Romney Marsh TN29 9ND, which serves fresh seafood

☎ 01797 321959
🌐 britanniadungeness.co.uk

Though the beach here may recall *Steptoe and Son*'s junkyard, there are still some working fishing boats enabling local families to earn a living. The various fishing and rowing boats, winches, ropes, nets, abandoned carriages and containers may look a mess, but they provide a history of the local fishing

The only currently operational Dungeness lighthouse

industry. You can still see some of the old, tanned fishing nets alongside the modern, brightly coloured nylon ones. Today this picturesque debris of a largely bygone industry provides a tempting foreground for landscape photographers.

Follow the obvious shingle track back to the main road in the direction of a house with a square white tower. Continue up the main road until you come to a coal-black tar-walled house with bright, primrose-yellow window frames. This distinctive dwelling is Prospect Cottage, the former home of the artist, theatre designer and filmmaker Derek Jarman (1942–94). In 1986, Jarman was diagnosed HIV positive and following the death of his father he bought Prospect Cottage, a Victorian former fisherman's hut, for £750 as a hideaway.

Although still a private residence, today it has become a site of pilgrimage for his many admirers. And gardeners are equally inspired by his rustic, upturned flints, driftwood and twisted iron sculptures, made from the flotsam and

jetsam washed up on the beach, and the tenacious plants Jarman planted to survive in this harsh maritime climate. Writing of his earliest days at Prospect Cottage, Jarman said it was the bleakness of Prospect Cottage that initially made him fall in love with it. He described the genesis of his garden:

When I came to Dungeness in the mid-eighties, I had no thought of building a garden. It looked impossible: shingle with no soil supported a sparse vegetation. At the back I planted a dog rose. Then I found a curious piece of driftwood and used this, and one of the necklaces of holey stones that I hung on the wall, to stake the rose. The garden had begun. I saw it as a therapy and a pharmacopoeia.'

'At first, people thought I was building a garden for magical purposes – a white witch out to get the nuclear power station. It did have magic – the magic of surprise, the treasure hunt. A garden is a treasure hunt, the plants the paperchase.

Continue along the road in the direction of the white lifeboat station. In 1940, the Dungeness lifeboat was one of 19 that took part in the evacuation of Allied troops from Dunkirk, and throughout the 1950s the station was famous for its so-called Lady Launchers – local women who hauled the lifeboat down to the sea. In front of the station on the right you'll see a black brick building, which was formerly a tanning copper, used to preserve fishing nets. Ahead is the Pilot Inn – recommended by Jarman as providing: 'Simply the finest fish and chips in all England'.

Follow the road as it bears left and crosses the railway tracks. Now head towards the row of white terraced coastguard cottages and just before you reach them you will see a green public footpath sign. Follow this to make your way across the shingle back towards the old lighthouse. About halfway there, you'll get a good view of the massive square blocks of the Dungeness nuclear power stations.

There were two nuclear power stations at Dungeness, the first built in 1965 and named Dungeness A and the second, Dungeness B, in 1983. Dungeness A closed down in 2006, and it was announced in June 2021 that Dungeness B would not resume operations after they had ceased in September 2018, and it would move into a defuelling phase.

Continue across the crunching shingle to make your way back towards the old High Light Tower lighthouse and your starting point.

Perhaps the last word should be left to Derek Jarman, who so loved this strange, almost magical place and who found his garden was 'therapeutic in its peacefulness':

Here at the sea's edge
I have planted my dragon-toothed
garden to defend the porch,

Steadfast warriors against those who
protest their impropriety
Even to the end of the world.

The Lego blocks of Dungeness Power Station

9.

Darwin's 'Thinking Path': Down House, Kent

BELOW Charles Darwin
RIGHT A winter shot of Darwin's Thinking Path

One of my most prized possessions is a simple flint, creamy-white on the outside crust but a beautiful, shiny jet-black in the centre. It had been split open at some time, as evidenced by the concentric 'bulb of percussion' marking its core. Just a stone, you might think, but it is one that reminds me of my East Anglian upbringing, where flint was the only stone I encountered as a child. But its importance to me lies in where I picked it up.

I was visiting Down House, the Kentish home of one of my personal heroes, the 19th-century naturalist and biologist Charles Darwin, famous for his revolutionary theory of the origin of species by natural selection, which later became known as the theory of evolution. It was, as the modern evolutionary biologist Richard Dawkins and others have called it, 'Darwin's Great Idea'.

Several recent revisionist writers have, with some justification, claimed that Darwin's theory owed much to previous work by his own grandfather, Erasmus Darwin, and fellow scientists such as Thomas Malthus, George Cuvier, Charles Lyell and Jean-Baptiste Lamarck. But it was Charles Darwin who first broke it to the world in his monumental,

ground-breaking and still best-selling 1859 book *On the Origin of Species by Means of Natural Selection*. The fact that an identical theory had also been suggested by a young naturalist, Alfred Russel Wallace, is also often overlooked. But Wallace's work encouraged Darwin to complete and publish his famous book, and he was gracious enough to initially present his momentous theory as a joint paper with Wallace to the Linnean Society in 1858.

After returning from an epic round-the-world voyage on HMS *Beagle* to South America, the Galapagos Islands, New Zealand and Australia between 1831 and 1836, Darwin formulated his theory in private. Down House, near Orpington in Kent, his home for the last years of his life. Despite declining health – he regularly suffered from what he called 'stomach catastrophes' – Darwin lived happily here for 40 years with his wife Emma and their large family of ten children, sadly only seven of whom survived to their teens.

While he was writing *Origin of Species*, every day at noon Darwin would take a walk five times round on what he called The Sandwalk, but which has been known since the 1930s as his 'Thinking Path', on the western edge of his property.

Down House

He had rented a narrow strip of land at the far end of Great House Meadow in 1846 from his neighbour, the local squire Sir John Lubbock. He planted a quickset hedge and bushes and a copse of trees at the southern end with alder, birch and hornbeam. And then he had laid the stone and sand path, which was to become his Sandwalk.

To do his daily mile, Darwin would take five of the locally abundant flints and pile them up at the start, kicking or knocking one off with his iron-tipped walking stick as he duly completed five circuits of The Sandwalk. Apparently, his mischievous children would delight in hiding in the trees and, hearing him coming from the click-click of his stick, would replace the stones on the pile after their father had passed, making him think he had further to walk. Unlikely I know, but I like to think that my little flint might have been one of Darwin's stony timekeepers.

Darwin had moved with Emma, and their then two young children, to the early 18th-century Georgian Down House on the outskirts of the village rather confusingly called Downe (spelt with a final 'e') six years after his return from the *Beagle* expedition in 1842. He described the house as 'ugly, looks neither old nor new' but it was 'at the extreme verge of the world' – the perfect distraction-free environment to complete his master work.

He wasted no time in extending Down House to suit his own needs and those of his fast-expanding family. But he also used the extensive 18 acre (6ha) grounds as an outdoor laboratory, making the lawns, kitchen garden, greenhouse and adjoining hay meadow the location for many of his experiments.

Darwin was often assisted in these by his children, whom, for example, he persuaded to record the flight paths of bumblebees as they buzzed to and fro when feeding on the red clover flowers in the Great House Meadow at the rear of the house. Darwin's fifth son, Horace, also helped him by coming up with his worm stone experiment, which measured the submersion of a stationary stone as the earth around it was slowly displaced by earthworms, all carefully tracked and recorded by father and son.

Some of the results of these experiments Darwin used in his last work: *The Formation of Vegetable Mould through the Action of Worms* (1881). He concluded: 'It may be doubted if there are any other animals which have played such an important part in the history of the world as these lowly orga   d creatures'. Darwin's worm stone is still embedded in the lawn as a circular concrete disc beneath a gnarled old Spanish chestnut tree, and the measuring device is displayed inside the house.

The Walk

To follow in the hallowed footsteps of Darwin on his 'Thinking Path', walk from the house through the kitchen garden, passing the remains of his concrete tennis court and the pale blue-painted wooden greenhouses. This was where in boiler-heated conditions Darwin investigated the behaviour of insectivorous plants, such as sundews, which had also held a life-long fascination for him.

The 15 acre (5ha) Great House Meadow on your left was named after a 17th-century manor house that once stood on the site and is where Darwin studied insect and plant activity. He generously allowed the villagers to use the southern end of the meadow for their cricket field, and in 2007, English Heritage, the current owners of the house, rebuilt the pavilion, thus preserving the long association of the village with Down House.

At the end of the well-stocked and beautifully maintained kitchen garden, a gate leads left onto the famous Sandwalk. The large, grassy meadow over the hedge to your right is called Great Pucklands and on my visit it was filled with an abundance of wildflowers including the bright golden stars of buttercups and white oxeye daisies, and was attracting clouds of those transient jewels of summer, butterflies.

The trees of the copse planted by Darwin soon appear ahead, looking like a dark tunnel and described by his little

Factbox

Location: Down House is just outside the village of Downe off the A21 or A233 Bromley-Westerham road, at Luxted Road, Downe, Kent (Tel: 01689 859119; Web: www. english-heritage.org.uk/visit/ places/home-of-charles-darwin-down-house)

Postcode: BR6 7JT

Length: An easy 1 mile (1.6km), but allow plenty of time for visiting the house

Terrain: Mostly on gravelled garden paths

Map: OS 1:25,000 Explorer OL146, Dorking, Box Hill & Reigate

Refreshments: The 16th-century Queens Head at 25 High Street Downe, Orpington BR6 7US is recommended, and even has a Darwin Bar, where the great man himself was said to have drunk

☎ 01689 852145
🌐 queensheaddowne.com

Darwin's greenhouse

The garden at Down House from the veranda

granddaughter Gwen as 'truly terrifying' and 'ominous and solitary' – which I suspect is exactly what Darwin wanted as he refined his theory during his cerebral strolls. Snowdrops, bluebells, violets and primroses bloom beneath the now mature trees in springtime, and Darwin noted the unexpected appearance of long-dormant yellow-flowered charlock (field or wild mustard) in one cleared area. More recently, a rare orchid known as violet helleborine, which is solely pollinated by wasps, was found thriving in the woodland. Holly forms an abundant understorey to the now mature trees as the level path winds peacefully through them, looping back on itself at the midway point after about 400 yards (366m).

At the far end, a small white-painted shelter stands where Darwin had built a summer house. It offers a quiet place to sit and reflect on how this simple woodland walk may have inspired Darwin's world-changing 'Great Idea'.

Retrace your steps to the house, where English Heritage have done a wonderful job in restoring the ground floor rooms to closely resemble how they were when the Darwin family lived there. In the surprisingly small, north-facing Old Study – described by Darwin as 'capital' for his purposes – you can still see his horsehair-stuffed mahogany armchair, rectangular wooden Pembroke table and his writing board, pocketbooks, microscope and string box, apparently just as he left them when he was writing Origin of Species nearly two centuries ago. The pigeon-holed shelves and partitioned 'privy' to the left of the marble fireplace were probably an unconscious reminder of the five seasick-haunted years in the cramped conditions he had experienced in his tiny cabin on The Beagle.

The beautifully light and airy dining room occupies the ground floor of the three-storey bay window extension, which Darwin had built shortly after he occupied it in 1842. Originally built as a drawing room, it gives lovely views out into the garden, across the Great House Meadow and beyond. The decoration of the dining room is based closely on an 1870s photograph of the room and contemporary wallpaper pattern books. Family portraits adorn the walls and the dinner service on display is period Wedgwood, a reminder of the family links to the famous Staffordshire pottery family of which Emma was a member.

The first-floor landing at Down House is now a gallery of many of the Darwin family's watercolours and photographs, while the former bedrooms on the first floor are now taken up with a modern exhibition about Darwin's life and work.

In conclusion, it is perhaps worth reflecting that in the last lines of *On the Origin of Species*, Darwin wrote: 'There is grandeur in this view of life, with its several powers, having been originally breathed into a few forms or into one; and that, whilst this planet has gone cycling on according to the fixed law of gravity, from so simple a beginning endless forms most beautiful and most wonderful have been, and are being, evolved'.

In view of his later close association with the theory, it's strange to realise that this was the only place in the book that he used any form of the word 'evolution'.

The kissing gate at the start of Darwin's Thinking Path

10.

The city that fell into the sea: Dunwich, Suffolk

BELOW The ruins of Greyfriars Friary
RIGHT The crumbling cliffs of Dunwich

It's an apocryphal story, of course. But in the not infrequent circumstance when the wind is from the east, ice-cold and howling direct from the Urals, churning the North Sea into a raging, spume-flecked storm, it's said you can hear the muffled sound of the bells of Dunwich's drowned churches chiming their everlasting death knell beneath the angry waves.

It's highly unlikely though, not least because the bells and other valuables of the city's eight churches would have been removed long before they disappeared under the waves of this fast-eroding coastline. To give just two examples, medieval parish records state that the bells of St Nicholas Church were sold to build a groyne to protect another of the town's churches as the sea continued its remorseless advance, while the bells of All Saints were sold for £70 8 shillings (£70.40) in 1826.

But the tall tales of the 'East Anglian Atlantis' persist, and an anonymous entry in Dunwich Museum visitors' book as recently as 2017 recorded a local man twice hearing 'a peal of six chimes' at about 2am during a 'very stormy' night.

Oft gazing on thy craggy brow,
We muse on glories o'er;
Fair Dunwich; thou art lowly now,
Renowned and sought no more.

Agnes Strickland

(In case you were wondering, the single automated bell of the last remaining 19th-century church of St James only tolls the hours).

Over the centuries Dunwich – dubbed 'the city that fell into the sea' – had possibly been the site of the Roman fort of Sitomagus. It has also been identified as Domnoc, the capital of the Saxon kingdom of East Anglia, and the 7th-century base from which St Felix, first Bishop of Dunwich, converted the kingdom to Christianity. It also survived three medieval sieges and, most notably, became one of the largest and most important medieval seaports in the country.

At the time of Domesday in 1086 Dunwich was one of the largest towns in England. It was granted borough and mayoral status in charters by King John in 1199 and 1215, and by the 13th century it had become one of the greatest ports on the east coast. It was used by crusaders and later as a naval base, and it boasted hospitals, schools, a large guildhall and other grand public buildings. It was also a notable religious centre with up to 18 churches, chapels and a Franciscan friary. In the troubled reign of King Stephen, it even had its own mint. A spiked paling enclosing an area of about 800 acres (324ha), contained at least 800 taxable houses and was guarded by five sturdy gates.

The beach at Dunwich

Its 5,000 citizens grew wealthy from trade, shipbuilding and a fishing fleet that numbered 70 vessels at its height. Its population was one-sixth the size of London, and as a parliamentary borough, it became one of the most notorious of the so-called 'rotten' boroughs. It elected two Members of Parliament to the House of Commons from 1298 until 1832, when the constituency, which by then numbered just eight residents, was finally abolished by the Reform Act.

But most of Dunwich's former glories have now been lost forever under the relentless waves of the North Sea, except for the still impressive ruins of the 13th-century Greyfriars Franciscan friary, now itself teetering on the edge of the cliff, and the chapel of the medieval Leper Hospital in the churchyard of the last remaining church of St James.

Loss of land to the insatiable sea at Dunwich is recorded as early as the Domesday Book, when over half the taxable farmland was reportedly engulfed between 1066 and 1086. Further major losses were subsequently reported in the great storms of 1287, 1328 and 1347, the latter resulting in the destruction of about 400 houses in the easternmost parts of the city.

The city continued to decline after more disastrous storms in 1560 and 1570 so that by 1602, it was a quarter of its original size. Further storms in 1740 destroyed large areas of the remaining city, so that only All Saints church, one of the largest in Suffolk, remained. Photographs record the gradual but inevitable fate of the forlorn flint-faced tower and aisle of All Saints during the early 20th century, before it too disappeared over the cliff edge in December 1919.

The Walk

Dunwich today is a tiny village of just over 120 people, a few fishing boats, the 17th-century Ship Inn and a scatter of redbrick cottages. This short stroll round the village takes you to most of the remaining features of this once great but now lost medieval city.

Park at the National Trust Dunwich Beach car park and walk back up Beach Road, past the site of the original Bridge Gate to the triangle in the road. A sign on your left leads to a footpath locally known as Lover's Lane, which climbs gently uphill, eventually taking you along the wooded clifftop for about 150 yards (137m), where it enters the former churchyard of All Saints. The church was abandoned as a place of worship as early as 1758, although burials continued for several years in the churchyard. All but one of these graves eventually fell victim to erosion and now lie beneath the North Sea.

A solitary headstone, standing forlorn in a snowdrop-starred spinney, is the last surviving grave of All Saints. The

Factbox

Location: Dunwich is on the Suffolk coast between Aldeburgh and Southwold, 4 miles (6.4km) south of Blythburgh and 7 miles (11.3km) north of Leiston, signposted off the B1125

Postcode: IP17 3EN

Length: 2 miles (3.2km), but allow a leisurely 1–2 hours, depending on how many stops you make

Terrain: Easy, on lanes, field paths and ending on a shingle beach

Map: OS 1:25,000 Explorer OL231, Southwold & Bungay

Refreshments: The Ship, St James Street, Dunwich, Saxmundham IP17 3DT is a traditional English pub

☎ 01728 648219
🌐 shipatdunwich.co.uk

There are excellent fish and chips at the Flora Tea Rooms, Beach Rd, Dunwich, Saxmundham IP17 3EN

☎ 01728 648433
🌐 floratearoomsdunwich.co.uk

Or try the National Trust Tea Rooms in the former Coastguard Cottages, Minsmere Road, Dunwich, Suffolk IP17 3DJ

☎ 01728 648501
🌐 nationaltrust.org.uk/visit/suffolk/dunwich-heath-and-beach

Jacob Forster's headstone

stone is inscribed: 'In memory of JACOB FORSTER who departed this Life March 12, 1796, Aged 38 years'. Now even this last reminder is under threat as it currently lies only 10 feet (3m) from the crumbling cliff edge. Poignantly, human bones recovered from the beach have sometimes been found placed beside Jacob's gravestone.

Just inland to the west of the former churchyard stand the late 13th-century ruins of Greyfriars Friary. The friary was founded by Richard Fitzjohn and his wife Alice. When it first appears in the historical record in 1277, it was home to 20 Franciscan friars, but was already being threatened by coastal erosion

and had to be moved inland, lock, stock and barrel, in 1290. At the Dissolution of the Monasteries by Henry VIII in 1538 most of the buildings were demolished by the Bishop of Dover, and the ruins were successively used as a house, a town hall and even a gaol for offending Dunwichians.

The only remains today are the still impressive flint and mortar ruins of two splendid gatehouses, a precinct wall, and in the eastern range, some two-storey walls believed to be the remains of a cloistered building that was possibly used as a refectory or infirmary. The popular Channel 4 archaeology programme *Time Team* visited Greyfriars in 2011, and its geophysical survey revealed a range

The Napoleonic anchor outside The Ship Inn

St James Church and village sign, Dunwich

of walls. The resultant trenches also revealed examples of carved medieval stonework and fragments of window glass. The surveys suggested that the original friary church may have been up to 200 feet (61m) long, with an aisled nave and choir. But the inexorable coastal erosion still threatens Greyfriars, and today the south-east corner of the friary wall has also started to collapse down the crumbling cliff of Norwich Crag.

Walk down through the ruins to Westleton Lane and turn left for a few yards then sharp right into Sandy Lane, which leads back down into the modern village of Dunwich. On your right after about half a mile (0.8km) you'll pass the insignificant mound of Leet Hill, where justice and community affairs were conducted for the town in Anglo-Saxon times. Adjacent is the flint-faced tower of the modern parish church of St James, which was built in 1832 on the site of the former Leper Hospital of St James.

The church itself is architecturally undistinguished but it includes some good 19th-century stained glass and a truncated 1576 wall brass to Thomas Cooper, a former bailiff of Dunwich, and his family, which was recovered from All Saints Church in 1928. But the chief interest of St James lies in its churchyard, and the enigmatic ruins of the 12th-century chapel of the Leper Hospital, now a private mausoleum to the local landowning Barne family and probably the oldest building still standing from medieval Dunwich. Also standing in the eastern end of the churchyard is a Victorian cast iron pedestal and urn, probably a product of the nearby Leiston

ironworks, and an isolated flint buttress re-erected from All Saints, the last medieval church in Dunwich.

Walk down to the crossroads and turn sharp right to re-enter the village on St James Street. The Ship Inn is on your left and on your right is the village museum fronted by its huge Napoleonic era anchor, trawled up by fishermen 4 miles (6.4km) offshore, and a 17th/18th-century ship's cannon.

The museum is devoted to the fascinating history of Dunwich and is highly recommended. It was founded in 1952 by the Dunwich Town Trust, and its exhibits include the mace and seal used by the former aldermen and councillors of Dunwich, the 16th-century Town Chest, a seal from Greyfriars, pilgrim badges and a Romano-British enamelled brooch, in addition to detailed reconstructions of the lost city.

Once you reach the end of the street, you might like to walk down to the beach to do some beachcombing yourself, and to take some time to ponder on the fate of the lost city of Dunwich, now lying beneath the remorseless waves of the North Sea.

11.

Secrets of the shingle:
Orford Ness, Suffolk

BELOW The beach at Orford
RIGHT Orford Castle from the air

You're not exactly made to feel welcome as you walk along the banks of the River Alde to visit Orford Ness, the 10 mile (16km)-long shingle spit on the constantly shape-shifting Suffolk coast.

Orford Ness is without doubt one of the strangest and most unsettling places in Britain, and official signs warn you that your unauthorised presence on the Ness is prohibited under the Official Secrets Act, and that any persons found there may be arrested. The military occupation of Orford, about 15 miles (24.1km) south down the Suffolk coast from Dunwich, astonishingly goes back nearly eight centuries. And as you look out from the crenelated battlements of Orford Castle,

built by Henry II in the late 12th century, and across to the spit of Orford Ness, the sinister mushroom shapes of what became known as The Pagodas are a chilling reminder that it was also at the front line in the Cold War of the 1950s.

The inexorable forces of longshore drift that took away the crumbling cliffs and buildings of the former medieval city of Dunwich (see page 64) actually created the ever-extending shingle spit of Orford

Ness. Known locally as 'The Island', this eventually blocked the estuary of the River Alde (or Ore) and the 13th-century port of Orford, which at its height in the Middle Ages handled more trade than neighbouring Ipswich.

The noble and unique keep of Henry's castle still dominates the quiet village of Orford, its revolutionary design an unusual 18-sided polygon with three square turrets at its corners. It was built to consolidate Henry's power in the region and to try to curtail that of the truculent East Anglian barons, who were led by Hugh Bigod, Earl of Norfolk, of nearby Framlingham Castle.

One of its more unusual occupants in the 12th century was the so-called Wild Man of Orford, a rare example of what was evidently a merman as he was described by an early chronicler as 'a Fish having the shape of a man in all poyntes' – except for what should have been the obligatory tail. He was caught in the nets of local fishermen and imprisoned in Orford Castle for some time, where he was fed on fish and allowed the occasional swim in the sea. But the Wild Man escaped and was allegedly responsible for the blocking of the harbour in revenge for his incarceration.

After its capture by Prince Louis of France, who invaded England in 1216 at

the invitation of the English barons fed up with 'Bad' King John, Orford Castle gradually lost its importance, partly due to the blockage of the port by the extension of the Ness – possibly at the fins of the merman.

The first military occupation of the Ness itself was between 1913 and 1916, when the southern half of the inshore expanses of the King's Marshes were drained and levelled to make an airfield. The site received its first 'stick-and-string' biplanes from the Central Flying School's Experimental Flying Section in 1913. This marked the beginning of 70 years of intense military occupation and experimentation on the Ness, which has left behind a number of crumbling sheds, bunkers, towers and

laboratories, some of which we will visit on our walk.

It was at the height of the Cold War that the Atomic Weapons Research Establishment arrived on the Ness, when purpose-built facilities were created for evaluating parts of nuclear weapons and for environmental work on the atomic bomb. Between 1953 and 1966 the six large test cells and other buildings were built on the shifting shingle to conduct the top secret tests. Some of these tests were designed to mimic the stresses a weapon might be subjected to before detonation. Although it was always claimed that no nuclear material was involved in these tests, an initiator agent for high explosives was used, and a failure could undoubtedly have

The menacing Pagodas on Orford Ness

Ness. The AWRE finally left the site in 1971, and the Cobra Mist station closed a couple of years later. In the late 1970s and early 1980s the site and buildings were re-commissioned as the Orford Ness transmitting station. This medium wave radio station – originally run by the Foreign Office and later the BBC – transmitted the BBC World Service to continental Europe from 1982 until 2011.

When the Ness was purchased by the National Trust from the Ministry of Defence in 1993, a team of bomb disposal experts scoured the site every day for eight weeks and found nearly 800 unexploded bombs – and somewhat worryingly, they are still being found. Suddenly the warning signs by the river became more relevant. But by then the unique importance of the landscape and wildlife of the Ness was being recognised, in particular the internationally rare and extremely fragile vegetation of the coastal shingle. Today the Trust protects the Ness' natural and historic features as managers of the Orford Ness National Nature Reserve (NNR).

resulted in a catastrophic explosion. For this reason, the tests were controlled remotely, and the huge laboratories were designed to absorb an explosion in the event of an accident. Perhaps the most impressive buildings from this period are two of the test labs – the so-called 'Pagodas' – which we saw from Orford Castle, and which have become such well-known landmarks on this part of the Suffolk coast. When he visited them for his 2015 book *Coastlines*, nature writer Patrick Barkham chillingly described them as 'psychotic cathedrals of Mutually Assured Destruction'.

In the late 1960s an experimental concrete, cobweb-like, Anglo-American military radar known as Cobra Mist was also installed at the northern end of the

The windmill-like Black Beacon, built in 1928

Factbox

Location: Orford is on the B1084, about 8 miles (12.9km) from Woodbridge. The ferry runs from Quay Street, Orford. Access to Orford Ness is seasonal and not every day. Ferry crossings must be booked up to two weeks in advance. The latest information is available on the National Trust website (Tel: 01394 450900; Web: www.nationaltrust.org.uk/visit/suffolk/orford-ness-national-nature-reserve)

Postcode: IP12 2NU

Length: The recommended red route is about 5 miles (8km)

Terrain: The route is mostly on tarmac roads, but there is some walking on shingle, which can be tiring

Map: OS 1:25,000 Explorer OL212, Woodbridge & Saxmundham

Refreshments: There are of two pubs in Orford: the 400-year-old Jolly Sailor, Quay Street, Orford, Woodbridge IP12 2NU

📞 01394 450243
🌐 jollysailororford.co.uk

The Kings Head, Front Street, Orford, Woodbridge IP12 2LW

📞 01394 450271
🌐 thekingsheadorford.co.uk

The Walk

If you want to explore this unique and still somewhat scary place, you'll need to book a ferry on one of the designated open days two weeks in advance from the National Trust at Orford Quay (details in the Factbox opposite). The 200 yard (183m) boat trip across the brown waters of the River Alde (or Ore) will take you to the jetty and information point near the site of the 1913 airfield on the King's Marshes.

You now have the choice of three routes to explore Orford Ness – the main and recommended red route is about 5 miles (8km) in length but can be easily shortened at any point. You can walk this route at any time in the spring or summer, but you'll have to wait until the end of the bird breeding season for the other trails to open. Easy going mostly on tarmac roads, it passes through the site of the First World War airfield, which is now the home to many marshland birds, such as the rare and beautiful marsh harrier. There is also a resident population of the small, dog-like Chinese water deer, which escaped from local ornamental deer parks, swimming across the river to reach their new home. Marsh-loving plants found here include samphire, sea purslane, sea aster and purple sea lavender.

The route then crosses Stony Ditch on a Bailey bridge, past the former Bomb Ballistics Building, to head straight for the wild expanses of the vegetated shingle facing the North Sea. The path here is on shingle, which can get tiring, but it leads due east to the site of the former land

The track to Orford Ness lighthouse

and sea mark of the candy red-and-white striped Orford Ness lighthouse on the seashore. This iconic building was finally demolished in 2020 when it became threatened by the approaching sea. If you take the route south from here, it will take you past the sinister-looking, windmill-like Black Beacon and closest to the weird shingle-capped Pagodas, at the southernmost limit of the site.

The unique plant life on the apparently inhospitable shingle includes the purple-flowered sea pea, whose seeds are able to withstand long periods in the sea; the buttercup-yellow horned poppy; and the white florets and fleshy grey-green leaved cushions of sea kale. You may also see here some of the Ness' population of unique, unusually large brown hares, bounding across the shingle. Sometimes claimed to be a separate breed, Orford's hares exhibit a common characteristic

of many island species in that they are noticeably bigger and fatter than their mainland cousins. Or maybe it was something they'd eaten...

The blue route, a half-mile (0.8km) extension to the red one, is open seasonally once young birds have fledged from the King's Marsh, as is the peaceful but more remote 8 mile (12.9km) green route, which will take you much further out into the King's Marsh and close to the Cobra Mist site. There is no access to the Cobra Mist site, but it can be seen in the distance at the route's northernmost limit.

Orford Ness, so close to the Suffolk Coast but strictly inaccessible to the public for the last eight decades, somehow manages to retain that brooding threat of what could have been a nuclear apocalypse. And it certainly makes for one of Britain's most curious walks.

12.

Ring of ritual:
Chanctonbury Ring, West Sussex

BELOW The stunted remains of Chanctonbury's beeches
RIGHT The view across the Sussex Weald from Chanctonbury

Award-winning nature writer Robert Macfarlane had an eerie, unearthly experience when he wild camped on a still summer's evening inside the iconic landmark of Chanctonbury Ring, 790 feet (241m) up on the South Downs near Washington, West Sussex.

'I heard the first scream at around two o'clock in the morning', he recounted in *The Old Ways* (2012), an account of his pilgrimage in the footsteps of his hero, the poet Edward Thomas. 'A high-pitched and human cry, protracted but falling away in its closing phase. It came from the opposite side of the tree ring to where I was sleeping.'

'.... Then I realised, with a prickling in my shoulders and fingers, that the voices had split and were now coming towards me: still at treetop height, but circling round the tree ring, one clockwise and one anticlockwise, converging roughly on where I was lying... The cries met each other almost directly above me, twenty or thirty feet up in the dark. After fifteen minutes they stopped and eventually, uneasily, I fell back to sleep.'

Macfarlane ruled out the obvious candidates for the spine-chilling night-time shrieks: the screech of a barn owl or that of a rabbit being taken by a weasel or a fox. It was only when he got home and researched the folklore of Chanctonbury that he realised it is considered to be one of the most haunted places on the South Downs.

Arthur Beckett in his *The Spirit of the Downs* (1909) had reported that...
'If on a moonless night you walk seven times around Chanctonbury Ring without stopping, the Devil will come out of the wood and hand you a basin of soup' in payment for your soul, which to Macfarlane sounded like a poor exchange. In 1944, Frank R. Williams, writing in *Sussex Notes and Queries*, claimed that the Devilish story derived from ancient pagan worship, which may have included a ritual dance ceremony followed by a sacrificial feast.

The occultist Aleister Crowley, self-styled 'Beast 666', and his friend Victor Neuburg, who lived in Steyning 2 miles (3.2km) from Chanctonbury, were reportedly convinced that the site was a place of power due to its pre-Christian religious significance. They imagined gruesome Druidic sacrifices taking place there.

Other persistent folk stories associated with Chanctonbury include that if a childless woman slept beneath the trees for one night it would increase her chances of conception, or that if you did the seven times walk around the circle, a Druid, a lady on a white horse or the ghost of no less a figure than Julius Caesar and his Roman army would appear. At least the reasoning behind the raising of the ghost of Caesar may have some historical basis in fact because Chanctonbury is virtually unique among prehistoric hillforts in having at least two Roman temples built inside its boundaries. The only other instance of anything like this happening is at Maiden Castle near Dorchester.

Even the distinguished archaeologist Jacquetta Hawkes had to admit there was 'something magical' about the little circular and single-ramparted 3.7 acre (1.5ha) late Bronze to Iron Age hillfort at Chanctonbury. She recorded traces of a small rectangular-walled Romano-British temple dating from AD 1 or 2, complete with a central cella (inner chamber or shrine) constructed from flint and mortar.

This was the larger of the two known temples and was constructed on a west-east alignment in the centre of the fort, on the highest point of the hill. A covered walkway enclosed it on the west, north and east sides, and it was paved with a rammed chalk floor about 10 feet

Twisted beeches in Chanctonbury Ring

(3m) wide. The walkway's external wall was covered in red-painted plaster, and entered from the east, aligning it with the original entrance to the hillfort.

Since Hawkes' day, a second temple has been found about 100 feet (30m) south-west of the first one. Its remains are more fragmentary as it appears to have been dismantled after falling out of use. Apparently, it was polygonal in shape, measuring about 26 feet (8m) on each side, with a rectangular annexe on the east side that had a tessellated floor made of cubes of greensand. Judging from the discovery of numerous bone fragments from the heads and jaws of pigs, archaeologists believe the temple may have been dedicated to a boar cult.

A small rectangular structure, which may have been an oven or furnace, was also found about 16 feet (5m) to the north-east of the temple. A large circular rubbish pit nearby revealed a variety of finds, including fragments of roof tile, window glass, oyster shells, pottery sherds and coins. These show that the temples were in use for about 350 years, from the mid-1st to the late 4th centuries AD.

It is thought that the bank and ditch of the original hillfort were reused by Romano-British people to form a *temenos*, or 'sacred precinct', on the Chanctonbury hilltop. The remains of the temples survive as buried wall footings of mortared flint rubble and are not visible on the surface today.

After a few centuries of use the hillfort, which could have been a defensive position, cattle enclosure or a religious

The track to Chanctonbury

shrine, was abandoned for about 500 years until it was reoccupied during the Roman period. It now forms part of a concentration of associated historical features created over more than 2,000 years, including round barrows dating from the Bronze Age to the Saxon periods and boundary dykes dating to Iron Age and Roman times.

After its final abandonment around the late 4th century, Chanctonbury remained unoccupied save for grazing sheep and cattle. It lies within the estate of prominent local landowners, the Goring family of Wiston House, which is about a mile (1.6km) away near Steyning. The ring of beech trees that gave it its distinctive crown was planted in 1760 by the enterprising 16-year-old heir to the family estate, Charles Goring. He decided to enhance the site by planting the circumference of the hillfort with beech trees. The story is that Charles carried water up the hill each time he visited to irrigate his trees, although another and probably more accurate version is that he had his footmen climb the hill each day with buckets of water.

In 1909, the Goring family decided that it would also plant trees inside the hillfort perimeter, and quantities of Romano-British pottery and building rubble were

The sun sets over Chanctonbury

found during these preparations, leading to the discovery of the two temples and a large number of other artefacts. But unfortunately, the planting damaged the archaeology within the hillfort due to the disturbance caused by tree roots. Further damage was sustained through quarrying and the hill's use during the Second World War as an anti-aircraft gun position, when four gun emplacements were constructed within its perimeter. Damage was also caused by Army training activities, which included the digging of practice slit trenches and rubbish pits on the site.

Even more catastrophic damage was to be inflicted on the famous local landmark by the Great Storm of 16 October 1987, which destroyed about 15 million trees in southern England, including over three-quarters of Chanctonbury's iconic clump of beeches. Thankfully it was decided to replant the ring, but the new trees are only just beginning to restore the hilltop to its former sylvan glory.

The Walk

Chanctonbury Ring stands in a commanding position on the edge of a steep natural escarpment looking across the Sussex Weald to the north. The view northwards extends for over 30 miles (48.3km) as far as Leith Hill in Surrey, and southwards towards the glittering waters of the English Channel.

Nearer at hand, the trig point just below the ring is the Chanctonbury Dew Pond, a Site of Special Scientific Interest. Constructed in about 1870, it was restored by the Sussex Society of Downsmen in 1970 and is maintained by them.

You could take in another of Sussex's hillforts by extending your walk by about 4 miles (6.4km) along the chalk ridgeway to Cissbury Ring, near Findon. Cissbury hillfort is famous for the 250 Neolithic flint mines – a kind of southern Grimes Graves – which have been found inside its 60 acre (24ha) circumference. The hillfort was constructed in around 400 BC and was in use for about 300 years, and just as at Chanctonbury, there is archaeological evidence of a settlement at Cissbury during the later Roman period. A group of buildings and two rectangular enclosures have been located near the eastern entrance to the hillfort.

Factbox

Location: There are two car parks at the base of Chanctonbury Ring: to the north-east on Chanctonbury Ring Road off the A283 Washington Road, and to the west on Washington Bostal just off the A24

Postcode: BN44 3DR

Length: It's just a short climb uphill from the car parks, but the suggested extension of the walk to Cissbury Ring will add a further 4 miles (6.4km), (8 miles/12.9km, there and back) to your walk

Terrain: Easy walking on chalky paths, but a stiffish climb to the summit

Map: OS 1:25,000 Explorer Map OL10, Arundel & Pulborough

Refreshments: The Red Lion Tavern, London Road, Ashington, Pulborough RH20 3DD is a country hostelry serving real ales and traditional pub food

☎ 01903 892523
ⓦ redlionashington.co.uk

The 15th-century Chequer Inn, High Street, Steyning BN44 3RE has period rooms and a cosy restaurant

☎ 01903 814437
ⓦ chequerinn.co.uk

The restored Chanctonbury Dew Pond

THE
MIDLANDS

The rocky summit of The Wrekin

13 — Green Knight pilgrimage: Lud's Church, Staffordshire **7 miles/11.3km**	14 — All round The Wrekin: The Wrekin, Shropshire **5 miles/8km**	15 — A little bit of Old England: Laxton, Nottinghamshire **4 miles/6.4km**
16 — One man went to Mow: Mow Cop, Cheshire **5.5 miles/8.9km**	17 — The oldest castle in England? Richard's Castle, Herefordshire **1 mile/1.6km**	18 — Rock of Ages: Bradgate Park, Leicestershire **4 miles/6.4km**
19 — The hills are alive with the sound of music: Malvern Hills, Worcestershire **2 miles/3.2km**	20 — Appointment with the Devil: The Stiperstones, Shropshire **3.5 miles/5.6km**	21 — 'Sistine Chapel of the Ice Age': Creswell Crags, Derbyshire/ Nottinghamshire **1 mile/1.6km**
22 — The Lair of the White Worm: Thor's Cave, Staffordshire **3.5 miles/5.6km**		

13.

Green Knight pilgrimage:
Lud's Church, Staffordshire

The Roaches and Hen Cloud

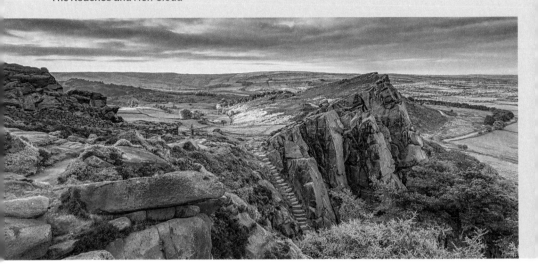

By bluffs where boughs were bare they passed,
Climbed by cliffs where the cold clung:
Under the high clouds, ugly mists
Merged damply with the moors and melted on the mountains;
Each hill had a hat, a huge mantle of mist.

Anon, 'Sir Gawain and the Green Knight' (c. 1300)

For anyone who knows the high moorlands of Staffordshire, that's a pretty accurate description of this 'Wild West' of the Peak District National Park. It is actually the account of the route of the 'comely knight' Sir Gawain and his guide, to his fateful rendezvous with the Green Knight, taken from the classic 14th-century Arthurian alliterative poem *Sir Gawain and the Green Knight*.

In a painstaking detective essay in literary geography, Prof Ralph Elliott of Keele University was able to pinpoint the scene of that monumental encounter to The Roaches in the Staffordshire Moorlands. Not only did the physical features described in the poem match the location almost uncannily, but it was also written with a native's eye for detail and in a dialect recognisably north Midland in origin.

The identity of the author, who must rank alongside Chaucer for this medieval masterpiece, has never been satisfactorily proven.

The Walk

Amazingly, you can still follow Gawain's route to the scene of the poem's dramatic beheading denouement through the Staffordshire Wildlife Trust's Roaches reserve, 4 miles (6.4km) north of Leek. The route starts between the beetling gritstone crags of The Roaches and the isolated outlier of Hen Cloud near Rockhall Cottage, where there is limited parking.

Rockhall Cottage, a former gamekeeper's hut partly built into the overhanging rocks of The Roaches, is now a climbers' bothy, rebuilt in memory of Don Whillans. Whillans has become something of a cult figure from the 'working-class revolution' in hard rock climbing of the 1950s. With friends like mountaineer Joe Brown, and equipped with nothing much more than plimsoles and allegedly their mothers' washing lines for a rope, they took the sport to new extremes of boldness and sustained difficulty. Their first ascents of climbs such as overhanging Sloth (named for the amount of time spent suspended upside down), The Mincer and Saul's Crack still test the modern rock jocks and astound passing pedestrians.

The walk makes for the col between The Roaches and Hen Cloud, the 1,345 foot (410m) summit of which looks from here like a miniature Rock of Gibraltar

Factbox

Location: The Roaches are just off the A53 Buxton to Leek road, about 4 miles (6.4km) from Leek and 9 miles from Buxton. There is limited roadside parking

Postcode: ST13 8UB

Length: The walk to Lud's Church and back is about 7 miles (11.3km); Allow at least 4 hours

Terrain: Starting with a quite strenuous moorland ridge, followed by forest paths and a short stretch of minor road

Map: OS 1:25,000 Explorer OL24, The Peak District – White Peak Area

Refreshments: The Roaches Tea Rooms, Paddock Farm, Roach Road, Upper Hulme, Leek ST13 8TY

T 01538 300345
W roachestearooms.co.uk

Ye Olde Rock Inn, Old Buxton Road, Upper Hulme, Leek ST13 8TY

T 01538 300324
W yeolderockinn.com

Or The Waterview Restaurant, Tittesworth Water Visitor Centre, Meerbrook, Leek ST13 8SW

T 01538 300180
W visittittesworth.co.uk

stranded far from the Mediterranean in the Staffordshire moors. A gentle scramble brings you to the crest of The Roaches, which get their name from the Norman-French *rochers* or rocks. These serrated summits, so well seen as you approach the Peak along the A53 Buxton road from Leek, must surely be the '...great crooked crags, cruelly jagged, the bristling barbs of rock seemed to brush the sky', described by the poet as Gawain sought out the Green Chapel. Here, he was due to face the Green Knight exactly a year after he had perhaps unwisely accepted the challenge for a return match after Gawain had beheaded him with a well-swung axe at a Christmas feast at the Camelot court of King Arthur.

This part of Staffordshire is as rich in myths and legends as the frequent mists that descend on these spiky summits. There are stories of a headless rider and a tall man dressed in green, which could all be folk recollections of the Gawain story.

Nearing the 1,675 foot (511m) summit of The Roaches ridge, with its fine views across the pastoral Cheshire plain to the glittering mirror of Tittesworth Reservoir and the glimmer of the distant River Mersey, you pass the dark, peaty hollow containing the murky waters of Doxey Pool. Inevitably Doxey Pool, which is said to be bottomless and have no inlet nor outlet, has attracted its share of legends. It's supposed to be the home of Jenny Greenteeth, a seductive siren or mermaid who tempted passing travellers to a watery grave. In 1949, a woman named Florence Pettitt claimed she saw a 'blue nymph' emerge from the pool, just before she was about to take her usual morning swim. The word 'doxey' refers to a harlot or prostitute in the local dialect, and it is thought that Christians used it to denigrate the Celtic goddess Brigid, in attempts to undermine her pagan power and influence. A cup has been carved into a gritstone boulder on the shore, which may have had herbs placed in it

The steps leading down to Lud's Church

A distant view of Shutlingsloe

as offerings to the spirit of the pool. Even today, flowers are occasionally left there.

The way now leads down a partly paved path through weirdly eroded pinkish gritstone tors to the road at Roach End, which is crossed, and a stile taken on the left leading down through scrubby birches into a beech-shaded bower, marking the entrance to Back Forest.

According to that unknown poet, 'Wonderfully wild was their way through the woods', and Gawain and his guide saw:

Brooks burst forth above them,
boiling over their banks
And showering down sharply in
shimmering cascades.

The description matches perfectly as the path descends to Forest Bottom, through the stately oaks, pines and beeches of Forest Wood to the dashing waters of the Black Brook, which joins the infant River Dane at Castor's Bridge. There's evidence here of the remains of a former smithy, which could have been where Gawain

heard a 'barbarous' noise, 'As if a great scythe were being ground on a grindstone'.

Now his way, and ours, leads up an engineered path through the trees to Castle Cliff Rocks, surely another candidate for those 'bristling barbs of rock' which had 'seemed to brush the sky'. Just up from here on the upper path lies the secret chasm of Lud's Church, Elliott's firm favourite for the legendary Green Chapel of the poem. It is much easier to find today thanks to waymarking, but when I first rediscovered it nearly 50 years ago, the way in was blocked by a fallen rock, since demolished by the National Park authority on the grounds of public safety.

Sir Gawain's 'hideous oratory',

... had a hole in each end and
on either side,
And was overgrown with grass in
great patches.
All hollow it was within, only
an old cavern
Or the crevice of an ancient crag...

ABOVE Inside Lud's Church (can you see the profile of the Green Knight?)

Lud's Church has a recorded history that also goes back to the 14th century, when Lollards held their illicit services here, far from the prying eyes of the authorities. Indeed, it was their leader, Walter de Ludank, who is thought to have given his name to the place. The legend is that his daughter, Alice, was mistakenly killed here when troops interrupted a service, and her tormented ghost is said to haunt the ravine.

Gawain could not explain it, but Lud's Church, although once marked on OS maps as a cave, is actually a huge dog-legged landslip formed in the uppermost gritstones of the now-forested valley of the Dane. About 50 feet (15m) deep and around 100 yards (91m) long, it is still an unaccountably eerie and spooky place, whose constantly wet walls drip with festooning mosses, ferns and grasses. It certainly retains its atmosphere of foreboding today, when even school parties troop through it in hushed, almost reverential tones.

See if you can spot the craggy, natural profile of the helmeted 'face' of the Green Knight at the upper end of the chasm, as I did on my first visit. I think I was the first to see it with my photographer friend Mike Williams, but since we revealed his presence, many hundreds more have seen and photographed it.

A pleasant way back to Rockhall Cottage is to climb up through the woodland and heather, bizarrely once occupied by herds of red-necked wallabies and yaks that escaped from the private zoo of the Brocklehurst family of nearby Swythamley Hall. Formerly a monastic grange and now a late 18th-century private country house, Swythamley is a candidate for Bertilak de Hautdesert's 'comeliest castle that ever a knight owned', where Gawain stayed before his fateful encounter with the Green Knight (who eventually turned out to be Bertilak himself, bewitched by Morgan le Fay). So perhaps it was appropriate then that for a decade up until 1987, Swythamley Hall became a training centre for Maharishi Mahesh Yogi's now-discredited Transcendental Meditation movement.

Reaching the ridge top you will be greeted with views of 'Cheshire's Matterhorn', the shapely cone of 1,660 foot (506m) Shutlingsloe, and a path which leads steadily back down to Roach End, then it's an easy level mile (1.6km) along the road that runs beneath The Roaches to return to your car.

14.

All round The Wrekin:
The Wrekin, Shropshire

A sunset view from the summit of The Wrekin

Walkers and climbers from the Midlands speeding west past Telford on the M54 towards Snowdonia always look out for the shaggy, wooded slopes of The Wrekin, towering away to the south.

But this modest 1,335ft (407m) summit is usually ignored by those seeking the greater heights and challenges provided by Welsh rock – it has become merely a gigantic milestone on the road to Wales. But by dismissing it so easily, those summit-baggers are missing one of the finest viewpoints not just in the Midlands, but in the whole of England.

Vincent Waite, author of *Shropshire Hill Country* (1970), was of the opinion that if

you climb no other hill in Shropshire, you must climb The Wrekin. Local writer HW Timperley agreed, reckoning that to the people of Shropshire, The Wrekin was 'as much a spirit as a hill', and 'when you go to it, the underlying mood or feeling is that of a pilgrimage'.

The Wrekin is both the symbol and the icon of the county, in much the same way that Yr Wyddfa has become the symbol of the Snowdonia National Park further west along the M54. If Shropshire had the honour of its own coin, The Wrekin would have to be on it. 'To all friends round The Wrekin' is still the rousing toast heard among Shropshire folk, and it remains the nostalgic symbol of home for all exiled Salopians.

The reason for all this affection for what is, after all, not even the highest summit in this beautiful border county, is that The Wrekin, which always proudly and significantly carries the definite article, is undoubtedly a hill with a presence. It rises so sharply and unexpectedly from the pastoral Severn Plain that it literally forces you to notice it.

There are few mountains, let alone hills, in Britain that have exerted the same powerful influence or sense of place on their surrounding communities. Perhaps Glastonbury Tor, towering over the willow-dotted Somerset Levels, or the volcanic plug of Arthur's Seat in Edinburgh, provide the nearest parallels.

Geologically speaking, The Wrekin is formed of some of the oldest rocks in Britain, and indeed the world. The lovely, purple-pink and green pastel shades of the Cambrian and Precambrian rocks date back to the very dawn of Earth, perhaps as much as 2,000 million years. In the case of the fossil-free Pre-Cambrian, that is before evidence of life itself.

The Wrekin takes its name from the British name of the Roman town of Wroxeter, known to the Romans as *Viroconium*, the still impressive remains of which lie about 5 miles (8km) to the west. The British people living near here were known as the Wrocensaetan, or the people of The Wrekin, and the earthworks that surround its airy summit enclose a 20 acre (8ha) hillfort dating from the Iron Age. You can imagine the Wrocensaetan watching in wonderment as the Romans constructed their ruler-straight imperial highway of Watling Street (now the A5) across the lowlands beneath. English Heritage have recently opened a new visitor centre on the site of the Roman town. For more information visit: www.english-heritage.org.uk/visit/places/wroxeter-roman-city.

You might expect a hill like The Wrekin to attract its fair share of legends, and you'll not be disappointed. Perhaps the most popular folk story of its origin involves a wicked Welsh giant (or in some versions The Devil) who had a grudge against the people of the county town of Shrewsbury. He set off with a great load of earth with which he intended to dam the River Severn and so flood the town and drown all its inhabitants. On his way, he met a cobbler carrying over his shoulder a sackful of boots to repair, and he asked him directions to Shrewsbury. The cobbler, realising the giant's evil intention, claimed that he'd just walked from Shrewsbury himself, and had worn out his entire load of boots in so doing. The giant groaned in despair and dumped his load of earth where he stood, thus forming The Wrekin.

Another legend tells of two warring giants who were building The Wrekin from soil they had dug from the bed of the River Severn. They quarrelled and one killed the other, burying him under the northern outlier of Ercall Hill from whence, it is said, he can still be heard groaning in the dead of night.

The Walk

We start our ascent of The Wrekin in the shadow of Ercall Hill, where there is limited lay-by parking at Forest Glen or in the disused quarry on Ercall Lane. Walk south on the lane, which links Cluddley and Little Wenlock, for about a mile (1.6km) until you see a stile on the right leading by the side of Wenlock Wood towards the wooded eastern slopes of The Wrekin.

The woodland path crosses a farm track and eventually you reach a broad forest track, which is followed left for about half a mile (0.8km) through avenues of stately beeches around the base of the hill. At a junction of paths at Little Hill, marked by a prominent yew tree, turn right and start the steep climb through the trees directly up the south-western spur of The Wrekin.

You will soon emerge from the trees on the broad, stony track formed of those ancient rocks, and head for the obvious rocky outcrop known as the Needle's Eye. Legend has it that this cleft in the rocks was caused when one of those warring giants threw his spade into the ground. There is a direct route from Eaton Constantine to the summit through this narrow slit, but it is only for the experienced scrambler.

You feel like you are on the roof of the Midlands, and the 360-degree view from the summit of The Wrekin, complete with toposcope, is breathtaking and said to

On the way to The Wrekin

Factbox

Location: The Wrekin lies about 5 miles (8km) west of Telford, on the minor road between Cluddley and Little Wenlock. Our walk starts in the shadow of Ercall Hill, where there is limited lay-by parking at Forest Glen or in the disused quarry on Ercall Lane

Postcode: TF6 5AL

Length: About 5 miles (8km); allow 3 hours

Terrain: Easy woodland walking, followed by a stiffish climb to the summit

Map: OS 1:25,000 Explorer OL242, Telford, Ironbridge & The Wrekin

Refreshments: The Huntsman of Little Wenlock, Wellington Road, Little Wenlock, Telford TF6 5BH

☏ 01952 503300
🌐 thehuntsmanoflilllewenlock.co.uk

The 'forest-fleeced' Wrekin

take in no less than 17 counties. In clear conditions, you should be able to make out the blue outline of the Malvern Hills 40 miles (64.4km) to the south; the neighbouring Shropshire summits of the Clee Hills, wooded Wenlock Edge and the whaleback of the Long Mynd, fronted by the shark's tooth of Caer Caradoc to the south-west; and the misty shapes of the Berwyns, the first hills of Wales, filling the western horizon 30 miles (48.3km) away.

Nearer at hand due south are the smoking cooling towers and chimney at Buildwas, which stand at the entrance to the Severn Gorge with Coalbrookdale and Iron Bridge, birthplaces of the Industrial Revolution, just downstream.

The well-trodden track now leads gradually down towards the northern end of the hill, passing a radio mast and through first Heaven's Gate and then Hell's Gate, which mark the entrances to the Iron Age hillfort that rings the summit. Significantly perhaps, it is Heaven's Gate which is the narrower.

Dropping down off the hill, you descend through the trees of Housman's 'forest-fleeced' Wrekin, past a cottage to return to Ercall Lane. Follow this back to the start near the small reservoir at the foot of Lawrence Hill, the third of the named Wrekin foothills.

15.

A little bit of Old England:
Laxton, Nottinghamshire

The tower of the parish church watches over Laxton village

It comes as a bit of a surprise to come across the broad, open fields of Laxton, to the east of Ollerton in north Nottinghamshire. All around are the hawthorn-hedged, tightly enclosed fields so typical of the Midland shires, punctuated here and there by copses of trees that often provide the last refuges for wildlife.

But as you climb up from the flood plain of the Trent to reach Laxton, which stands at just under 300 feet (91m), it feels as if you have been suddenly transported from the East Midlands to the prairies of East Anglia. Horizons broaden, the hedges disappear, and the sky opens up as you step back a thousand years into a unique little bit of Old England.

Laxton is the only village in the UK that still practises the open field system of agriculture, common throughout the country during the Middle Ages. This amazing survival is thought to be due to the two major landowners in the area, Earl Manvers and the Earl of Scarborough, failing to reach an agreement on how and where the enclosures should take place during the early 19th century.

Although some partial enclosure occurred by the start of the 20th century, Laxton's importance as a unique historical landscape was recognised, and the emphasis changed to the preservation of the old system, encouraged by a Higher Level Countryside Stewardship scheme set up by the Court Leet and Natural England.

Laxton (or Laxintune, or Lexington as it has also been known) was already a well-established village by the time of the Norman Conquest. Roman remains have been found at Fiddler's Balk in the West Field, and many of the names still in use, such as toft, flatt, gate and syke, are all of Danish origin, showing that Scandinavian invaders also left their mark on this ancient landscape. The name comes from the Old English and means 'the settlement of Leaxa's people'.

In William the Conqueror's great land register, the Domesday Book of 1086, 'Laxintune' is shown to be a cultivated and populous village, consisting of an adult population of around 35 villeins and serfs (including, unusually, one female serf or ancilla), supporting a total population of perhaps 100-120 people. The Domesday entry also shows that the people of Laxton were cultivating about 720 acres (291ha) of arable land, with about 40 acres (16ha) of pasture for mowing, and woodland providing pannage (acorns and beechmast) for pigs, and for fuel and building timber.

The well-preserved earthworks of the Norman motte and bailey castle on the northern edge of the village date from the late 11th century and feature an

A sign points towards Laxton's open fields

unusual extra cone on the summit of the 'motte', the mound on which the original timber tower was built. It was from here that the 'Bad' King John of 1066 and All That enjoyed many weeks of hunting in the royal Forest of Sherwood, although whether he had any encounters with his traditional local enemy, Robin Hood, is not recorded. What is recorded is that King John signed documents while staying at Laxton on several occasions from 1205 to 1213.

One of these, dated 1207, shows that the serfs and villeins of Laxton must have done something to seriously upset the notoriously bad-tempered monarch. It records that: 'The men of Laxton had...to give the lord the King 100 pounds to have the King's peace, and to spare their town from being burnt to the ground'.

The castle was also the home of one of history's most impressive but least known female leaders: Matilda of Laxton, Constable and Keeper of the King's Forest of Sherwood. During the First Baron's War, which took place following the signing of the Magna Carta from 1215 to 1217, Matilda and another female leader, Nicholaa de la Haye, Constable of Lincoln Castle, were key figures in the loyalist side against the barons, who wanted to replace John with a French prince. When Lincoln Castle was besieged by the rebels in 1217, Matilda and her Saxons acted as scouts for the loyalists, safeguarding access to the castle. This ultimately allowed the English army to relieve the castle and break the siege.

Laxton Castle later proved to be a popular lodge for a succession of medieval monarchs who hunted in Sherwood Forest, which was then populated by herds of deer and wild boar, and packs of wolves. Other royal visitors to Laxton Castle included Henry II and Edward I. The castle fell into decay in the 14th century, but the Roos family built a three-gabled manor house, now also since disappeared, to the south of the site in the 17th century. Today, there are spectacular views from the tree-topped motte across the marching pylons towards the great billowing cauldrons of the power stations of the Trent Valley to the east, and over the village of Laxton and its West Field.

The village's open field system was probably already in place by the time of Domesday. Basically, it relies on a three-field rotation system, where every year, one field is sown with winter wheat, the second a spring-sown crop such as barley, and the third is left fallow. All village farmers have the right to use the land in strips or furlongs in the three great open fields of Laxton: the West Field, the Mill Field and the South Field.

Uniquely, Laxton's open field system is still administered by the Court Leet, a form of manorial government that survives from medieval times. On Jury Day, usually held in December, an inspection is made of the open fields, checking that everything is in order. This is followed a week later by the Court Leet held in the Dovecote Inn, where officials and a new jury are appointed and, where deemed necessary, fines are imposed.

An aerial view of the remains of Laxton's Norman castle

The Walk

Our walk starts from the village car park, near the Visitor Centre. Turn left onto the road past the Dovecote Inn, passing the site of the walled pinfold (for impounding stray animals) in Kneesall Road. Bear right at the junction with the Moorhouse Road and after about 200 yards (183m) turn right by the second wooden footpath sign onto the broad, muddy trackway known as the Langsyke ('long stream' in Old English).

This leads up through a gate and an avenue of young beeches into a holloway and out onto Mill Field, the largest of the three great open fields of Laxton. In the summer, if the field is in arable use, you will be able to see different crops growing in the separate strips, and there are fine views right back towards the village and the church tower.

Ascend the broad green headland for about 500 yards (457m), towards a prominent interpretive sign from which views extend, on a clear day, as far as the triple towers of Lincoln Cathedral, about 20 miles (32.2km) away to the east. Turn sharp right at this junction onto a metalled farm track, which leads out to the Ollerton Road. This is crossed and you follow a grassy, often wet holloway, turning right at the junction with another towards the end of the main street of the village, with the church tower ahead.

Factbox

Location: Laxton is about 5 miles (8km) east of Ollerton, just off the A6075 Ollerton-Tuxford road

Postcode: NG22 0NX

Length: About 4 miles (6.4km)

Terrain: Mainly on field paths and holloway lanes, which can be very wet and muddy, especially after rain

Map: OS 1:25,000 Explorer OL271, Newark-on-Trent

Refreshments: Good pub food can be obtained at the Dovecote Inn, Crosshill House, Laxton, Newark NG22 0SX

☎ 01777 871586
🌐 thedovecoteinnlaxton.co.uk

A holloway near Laxton

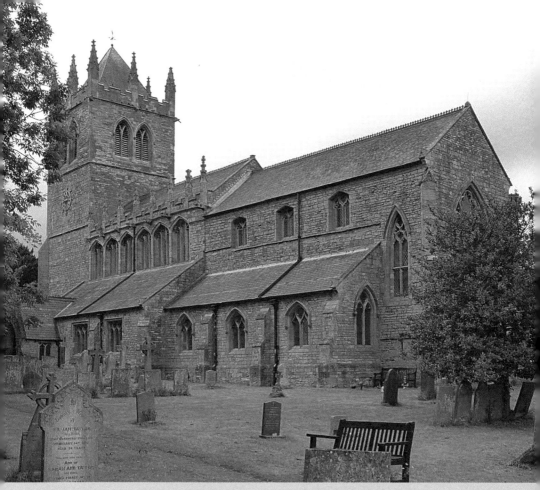

The pinnacled tower of the 13th-century church of St Michael the Archangel, Laxton

Just before reaching the street, turn left onto a farm track. After about 150 yards (137m), leave the track, turning left over a stile by a footpath sign partly hidden by the hedge. Cross another stile, which leads across the West Field via Hall Lane, another wet, deeply hedged green track. Follow the lane for about 500 yards (457m), where a gate and sign leads left across a field towards the earthworks of the castle, once the home of Matilda, surrounded by ageing hawthorn trees.

Retrace your steps to the lane, where you go straight ahead, arriving back into the village nearly opposite the church. The beautiful, Decorated, mainly 13th-century Parish Church of St Michael the Archangel had, like the castle, fallen into disuse and impious neglect until it was remodelled by Earl Manvers, the lord of the manor, in 1854. He dismantled and rebuilt the tower, shortening the nave by one bay. Note the grotesque gargoyles on the battlements of the nave, and the remains of a medieval preaching cross in the churchyard.

Turn left here to walk down the Main Street and back to the Dovecote Inn. If you have time, the National Holocaust Centre and Museum (formerly the Beth Shalom Holocaust Centre) in Acre Edge Road, Laxton is also well worth a visit.

16.

One man went to Mow:
Mow Cop, Cheshire

BELOW The Old Man of Mow
RIGHT The romantic folly that tops Mow Cop

One cold May Sunday in 1807, a Stoke-on-Trent wheelwright named Hugh Bourne climbed to the windswept 1,165ft (355m) summit of Mow Cop, on the borders of Staffordshire and Cheshire, to launch the Primitive Methodist movement.

Bourne and his friend William Clowes of Burslem were anxious to return to a far simpler form of religious observance, and they invited a number of like-minded friends to that first 'camp meeting' of the new order, an offshoot of Wesleyan Methodism. The meeting, held in a field at School Farm, south-west of the hill top and attended by 4,000 people, is said to have lasted for between 12 and 14 hours. It was the precursor of many similar mass gatherings on this well-known viewpoint.

In their *New History of Methodism* (1909) John Townsend, HB Workman and George Eayrs explained: 'Men naturally turn to Mow Cop rather than to Norton (scene of the third Methodist camp meeting, now a neighbourhood of Stoke-on-Trent) for there is more to engage and impress the imagination in the former...'

Primitive Methodism was guided by Bourne's equal and burning concerns for the spiritual salvation and the social

welfare of ordinary working people. In the face of stubborn establishment opposition, Bourne promoted working-class education – including instruction in 'the Three R's' (reading, writing and arithmetic) – in addition to religious studies at the Primitive Methodist Sunday Schools.

This socialist attitude was reflected in the fact that many early trade union pioneers were drawn from the ranks of Primitive Methodist preachers, and a basic 'welfare state' operated among chapel goers, their families and friends. And in common with some other non-conformists, Bourne always accepted women as of equal status to men by, among other things, appointing women preachers.

While he was still working as a wheelwright, Bourne built a chapel at Harriseahead, north of Stoke on-Trent, with his own money and found time to conduct similar meetings all over Britain and as far away as the United States. Before his death in 1852 at the age of 80, he had seen over 5,000 chapels established, including the large red-brick building in the village of Mow Cop in 1860, and a total congregation of Primitive Methodists of over 100,000 souls extending far beyond the British

The memorial stone marking the birth of Methodism at Mow Cop

Isles to Canada, the USA, Australia, New Zealand, Nigeria and South Africa. By the time of his death, Bourne was regarded as a father figure for the movement and his funeral procession was attended by more than 16,000 people.

Over 70,000 of Bourne's disciples gathered to worship at Mow Cop for a centennial meeting in 1907 at what had become their 'Holy Mount'. A typically rugged memorial stone on the hillside, inscribed 'to the Glory of God', was unveiled by the president of the Methodist Conference in May 1948 and records the beginning of the religious revival of Primitive Methodism on the spot 141 years before. In 1932, the movement merged with the parent church by an act of union, and five years later, over 10,000 Methodists attended a service at Mow Cop when the summit was formally handed over to its present owners, the National Trust.

Mow Cop is the southernmost gritstone outcrop in Cheshire and is certainly an inspiring and inspirational place. It has extensive westward views over the broad Cheshire Plain as far as the Berwyn Mountains of North Wales, north-east to the hills of the Peak District and south as far as the dark conifers of Cannock Chase

and the dim outlines of the Shropshire Hills. Nearer at hand the huge, usually upturned white saucer of the Jodrell Bank Radio Telescope is prominent in the broad green plain below, with the tower blocks of Stockport and Manchester in the north, beyond wooded Alderley Edge, and the airliners coming in and out of Manchester's international airport.

The strange mock-Gothic folly castle that tops the hill was built in 1754 by the local squire, Randle Wilbraham, to adorn the eastern skyline as seen from his home 3 miles (4.8km) to the west at Rode Hall. The folly takes the form of a two-storey circular tower alongside a Gothic-arched curtain wall, which steps down the hillside. Wilbraham used the tower when it was roofed as a summerhouse, gazebo or prospect tower for guests visiting his home in the plain below – literally the monarch of all he surveyed.

Before that, the prominent hilltop of Mow Cop had been used as the site for a beacon, lit to warn of the coming of the Spanish Armada in 1588, linking The Wrekin in Shropshire to the north with the next beacon south, on Alderley Edge.

The nearby gritstone quarries just to the north of the tower contain an isolated leaning tower left by the quarrymen and known as the Old Man of Mow. It is strange how many prominent British hills – such as the Old Man of Coniston in the southern Lake District and the Old Man of Storr on Skye – take the epithet 'Old Man'. Perhaps it is a recognition of the measure of affection that local people have for these important and familiar local landmarks.

The Walk

Our walk starts at the car park near the summit and descends through woodland to the Ackers Wood railway crossing in the plain below the hill, following the towpath of the Macclesfield Canal, before climbing up to Mow Cop again via the hamlet of Mount Pleasant.

From the car park, head north for a few yards following the Gritstone Way and Mow Cop Trail signs on the broad track towards residential Wood Street. Turn right on crossing the road and then immediately left, where a signpost points towards the Old Man of Mow.

Take this track, which leads past the strange pinnacle of the Old Man on the right, and in a few yards, just before an ugly radio mast, a yellow waymark points downhill to the left, across a muddy field and then steeply down through the oaks and hollies of Roe Park Woods. Emerging from the woodland at a stile, bear right around a farm to eventually reach a metalled lane, which leads to the Ackers railway crossing.

Take care crossing the line and enter Yew Tree Lane, turning right at the junction into New Road to reach the bridge over the Macclesfield Canal. Descend left down to the towpath on the far side of the bridge (No 85).

Turn right and follow the canal towpath south for about 1.5 miles (2.4km), with the tower of Mow Cop prominent on the hill away to the left and passing the fine, red-brick Georgian façade of Ramsdell Hall on the opposite bank. Just past the Heritage Narrow Boats Marina at Kent Green, take the stile on the right just before bridge No 87 and turn left on reaching the road. Follow this road under the railway line and up the hill towards the village of Mount Pleasant. At the top of the hill, the road (Mount Pleasant Road) turns sharply right. After about 100 yards (90m) take the track on the left known as The Brake.

Factbox

Location: The National Trust car park is beneath the folly at Mow Cop, which is about 2 miles (3.2km) west of Biddulph

Postcode: ST7 3PA

Length: About 5.5 miles (8.9km)

Terrain: The walk involves a descent and ascent of about 600 feet (182m) and is mainly on field and woodland paths, lanes and canal towpaths. The paths, especially when descending to the canal, can get very muddy

Map: OS 1:25,000 Explorer OL258, Stoke-on-Trent & Newcastle-under-Lyme

Refreshments: Try the thatched and unusually named Bleeding Wolf, 121 Congleton Road N, Scholar Green, Stoke-on-Trent ST7 3BQ

☎ 01782 782272
🌐 bleedingwolf.pub

17.

The oldest castle in England?
Richard's Castle, Herefordshire

Richard's Castle standeth on the top of a very rocky hill, well wooded. The keep, the walls and the tower yet stand but are going to ruin.
John Leland, *Itinerary* **(c. 1538)**

BELOW A half-timbered house in Richard's Castle
RIGHT The ruined walls of Richard Scrob's castle

The ruins of what is claimed to be the oldest castle in England, built by a Norman knight before the Conquest, stands on the summit of a hill to the north-east of the village of Richard's Castle in the old county of Herefordshire. The castle enjoyed commanding and strategic views south over the Teme valley to the Malvern Hills and west to the Black Mountains. It is situated next to the beautiful, but now redundant, 12th-century church of St Bartholomew.

Richard's Castle was certainly one of the earliest Marcher castles, built in the mid-11th century by Richard Scrob (or Fitz Scrope), most probably Sheriff of Worcester and a bodyguard to the Saxon King Edward the Confessor, to defend the Anglo-Welsh border. Richard was a Norman knight who had been granted lands in Herefordshire, Worcestershire

and Shropshire by King Edward as recorded in the Domesday Book. He built the castle ,which takes his name, sometime before the year 1051.

The castle was originally of the motte and bailey type of construction, one of only three or four castles of this type known to be built in England before the

Protective walls

Conquest. The vast majority were built by the Norman overlords to overawe the native population after the Conquest. After being crowned King of England on Christmas Day 1066, William the Conqueror returned to Normandy, leaving his brother Odo and his cousin William Fitz Osbern as governors of England, with orders to build strong castles in suitable places. It is believed that in the first 20 years of William's reign, as many as 700 motte and bailey castles were built throughout England.

Soon after Richard's Castle was built, Edric Silvaticus, better known to later generations as Edric the Wild (see also the Stiperstones walk, page 120), was attacked and had his lands ravaged by the Norman garrison of Hereford alongside Richard Scrob and his retinue. The strange thing about this is that Edric had recently submitted to the Conqueror. Possibly, he had gone back on his word when reaching the Marches and was still loyal to the old order that had perished with King Harold at Hastings, and Richard was therefore instructed to attack Edric as a traitor. As Edric's lands lay mainly around Wigmore and Clun we can be sure that Richard used his castles along the Teme valley as strategic bases during this campaign. However, the Norman attacks did not prove successful, and they suffered great losses.

An old cast iron milepost in Richard's Castle

In 1067 Edric summoned the Welsh kings Bleddyn of Gwynedd and Rhiwallon of Powys to form a united front against his bitter Norman enemies. The allies laid waste to Herefordshire and attacked Hereford Castle, inflicting serious injury to many of the castle garrison, but without overthrowing the castle.

Whichever side Edric was on, by 1067 he certainly became a veritable thorn in the side of King William over the next two years. His position in the west was gradually contained until 1070, when he surrendered to William, who then rather opportunistically made use of his military prowess in his wars on the Continent. But it is thought Edric may have finished his days in a royal prison after rebelling with his lord, Earl Roger of Hereford,

and defending Wigmore Castle against Ralph Mortimer, who was fighting for the king.

Today Richard's venerable castle is mainly reduced to earthworks and crumbling, ivy-covered and overgrown foundations. The original polygonal keep stood on the steep-sided motte or mound, which is still visible. The keep was 44 feet (14.4m) in diameter and had walls that were 12 feet (4m) thick. A D-shaped forebuilding, probably reached via a semi-circular barbican, faced east into the extended, kidney-shaped bailey. The bailey wall still stands 20 feet (6m) high in places and there are remains of several towers and an early gatehouse around the perimeter, which may have enclosed a later failed medieval township.

The castle was built on a solid rock foundation as can be seen in the rock-cut ditch around it. The motte ditch within the bailey was filled in during the 12th century. The bailey was entered from a large outer ward, which may have included what is now the bell tower of the church as a gate tower to the south-east. Subsequently a curtain wall was added to the north and south, which also contained small D-shaped towers.

The final addition to the castle site was a rectangular keep-like structure, possibly built after the original keep had collapsed or become unsafe. This measured 45 x 33 feet (14 x 10m) and had an internal spiral staircase in its south-western corner as well as garderobes. It would have been similar in size to the keeps at Criccieth and Dolwydellan in Gwynedd, and Hopton in Shropshire.

Richard was last mentioned in 1067 when his castle passed to his son, Osbern Fitz Richard, who married Nesta, the daughter of King Gruffydd ap Llywelyn of Wales. Osbern died around 1137 and was succeeded by his grandson, Osbern Fitz Hugh, who died in 1187. Richard's Castle then passed to his marital brother-in-law, Hugh de Say, who died in 1190, leaving the barony to his son, another Hugh Say, eventually passing the castle out of the line of direct descent from Richard Scrob.

In 1196 Hugh Say fought at the battle at New Radnor and it is believed he was killed there, his castles eventually passing to Robert de Mortimer of Attleborough. In 1264 his son, Hugh Mortimer, was forced to surrender himself and Richard's Castle to Simon de Montfort, 6th Earl of Leicester. His grandson, the last Hugh Mortimer of Richard's Castle, was apparently poisoned by his wife in 1304.

The castle then passed to the Talbots through Richard Talbot's marriage to Joan Mortimer. In December 1329, Joan, the late wife of Richard Talbot, had noted in the Patent Rolls that she planned to leave Richard's Castle to John de Wotton, chaplain, and William Balle of Underlith. However, the Talbots were still living there in the late 14th century, but by the 16th century and Leland's visit quoted above, it was in ruins.

The adjacent church of St Bartholomew was founded either by Richard Scrob or his son and the chancel was probably built around 1362. The north transept

The interior of St Bartholomew's Church

All Saints Church, Richard's Castle

was the Chantry Chapel of the local Knights Templar and was consecrated in 1351. The south aisle was built between 1310 and 1320 and there is a detached plaster-rendered bell tower, one of few in the county, which dates from the early 14th century and once possibly formed part of the defences of the adjacent castle.

Inside, the church has hardly changed since Georgian times. Its muted pastel colours and striking architectural details make this building an atmospheric haven of peace and quiet. The furnishings include Georgian box pews, a gallery and a 17th-century canopied box pew for the

Salweys, latterly Lords of the Manor of Richard's Castle. It is still used by them at the two or three services held in the church each year.

The modern parish church of All Saints is situated to the north of the village at Batchcott, across the border in what used to be Worcestershire. Designed by the notable Victorian architect Norman Shaw and opened in 1892, it is a Grade I listed building. In a nice gesture to the past, the flowing window tracery was copied from the former parish church of St Bartholomew and the reredos is a masterpiece in medieval Burgundian style by Charles Edgar Buckeridge.

The Walk

To reach the castle, turn off the main road at the corner with The Castle Inn. Walk up the hill until you get to the church. There is a path that takes you into the churchyard via a gate. As you walk up this, turn left and follow the path down the graveyard, and you will find yourself at the castle remains.

Allow plenty of time to visit the old church and to wander round the remains of this unique ancient fortification, built by a Norman knight before William the Conqueror invaded England on the date that every schoolchild remembers.

Factbox

Location: Richard's Castle is on the Herefordshire/Shropshire border, about ten minutes' drive from Ludlow on the B4361

Postcode: SY8 4EL

Length: 1 mile (1.6km), there and back; allow about 1 hour

Terrain: Easy going but sometimes overgrown paths

Map: OS 1:25,000 Explorer No 203, Ludlow

Refreshments: The Castle Inn, Castle Road, Richard's Castle, Ludlow SY8 4EW is at the start of the walk and has a welcoming public bar – complete with a real fire

☏ 01584 831678

The track to Richard's Castle

18.

Rock of Ages: Bradgate Park, Leicestershire

BELOW 'Little Matlock,' Bradgate Park
RIGHT Former home of the 'Queen for Nine Days'. The ruins of Bradgate House

Few motorists even notice it as they speed headlong north from the capital on the M1 motorway. But as the road climbs to reach its highest point between Junction 22 and 23 to the north of Leicester, it passes through a shallow rocky cutting.

The pale pastel colours of the slaty Precambrian bedrocks – among the oldest anywhere in the world – are exposed in the walls on either side, decorated by a necklace of golden-yellow gorse bushes and the usual motorway detritus.

The Precambrian era marks the very dawning of life on our planet, dating from around 4.6 billion to about 500 million years ago. It received its name because

it came before the Cambrian era, which in turn takes its name from the Latin for Wales, where the stratified rocks from this period were first identified.

Astonishingly, the Precambrian period accounts for nearly 90 per cent of the Earth's geological time, but in Britain, its complex-structured rocks only surface here in what was the medieval Charnwood Forest, in Pembrokeshire

and Anglesey in Wales, in the North West Highlands of Scotland, and in the Yorkshire Dales, Shropshire Hills (see pages 89 and 120) and Malvern Hills (see page 114).

It was among these ancient rocks of Leicestershire where TV naturalist Sir David Attenborough's love of nature first blossomed. David was six when he moved to Leicester when his father, Frederick, became principal of Leicester University College. David lived on campus for the next 12 years before his studies took him from Leicester to Cambridge and then on to the BBC, where he made his name as the second director of BBC2 and latterly through his enormously popular natural history programmes. As a 12-year-old, Attenborough spent his free time as a volunteer in the geology department of the New Walk Museum, now known as Leicester Museum & Art Gallery. Or he'd get on his bike and pedal to places such as Bradgate Park, Tilton and Billesdon to do a spot of fossil hunting.

In 2008, Attenborough came back to the county to film the *First Life* TV series. Looking at the oldest multi-cellular organisms on Earth, he described Charnia masoni, a 560-million-year-old fern-like fossil that was found by a 15-year-old schoolboy in a Precambrian rock outcrop near Woodhouse Eaves in Charnwood Forest in 1957. Charnia masoni is significant because it was the first life form in the Precambrian period to be identified. Its finder, after whom it was named, was Roger Mason, a Leicester schoolboy who later became a professor of metamorphic petrology in China.

In 1957 Roger and his friends were exploring in Charnwood Forest, in what is now a strictly protected fossil site. They noticed this unusual fossil, and Roger took a rubbing of the rock. He showed it to his father, a Unitarian minister who also taught at the local university and who knew Dr Trevor Ford, the respected local geologist. Roger took Ford to the site, and he wrote up the discovery in the *Journal of the Yorkshire Geological Society*. You can see the holotype (the example from which the species was first described), along with a cast of its sister fossil Charniodiscus, in the Leicester Museum & Art Gallery.

Later it was discovered that a 15-year-old schoolgirl named Tina Negus had seen this fossil a year before the boys – but her geography teacher did not believe her and had dismissed the possibility of fossils in the Precambrian. Roger Mason later acknowledged that the fossil had been discovered earlier by Tina but admitted: 'No one took her seriously'. She finally received long overdue formal recognition in 2007, at the 50th anniversary celebrations of the official discovery.

The silhouette of the Old John folly tops this view

The Walk

Far be it for me to suggest the hazardous notion that you should stop on the M1's hard shoulder to investigate Charnwood's Precambrian past. Our walk instead starts in the much safer environment of one of Leicester's most popular playgrounds, the 830 acre (336ha) Bradgate Park, where deer still graze in the remains of the medieval Charnwood Forest. The first recorded reference to a deer park at Bradgate comes from 1241, and the park still supports a herd of about 550 both red and fallow deer, of which about three-quarters are fallow.

Bradgate Park is now a country park which was gifted to the citizens of Leicester by wealthy local industrialist Charles Bennion in 1928, with the philanthropic instruction that it was 'for the quiet enjoyment of the people for all time'. Many thousands of local people have been grateful for that act of benefaction, and have come to value the moorland, ancient pollarded woods and lakes as a vital escape from the hosiery and footwear factories that formed the basis of Leicester's industrial fortune.

In the heart of the Bradgate Park near the southern end of Cropston Reservoir are the ruins of Bradgate House, built as a hunting lodge by Thomas Grey, 1st Marquis of Dorset, in 1490. Only the skeletal ruins remain of the house today except for the chapel, but when it was built, it was one of the first English country houses to be constructed

Factbox

Location: Bradgate Park is situated 7 miles (11.3km) north-west of Leicester on the Cropston Road. Park in the Newton Linford car park

Postcode: LE6 0HE

Length: About 4 miles (6.4km)

Terrain: A little gentle climbing but all on easy or well-made paths

Map: OS 1:25,000 Explorer OL246, Loughborough

Refreshments: Bradgate Park Conservatory Tearoom, Bradgate Road, Newtown Linford, Leicester LE6 0HE or the Deer Barn Tearoom, Bradgate Park, which is close to Cropston Reservoir

☎ 01162 341815
Ⓦ www.bradgatepark.org/eat-drink-shop

Another view of 'Little Matlock'

Inside the ruins of Bradgate House, where Lady Jane Grey was brought up

entirely from brick as an unfortified residence.

Undoubtedly the most famous resident of Bradgate House in her childhood and early years was Lady Jane Grey, the tragically uncrowned 'Queen for Nine Days' following the death of Edward VI in 1553. Sixteen-year-old Jane was placed on the throne by her scheming father-in-law, the Duke of Northumberland, only to be executed the following year by order of Mary Tudor, who eventually succeeded her as queen for her own brief (five-year) but notoriously 'bloody' reign.

No less an authority than Leicestershire's greatest geologist, Dr Trevor Ford, described the rocks exposed in Bradgate Park as 'a variety of rock types representative of the most ancient in England'. So we'll start our walk back at

the very Genesis of planet Earth from the Newtown Linford car park at the south-western tip of Bradgate Park. At just over 10 miles (16km) in length, the River Lin is Leicestershire's shortest river, and it runs through the southern part of the park before running into the Cropston Reservoir and eventually reaching the Soar in the hunting country of Quorn. Its banks are a popular picnic spot, especially at weekends and on Bank Holidays.

The landscape of this part of the park, with its series of shallow waterfalls and exotic tree plantings, was designed in Victorian times and is somewhat hyperbolically known as Little Matlock. The igneous rocks exposed here in what is rather grandly known as the Little Matlock Gorge are known as Markfieldite and take their name from the nearby village where they were once quarried. They are formed of very hard crystals of pink feldspar, white quartz and green hornblende, which emanated from magma deep within the Earth's crust over 600 million years ago.

In less than a mile (1.6km) you will come to the romantic ruins of Bradgate House. The path leads along the western shore of the reservoir until you reach a small group of trees known as Coronation Wood, where you turn left towards Coppice Wood. Here, fine and coarse-grained rocks of volcanic dust are cleaved into slates, giving a zig-zag appearance on the rock faces. At the end of the plantation, turn left and join the track following the deer park wall west, leading up to Old John.

You soon come across the jagged and splintered Sliding Stones outcrop, which is formed of 600-million-year-old Slate Agglomerate. This mass of volcanic debris was formed when a heavy shower of ash fell into the sea and slithered along over a bed of mud, to be later exposed by glacial action during the Ice Ages. An ancient and wizened oak tree sprouts tenaciously from one of the larger joints of the crag, which it is gradually forcing apart. This Slate Agglomerate formation continues in a succession of crags, which run across the park to the prominent chimney-like Leicestershire Yeomanry War Memorial, erected in 1924 on the park's highest point to commemorate those who died in the Boer and the two World Wars.

It's now just a short step across to the folly known as the Old John Tower, which bears a striking resemblance to the Mow Cop folly we met earlier on (see page 98). The 18th-century tower is one of Leicestershire's most famous landmarks and is sometimes referred to as the icon of the county. It commemorates a loyal retainer of the 5th Earl of Stamford, who was apparently accidentally killed by a falling tree. The interpretation inside the tower is dedicated to George Harry, the 7th Earl of Stamford, and the racetrack they once had built in the park.

Old John stands on a 700 foot (213m) hill composed of the Beacon Beds, which are thin, slaty layers of volcanic rock known as Felsitic Agglomerate. These rocks form part of the Maplewell Group, in which many important Precambrian fossils, such as Charnia masoni, have been found. Head south down the hill from the Old John Tower past the War Memorial to return to the Newtown Linford car park.

A close-up of Old John

19.

The hills are alive with the sound of music:
Malvern Hills, Worcestershire

BELOW Edward Elgar at work in his study
RIGHT Rising like the Himalaya. A distant view of the Malvern Hills from the Severn Valley

Edward Elgar, surely the most supremely English of all our composers, on his deathbed is said to have remarked to a friend: 'If ever you're walking on the Malvern Hills and hear my "Cello Concerto", don't be frightened, it's only me'.

That thoughtful, elegiac work has become a test piece for the solo cellist and was perhaps most passionately performed by 20-year-old Jacqueline Du Pré in a recording with Sir John Barbirolli and the London Symphony Orchestra in 1965. On hearing that recording, Mstislav Rostropovich, the great Russian cellist, is said to have removed it from his personal repertoire. When asked why, Rostropovich replied: 'My pupil, Jacqueline du Pré, played it much better than I'. Barbirolli himself had an early association with the Cello Concerto: he was a member of the cello section of the London Symphony Orchestra in the disastrous, grossly under-rehearsed premiere of the work in October 1919.

But if anything can conjure up a vision of the view of the essentially English patchwork-quilt countryside of Elgar's beloved Worcestershire and the Severn Plain from the Malvern ridge, it must

surely be this gently pastoral yet emotionally charged piece. As Elgar's daughter, Carice Irene, said: 'No one was more imbued with his own countryside than my father'.

Everest mountaineer Wilfred Noyce once claimed that of all British hills, the miniature mountain range of the 10 mile (16km) ridge of the Malverns came the closest to the Himalaya in the way that they rise so suddenly and steeply from the plain. They may be modest in height – the highest summit of the Worcestershire Beacon only reaches 1,394 feet (425m) – but, especially after a dusting of winter snow, the Malverns can belie their

relatively low altitude. And the traverse of that roller-coaster ride is an exhilarating day's outing for any hillwalker, even those, like Noyce, who are used to far greater hills.

The name of the Malvern Hills is probably derived from the ancient British *moel-bryn*, meaning 'bare-hill', which is similar to the Welsh *moel fryn*, which also means bald hill. And the Malverns are kept 'bald' today by grazing sheep and cattle licenced by the Malvern Hills Trust, formerly the Malvern Hills Conservators. The Conservators are one of the oldest conservation groups in the country, and have kept a watchful eye over the hills since their formation by Act of Parliament in 1884. They changed their working name to the Malvern Hills Trust in 2017.

Official government recognition of the scenic and natural beauty of the Malverns was made in 1959, when over 40 square miles (103 sq km) of the hills were designated as an Area of Outstanding Natural Beauty (AONB). They are also a biological and geological Site of Special Scientific Interest (SSSI).

Straddling the border between the old counties of Herefordshire and Worcestershire, the Malverns represent some of the oldest rocks in Britain.

Dating from the Precambrian period between 4,600 and 500 million years ago, their incredibly hard, pastel-shaded pink and mauve diorites, granites, metamorphic schists and gneiss rocks were tempting to Victorian quarrymen. But we have to thank the Malvern Hills Conservators that the distinctive skyline of the Malverns, seen to such striking effect from the M5 or the Birmingham–Bristol railway line, is still intact. I always eagerly looked forward to seeing their smoothly undulating skyline when I was a regular rail traveller between Birmingham and Cheltenham.

An aerial view of the winding Malvern ridge

'.. a fair field full of folk'– the view across the Severn Plain from the Malverns

They have long marked the border country between Middle England and the first blue foothills of Wales to the west. The Red Earl's Dyke, or Shire Ditch, still runs from the Herefordshire Beacon to the terminal summit of Midsummer Hill at the extreme southern end of the range. It was constructed in the 13th century by Gilbert de Clare, the eponymous and apparently fiery red-haired Earl of Gloucester.

William Langland, one of our earliest English poets, may well have been dozing 'under a broad bank' of the Red Earl's Dyke one bright May morning in the 14th century when he dreamed his dream of 'a fair field full of folk... the rich and the poor, working and wandering', in his 'Vision of Piers Plowman'. In this classic alliterative poem, partly theological allegory and partly political satire, Piers embarks on a search for the true Catholic Christian life through a series of the dreams he experienced on the Malvern Hills.

The Herefordshire Beacon towards the southern end of the range is the second highest of the Malvern Hills at 1,109 feet (338m). It is encircled by the sinuous, curving earthworks of a 32 acre (13ha) hillfort dating from the Iron Age, one of the most spectacular and complete hillforts in Britain. Popularly known as the British Camp, traces of 120 hut circles have been found within its contour-hugging earthworks. At its centre and on the highest point are the remains of a circular Norman motte and bailey castle, named by the overly romantic Victorians as The Citadel.

Legend claims that this was the site where the Celtic guerrilla leader Caractacus fought his last battle against the Romans – although this is also claimed for Caer Caradoc in the Shropshire Hills. Wherever the battle took place, Caractacus was captured and whisked off to Rome to be exhibited as a spoil of war by the Emperor Claudius. Which brings us back to Elgar and his 1898 cantata *Caractacus*, which was also set in the Malverns and describes the defeat and capture of the defiant rebel chieftain.

Factbox

Location: The British Camp car park is on the south side of the A449 Malvern to Ledbury road, about 4 miles (6.4km) from Great Malvern. Space is limited, so on fine days or Bank Holidays you'll need to get there early if you want to find a parking spot

Postcode: WR13 6DW

Length: 2 miles (3.2km), but can be extended along the ridge

Terrain: A little climbing but on grassy or well-made paths

Map: OS 1:25,000 Explorer OL190, Malvern Hills & Bredon Hill

Refreshments: In summer, there is usually a mobile café, Sally's Place, serving refreshments and ice cream on the opposite side of the road to the British Camp car park. Otherwise, there are numerous hostelries in Great Malvern

T 07790 209288
W facebook.com/sallysplacemalvern

The Walk

This short, family-length walk climbs to the summit of the Herefordshire Beacon and explores its still substantial earthworks. It starts from the car park on the south side of the A449 Malvern to Ledbury road at British Camp. Near the entrance to the car park is an information board interpreting the history of the hillfort, which dates back to around 200 BC.

Leave the car park by the metalled path, which leads gently uphill on to the Herefordshire Beacon, taking the higher path to the right where the path forks. This climb offers some excellent views along the sinuous main ridge of the Malvern Hills to the north, starting with Pinnacle Hill and culminating in the reigning summit of the Worcestershire Beacon at its northern end. You now have the chance to explore the substantial concentric banks and ditches of the British Camp. The summit of The Citadel is easily reached and offers a grandstand view of the Malvern Ridge, the Severn Plain below to the east and beyond that the outline of The Cotswolds, and to the west, the first misty blue hills of the Cambrian Mountains of Central Wales.

To continue the walk, descend south from the summit, still inside the ramparts of the hillfort, and cross Millennium Hill, which was anonymous until the Malvern Hills Trust decided to give it a name to mark the beginning of the Third Millennium in the year 2000.

A welcome resting spot and a glorious view

The British Camp Reservoir

Leaving the earthworks of the British Camp, you cross Broad Down. Directly below to your right is the now disused British Camp Reservoir, which was opened by the Duchess of Teck in 1895 and built to supply Malvern with clean drinking water. Below the western side of the ridge is a small human-made cave excavated in the 600-million-year-old volcanic pillow lavas, which is known as Clutter's or Giant's Cave. Legend links it with the 14th-century Welsh prince Owain Glyndŵr and the 15th-century Lollard rebel John Oldcastle, but it is more likely to have been occupied by a simple hermit.

Stay on the main ridge following the Red Earl's Dyke and continue south to eventually reach Hangman's Hill, whose name seems to indicate it may have had a rather grisly use in times past. Unless you want to extend the walk beyond the Wyche Cutting to take in the southernmost summits of Perseverance Hill, Black Hill and Midsummer Hill (which is also crowned by an Iron Age hillfort), you should retrace your steps to the Herefordshire Beacon. And if you are not revisiting the summit, fork right from the ridge path to take the lower path that traverses the flanks of the Beacon and leads easily back to the car park.

The view north along the Malvern ridge from the earthworks of the British Camp

20.

Appointment with the Devil: The Stiperstones, Shropshire

BELOW Heather carpets The Stiperstones in late summer
RIGHT The Devil's Chair, Stiperstones

The shattered 480-million-year-old Ordovician quartzite crags of the Stiperstones in the Shropshire Hills seem to attract myths and legends as easily as the mists which so often wreath their heathery summits.

One of the most common is that if you sit on The Devil's Chair - the fanciful name given to the most prominent rocky summit - at midnight on Midsummer's Eve, you will encounter Old Nick himself. The late Vivian Bird, a Birmingham walker/journalist friend of mine who came up with the classic Six Shropshire Summits walk, once decided to put the legend to the test, timing his ascent to reach the Chair at exactly the appointed hour.

Midsummer's Eve of course also marks the ancient Celtic festival of Lughnasadh when barriers between mankind and the supernatural are said to be lowered. Locals believe this is the night when the Devil sits in his chair and summons all his local followers - the witches, ghosts and evil spirits of Shropshire - to gather to elect their king for the year.

However, my gentle, God-fearing friend Vivian was disappointed in his promised

rendezvous with Satan. As he recounted in his book *Exploring the West Midlands* (1977): 'As I sat on the rock of the Chair it was just midnight. Michael (his son) joined me, and a disturbed lapwing circled before the moon like a witch on a broomstick as we drank coffee'. Maybe my friend, on Lughnasadh night, that's exactly what it was.

The association of the Stiperstones with the Devil goes back a very long way. According to one account, he is supposed to have dropped an apronful of stones from Ireland on the summit, which he had intended to use to fill up the appropriately named adjacent ravine

of Hell Gutter, on the lower slopes of the hill. Another story is that the Devil hated England so much that he declared when the Stiperstones sink down into the plain, England will perish. Local people still say that when the frequent mists cover the Stiperstones, 'the Devil's on his throne', hoping that his weight will sink the hill and bring about the downfall of the nation.

Yet another persistent tale centred on the bristling summits of the Stiperstones is that of Wild Edric, a Saxon noble who was buried beneath the hill having eventually submitted to William the Conqueror after the Norman invasion in 1066. There may be some truth in this one, because Edric Silvaticus, Lord of the Manor of Lydbury North at the time of the Conquest, did initially resist the Norman invaders, and was the subject of a curse when he finally reached agreement with them in 1070. The story goes that because of the curse, Edric, his wife and followers were imprisoned in one of the lead mines that abound in this area. Local lead miners reporting knocking sounds coming from deep in the mines claimed that this was the ghost of Edric, guiding them to where richer deposits of the galena ore could be found.

Echoing the legend of King Arthur, it was said that when danger threatens England, Edric and his 'Wild Hunt' will rise up to meet the challenge. It was claimed that Edric's Hunt was seen galloping across the hills just before the start of the Crimean War and also the First and Second World Wars, before disappearing to return to their underground prison once more.

In literature, the Stiperstones most famously featured prominently in *The Golden Arrow* (1916), the first and perhaps best-known of the romantic novels of Mary Webb (1881–1927), who lived in the village of Pontesbury at the northern end of the ridge. She named the range Diafol (Welsh for Devil) Mountain and described it thus: 'It drew the thunder, people said. Storms broke suddenly round it out of a clear sky. No one cared to cross the range near it after dark... It remained inviolable, taciturn, evil'.

The Devil's Chair was the focus of her drama, and she writes: 'The Devil's Chair loomed over them – for all the distance between – like a fist flourished in the face. It was dark as purple nightshade. The cobalt shadows of clouds swept across the hills in stealthy majesty'.

DH Lawrence was another novelist who used the Stiperstones as a setting for his

The rocky track to The Devil's Chair

The Bog Visitor Centre – once a school

1925 novella *St Mawr*. In particular he said he found the Devil's Chair 'had a strange effect on the imagination'. He wrote: 'It was one of those places where the spirit of aboriginal England still lingers, the old savage England, whose last blood flows still in a few Englishmen, Welshmen, Cornishmen'. It is disappointing to learn that *St Mawr* was actually written on the Lawrence ranch near Taos in New Mexico.

We start our exploration of the Stiperstones at the unattractively named The Bog Visitor Centre, which was once the school at the heart of a thriving lead mining community. Lead has been mined here on the Shropshire Hills at least since Roman times, because a 198lb (90kg) lead ingot (or pig) bearing a Roman inscription was once found near here. At their peak in the 1870s, lead mines in the area employed over 1,000 men, attracting mining families from Cornwall and Wales, but cheap imports caused prices to drop, and the last mine went out of business in the 1940s. The centre retains its schoolroom-like interior and provides historical information about past miners, their mines, and the present-day work to restore the landscape.

The Stiperstones was officially unveiled as a National Nature Reserve (NNR) by the naturalist the late Dr David Bellamy and children from the Stiperstones Primary School in 1982. Thankfully, the Stiperstones is now well protected because it is also a Site of Special Scientific Interest (SSSI) and lies within the 310 square mile (803 sq km) Shropshire Hills Area of Outstanding Natural Beauty (AONB). The Shropshire Hills AONB was designated in 1958 and also covers the Long Mynd, Clun Forest, the Clee Hills and the hillfort-topped volcanic outlier of Shropshire's iconic symbol, The Wrekin, above Telford (see page 89).

The Stiperstones is exceptional not only for its unique geology but also for its birdlife. It provides a haven for birds that are normally associated with upland Britain, such as red grouse, curlew, peregrine falcon and that rare 'mountain blackbird', the ring ouzel.

In 1998 the Back to Purple project, a partnership of Natural England, Forest Enterprise and the Shropshire Wildlife Trust, started removing the alien conifer plantations and restoring the heather moorlands on and around the Stiperstones. This involved felling trees and re-establishing the heather and bilberry moorland, revealing previously hidden features such as the Nipstone Rock, which is just to the south of the visitor centre. Thousands of heather seedlings have been planted to supplement natural regeneration and further work below the summit ridge has aimed at restoring herb-rich grasslands, hay meadows and wet flushes to encourage bog cotton, heath bedstraw, the rare mountain pansy and native woodlands.

The Walk

To start our walk, go up the hill at the back of the car park and after about half a mile (0.8km) take the gate on your left. Keep to the left side rocky track, which leads towards Cranberry Rock, named after the dark-pink flowered evergreen shrub that has distinctive large bright red berries in the autumn. Bear right at the rock and follow the heathery path as it runs along the ridge until you reach a cairn, where you continue straight on towards the prominent Manstone Rock, topped by its trig point. At 1,759 feet (536m), Manstone Rock is the reigning summit of the Stiperstones.

Continue north along the main ridge and you will soon pass the upstanding crag known as the Devil's Chair, the largest and best known of the Stiperstone tors. It's a bit of a scramble to follow my friend Vivian and sit in Satan's seat, but worth it for the view, which extends across the Shropshire Hills, with the great whaleback of the Long Mynd particularly prominent to the east. There are also extensive views across the North Shropshire plain and towards AE Housman's 'blue remembered hills' of Mid Wales to the west.

Continue north to a crossroads of tracks through the heather, where you turn left and then downhill to a small waterworks. Here you turn left again and follow the track through a series of gates across fields until you reach your starting point at The Bog Visitor Centre.

Jagged quartzite crags punctuate
The Stiperstones

Factbox

Location: The Bog Visitor Centre is 2.5 miles (4km) east of the A488 between Bishop's Castle and Shrewsbury

Postcode: SY5 0NG

Length: About 3.5 miles (5.6km)

Terrain: This is a hill walk in rocky terrain on stony and uneven paths

Map: OS 1:25,000 Explorer OL216, Welshpool & Montgomery

Refreshments: Information, refreshments and toilets are available at The Bog Visitor Centre, The Bog, Stiperstones, Shrewsbury SY5 0NG

T 01743 792484
W bogvisitorcentre.com

Or try The Bridges Pub, Ratlinghope, Shrewsbury SY5 0ST

T 01588 650260
W thebridgespub.co.uk/

The village, on the eastern side of the Stiperstones, is locally pronounced 'Ratchup' and is well known for its live Irish music

21.

'Sistine Chapel of the Ice Age': Creswell Crags, Derbyshire/ Nottinghamshire

An aerial view of the now lake-filled Creswell Crags gorge

The short, stocky man with deep-browed eyes peered out from the dark recesses of the cave entrance onto a world far different from that of today.

The same creamy-white Magnesian limestone crags frowned down onto a meandering marshy riverbed, and ivy trailed down from the escarpment lip. But there was no placid, reed-fringed lake filling the valley bottom, and there were far fewer trees than those which now generously cloak the sides of the gorge.

The biggest difference, however, was in the animal life with which he shared his valley home. Great herds of reindeer and bison passed through the limestone portals of the gorge as they followed the ever-retreating ice northwards in search of good grazing. They were joined by the massive, lumbering forms of woolly mammoths, their huge inward-sweeping tusks meeting in front of their swinging trunks and glinting in the imperceptibly, ever-strengthening sun. Occasionally, rusty-red, shaggy-coated woolly rhinoceros joined the peaceful grazers on the valley bottom, while packs of whickering spotted hyenas shared some

Steps lead up to Church Hole Cave

caves with the first human settlers, picking up their scraps just like modern urban foxes.

This idyllic scene took place at Creswell Crags, on the former coalfield borders of modern Derbyshire and Nottinghamshire. It was some 12,000 years ago towards the end of the last Ice Age and at one of the northernmost places on earth to be visited by these early humans. For those Palaeolithic hunter-gatherers, life must have been pretty good, at least it seems to have allowed them plenty of free time. Because in a ground-breaking discovery made in 2003 by a team of British and Spanish archaeologists, the caves that line the gorge were found to be the earliest place in Britain where humans produced a recognisable and verified form of art. A clue to its presence was made in 1878, when a tiny bone was found in Robin Hood's Cave, which

showed the unmistakeable engraving of a shock-maned horse's head.

Even if you take the organised tour of Church Hole Cave from the Creswell Visitor Centre, it still takes what archaeologists call 'the eye of faith' to make out the inscribed bas-relief figures high on the cave walls. They include, among more than 50 carvings so far discovered, a beautifully proportioned red deer stag, a horned bison, and the head of what has been described as an ibis-like bird with a delicately curved bill. Church Hole Cave has even been dubbed by one perhaps over-excited archaeologist 'the Sistine Chapel of the Ice Age'.

The cave floor had been lowered by about 7 feet (2.1m) by treasure-seeking Victorian antiquarians, so the carvings are now high up near the roof of the cave and only reached today via a stepped viewing platform. Later they were covered by generations of graffiti 'artists' who added their names and dates to the surface. One even added a beard to the stag's chin, thinking it might be a billy goat!

More recently, in 2019, Creswell Crags revealed yet another previously unnoticed and undiscovered mystery, when hundreds of so-called 'witches' marks' – the most ever found together in Britain – were discovered on the walls of several of the caves. These so-called 'apotropaic' marks (the name comes from the Greek *apotrepein*, meaning 'to turn away'), were discovered by two keen-eyed enthusiasts, inscribed into the walls and ceilings of the caves, over dark holes and large crevices. Such ritualistic protection marks were designed to ward away witches and other evil spirits and are most commonly found in historic churches and houses, near entrance points such as doorways, windows and fireplaces.

The way to the caves

Creswell Crags, now run by a Heritage Trust and still on the 'tentative' list to become a British World Heritage Site, describes itself as the Home of the Ice Age Hunter, and is a must for anyone interested in our prehistoric past. Pre-booked tours of the caves are highly recommended and can be combined with a pleasant family-length stroll through the dale.

Peace returned to the gorge in 2007, when the single-lane, traffic-light controlled B6042 road was re-routed about 160 yards (146m) to the north by Derbyshire County Council in order to minimise the impact of traffic on the site. A former sewage works was also demolished and the present heritage centre was built.

The view from the dam of the Crags lake

The Walk

Start from the Creswell Crags Museum and Heritage Centre, where there is ample parking, toilets and a convenient café. You walk through the flower-filled Crags Meadow and a children's play and picnic area and into a woodland, which is carpeted with bluebells, primroses and pungent wild garlic in spring.

The easy path then takes you up to the embankment holding back the water of the placid lake that now fills the bottom of the valley. This was constructed by the local landowner, the Duke of Portland from nearby Welbeck Abbey, in the 19th century. Originally conceived as a boating lake, hence the Boat House name of the first cave you pass, it is now the home of a variety of wildfowl, including some resident swans, kingfishers and herons. Overhead, you may hear the guttural 'kronk' of a raven.

Turn left here to take the path which soon leads past the low, ivy-hung entrance of Boat House Cave on your left. It is a short step from here under the overhanging crags, also festooned with ivy, to reach the entrance to Church Hole Cave, where the great discovery of Ice Age art was made in 2003. Wooden steps lead up to the grilled entrance, and if you have booked a tour to see the art, you'll have to don a helmet and face another short climb up the steps to the viewing platform. And remember, you'll have to use that 'eye of faith' to see the faint engravings.

You soon reach the marshy end of the lake, where threatened water voles – the 'Ratty' of *The Wind in the Willows* – have made their home. Cross the stream that issues from the lake and make your way down the opposite, southern side of the gorge. The first two named caves are Dog Hole and Pin Hole, and there is also a series of fissures in the beetling limestone crags before you reach the next large cave, which takes its name from Robin Hood, the local folk hero of nearby Sherwood Forest.

This was the largest and most important Palaeolithic cave dwelling at Creswell,

Factbox

Location: Creswell Crags Museum and Heritage Centre is 5 miles (8km) from the M1 (exit 30) and within easy reach of Nottingham or Sheffield. Follow the brown tourist signs on the A60 or the A616

Postcode: S80 3LH

Length: An easy 1 mile (1.6km), which with stops should take no more than 1 hour

Terrain: Easy going on well-maintained paths

Map: OS 1:25,000 Explorer OL270, Sherwood Forest

Refreshments: The Creswell Crags Museum and Heritage Centre, Crags Road, Welbeck, Worksop S80 3LH has a convenient café, or there are pubs in Clowne and Creswell

📞 01909 720378
🌐 creswell-crags.org.uk

The Creswell Crags Visitor Centre

floor revealed animal bones and flint tools, indicating human occupation some 8,000-6,000 years ago.

As you make your way past the series of grilled cave entrances at dusk, you may be lucky enough to see some of the modern residents of the caves, as nine species of bats have been recorded here, including Daubenton's, whiskered, natterer's and brown long-eared. And the crags also boast one of the most northern populations of barbastelle bats in Europe. In spring the earliest butterflies, such as brimstones, small tortoiseshells and red admirals, emerge from their winter hibernation in the caves. An astonishing total of 20 different species of butterflies, including rarities like the unfortunately named dingy skipper and the white-letter hairstreak, have been recorded in the gorge.

and where the horse's head carving and other carved bones were found in 1878, along with numerous flint tools such as awls, hammers and scrapers. The range of tools found here is unique and so distinctive that they have given their name - Creswellian - to this style of Stone Age artefacts.

The last cave you pass is Mother Grundy's Parlour, which is again reached by a flight of wooden steps. It is thought to take its name from a woman who is said to have lived in this cave in the 19th century. It's not hard to believe that she might have been suspected of being one of the witches against whom those apotropaic marks were guarding. Excavation of the deposits on the cave

Birdsong is perhaps the defining feature of springtime at Creswell, as resident birds are joined by rare migrants such as spotted flycatchers who return here all the way from sub-Saharan Africa to breed. In winter, siskins, goldfinches and redpolls are often seen and ringing has shown that many of them travel from as far away as Scotland. You can make use of the bird hide along the way to spot these rarities.

It's humbling to think that our Palaeolithic forbears might have stared out from the caves of Creswell and enjoyed exactly the same glorious birdsong chorus to the coming of spring as they listened for the thundering hooves of the approaching herds of migrating reindeer and bison.

22.

The Lair of the White Worm: Thor's Cave, Staffordshire

BELOW A distant view of Butterton village
RIGHT The impressive maw of Thor's Cave

Thor's Cave is surely the archetypal caveman's home – a gaping 60 foot (18m)-high void in a limestone crag 250 feet (76m) above the winding valley of the River Manifold in the Staffordshire Peak District.

As you gaze up at it from the Manifold Track, you half expect Fred Flintstone and Barney Rubble from the 1960s Hanna-Barbera hit cartoon *The Flintstones* to emerge, and Fred's trademark bellow 'Wilma!' to come echoing from its Stygian depths. Sure enough, firm evidence of prehistoric occupation has been discovered here, but so far, no sign of Fred, Wilma, Barney nor Betty! Archaeological excavations in the 1860s and the 1920s uncovered both human and animal remains, stone tools, pottery, amber beads, and bronze and antler artefacts in both Thor's Cave and the adjacent Thor's Fissure and Elderbush Caves.

It was estimated that the caves contained the burials of at least six people, and it is assumed they were occupied from the end of the Palaeolithic period, with apparently more intensive use being made of them during the Iron Age and

Unsurprisingly in view of its spectacular location, Thor's Cave has also attracted the attention of filmmakers over the years. Probably the most memorable was Ken Russell, whose 1988 cult horror movie *The Lair of the White Worm*, was loosely based on the 1911 Bram Stoker novel of the same name and drew heavily on the Durham legend of the Lambton Worm (see page 167). The film stars movie megastars Hugh Grant, Amanda Donohoe and Peter Capaldi in one of their earliest film appearances, Grant playing his usual upper-class, cut-glass accented English toff in the form of the monster-slaying Lord James D'Ampton.

Ken Russell had always been an admirer of the Irish novelist Bram Stoker, who wrote his horror novel *The Lair of the White Worm* a year before his death in 1912. Russell said he took '...the spine of the novel and used that as the film's backbone, and that is the snake-worshipping cult. The worm really is the character that steals the show.

And as with the Loch Ness monster... there is the assumption that a land-based creature of this sort could still exist under the right conditions... which in the story is this huge cavern called Thor's Cave in Derbyshire (sic), located next to a snake-like river.' The cave features prominently

ABOVE A walking party reaches the entrance to Thor's Cave
RIGHT Sign to the cave

in the film, where it is known as 'Stone Rigg Cavern' and is home to the fabled White Worm.

Thor's Cave was also used in the filming of rock band The Verve's 1993 video for their single 'Blue', and it is pictured on the cover of the band's first psychedelic-influenced album, *A Storm in Heaven*, released in the same year.

The Walk

We start our exploration of 'The Lair of the White Worm' in Wetton, a typically nucleated White Peak village, attractively set around its tiny green nearly 1,000 feet (30.5m) up on the limestone plateau and overlooking the deep valley of the Manifold. The Royal Oak public house welcomes walkers, and the parish church of St Margaret's, although severely re-built in 1820, retains its venerable 14th- century tower.

Start from the car park south of the village and turn right to where the road to Wetton Mill enters, then turn left along Carr Lane, which gradually descends towards the valley of the Manifold. As you drop down through trees to the river you have views of Beeston Tor, where further evidence of early human habitation has been found.

In the prominent cave in the tor known as St Bertram's Cave, antiquarian the Rev George H Wilson discovered a hoard of Anglo-Saxon jewellery and 49 coins in 1924. The hoard included two decorated silver brooches, three gold rings and other fragments. The coins dated the burial of the hoard to approximately AD 875 at the time when the Great Viking Army was encamped at nearby Repton in Derbyshire, which could suggest a possible reason for it being hidden away here.

St Bertram himself was an interesting figure. According to an account from the 14th century, he was said to have lived sometime in the 8th century and was the son of a Mercian king. After his Irish wife and new baby had tragically been killed by wolves in the Mercian forest, he relocated to a hermitage at Ilam at the entrance to Dovedale, where he died. He may also have used the Beeston Tor cave, which takes his name as a refuge. Bertram was said to have converted

Factbox

Location: Wetton is signposted on a minor road about 1 mile (1.6km) west of Alstonefield off the A515 Ashbourne-Buxton road in the Staffordshire Moorlands. Car park, with toilets, in Wetton village

Postcode: DE6 2AF

Length: About 3.5 miles (5.6km), so you should allow 1½-2 hours

Terrain: Some steep climbs in and out of the Manifold Valley, but nothing too strenuous

Map: OS 1:25,000 Explorer OL24, The Peak District - White Peak Area

Refreshments: The 400-year-old Royal Oak, Royal Oak Road, Wetton, Ashbourne DE6 2AF is a real family-run pub with a list of landlords dating back to 1760

☎ 01335 310287
🖥 royaloakwetton.co.uk

There's also a lovely little tea room Wetton Village Hall and Tearooms, Wetton, Ashbourne DE6 2AF

☎ 07801 683546
🖥 facebook.com/oldschooltearoomwetton

many pagan Saxons to Christianity, and reputedly was able to work miraculous cures through his prayers. His altar tomb in St Bertram's Chapel, in the originally Saxon Church of the Holy Cross at Ilam, dates from the 13th century. It became a place of pilgrimage in the Middle Ages and many visitors still leave their prayers there. St Bertram's Well, a spring just south of the church, is said to have been a source of fresh water since Saxon times.

Cross the River Manifold by the footbridge near Beeston Tor Farm, then it's an easy mile (1.6km)-long stroll along the level Manifold Track, which winds peacefully down the Manifold Valley. This is usually much quieter and less visited than Dovedale, its better known and more populous neighbour across the border in Derbyshire.

The Manifold also exhibits that strange peculiarity of some limestone rivers in that, for most of the year, it disappears through fissures in the limestone bed to run for much of its course underground. In the case of the Manifold, this happens at Wetton Mill, and it bubbles to the surface again over 3 miles (4.8km) downstream in the grounds of Ilam Hall.

The valley is threaded by the 8 mile (12.9km) Manifold Track or Way, a walking and riding route converted by Staffordshire County Council in 1937 from the former track bed of the Leek and Manifold Light Railway. The railway, which used attractive primrose-yellow carriages obtained from India, was a short-lived enterprise that opened in 1904 to serve the Duke of Devonshire's nearby copper

The steps leading up to the cave

mines at Ecton Hill, and it closed in 1934. As a local person was heard to remark: 'It starts from nowhere and finishes at the same place'. Thor's Cave even had its own tiny station at the foot of the crag, and there are delightful archive photographs of the steam-driven trains of the Leek and Manifold Light Railway disembarking passengers at this beautiful spot.

The gaping maw of Thor's Cave now appears in its imposing limestone crag above the trees. Go over the footbridge and then steeply up the path through the woods via numerous sometimes slippery steps, until you eventually reach the impressive entrance to the cave. Formed from the harder reef limestones of the Carboniferous age, Thor's Cave is the remnant of a much older cave system which was finally exposed by the grinding Ice Age glaciers that originally carved out the valley. Further fissures lead on from the back of the cave, and others such as Elderbush and Thor's Fissure Caves exist close by, where the prehistoric and Romano-British remains were discovered, but these are only accessible to experienced cavers.

The origin of the name is uncertain, but it possibly comes from the Old English *torr*, which simply means a 'high, rocky peak'. Some authorities think it originates from the paganism of the early Anglo-Saxons and takes its name from Thor, the hammer-wielding Norse god of thunder and lightning, who is also associated with sacred groves, strength and fertility.

As you enter the cave, you must take care exploring this stupendous void. The polished bare limestone floor slopes upwards from the entrance and can be very slippery when wet. The cave is a favourite spot for rock climbers, with the Thormen's Moth route perhaps being the classic. It climbs around the central lip of the entrance and is only accomplished with the assistance of artificial climbing aids. That's the reason why abandoned climbing gear can sometimes be seen hanging from the roof, somewhat spoiling the view.

And it is a breathtaking, panoramic view looking out from the cave, framed by the great rock oval void of the entrance, across the Manifold Valley towards Ossom's Hill on the opposite bank, which is usually clad in golden gorse. It has been the subject of many memorable photographs and certainly makes that steep climb and the visit worthwhile.

When you have finished exploring the cave, it's just a short walk across a sometimes muddy path to reach Carr Lane, which leads back to your starting point in Wetton village.

The wonderful view from the cave

NORTH
of England

23

Rock idols: Brimham
Rocks, Nidderdale,
Yorkshire

3 miles/4.8km

24

Crossing the 'Wet
Sahara': Morecambe Bay,
Lancashire

8 miles/12.9km

25

'Out on the wily, windy
moors': Brontë Moors,
West Yorkshire

7.5 miles/12km

26

Yorkshire's ghost village:
Wharram Percy,
Yorkshire Wolds

1 mile/1.6km

27

The bloodiest battle:
Towton, Yorkshire

3 miles/4.8km

28

Chasing the Lambton
Worm: Penshaw
Monument, Tyne & Wear

2.5 miles/4km

29

Kinder surprise:
Kinder Scout,
Derbyshire

5.5 miles/8.9km

30

Castles in the air:
Alport Castles,
Derbyshire

7 miles/11.3km

31

First settlers in Settle:
Attermire Caves,
Yorkshire Dales

4 miles/6.4km

32

Cumbria's Grand
Canyon: High Cup Nick,
Cumbria

8 miles/12.9km

33

A curious encounter
with Wainwright: Cautley
Spout, Howgill Fells,
Cumbria

3 miles/4.8km

34

Monolithic maidens:
Long Meg and her
Daughters, Cumbria

5 miles/8km

35

Land's End of
Yorkshire: Spurn Head,
Humberside

6 miles/9.7km

36

From industry to
tranquillity: Lathkill Dale,
Derbyshire

4.5 miles/7.2km

37

Finding Cuddy's Cave:
St Cuthbert's Cave,
Northumberland

3 miles/4.8km

23.

Rock idols: Brimham Rocks, Nidderdale, Yorkshire

BELOW Aerial view of Brimham Rocks
RIGHT Brimham's bizarre rock garden

Eighteenth-century antiquaries could not believe that the fantastic natural sculpture park of gritstone rocks and tors at Brimham, overlooking Nidderdale in North Yorkshire, was not the remains of some ancient, long-forgotten civilisation.

The pioneer archaeologist Major Hayman Rooke, nicknamed the 'Resurrection Major' by his contemporaries for his prodigious programme of barrow-digging, actually concluded in a paper presented to the Society of Antiquaries in 1786 that they were the work of 'artists skilled in the power of mathematics'. Inevitably, it was the Druids who were favoured as the 'builders' of this amazing natural phenomenon, although we now know that the fabled priesthood emerged relatively late on the British scene during the pagan pre-Roman, Celtic period, around 2,000 years ago.

The truth is that during the 18th and 19th centuries, the Druids were attributed with just about every freak of nature and prehistoric monument, especially the famous stone circles like Wiltshire's Stonehenge and Avebury, and Castlerigg

in Cumbria, which could not be otherwise explained. As an 18th-century parson once commented: 'On no subject has fancy roamed with more licentious indulgence than on the Druids and their institutions'.

So it comes as no surprise to find that many of Brimham's bizarre rock formations were named after those sickle-wielding, white-robed and bearded priests of the oak groves. There's the Druid's Writing Desk, for example – a flat, table-topped tor which overlooks Nidderdale towards the distant heights of Great Whernside; the Druid's Coffin – a body-shaped crevice; the astonishing

Druid's Idol – a massive 200-ton boulder precariously perched on a tiny 12in (30.5cm) diameter pedestal; and the Druid's Pulpit – which stands silently awaiting a preacher brave enough to clamber up to its vantage point. Journalist Herbert W Ogle (1871-1940) of Otley in his 1920s book *Brimham Rocks: The Wonder of Nidderdale* also lists the Druid's Head, Druid's Castle, Druid's Parlour, Druid's Kitchen and even a severely anachronistic Druid's Telescope.

The imagination of the early explorers of Brimham's rock garden was not confined to Druidism, however, and other rocks go under such fanciful zoological names as the Sphinx, the Turtle, the Dancing Bear, the Eagle, the Camel, the Cow, the Yoke of Oxen, the Baboon's or Monkey's Head, the Gorilla, the Watchdog, the Porpoise, and the Crocodile. For good measure, there are also two Anvils and a Blacksmith, two Cannon rocks, the Castle, the Crown, the Indian's Turban, the Flowerpot, and on the edge of the moor, a Lovers' Leap.

The rangers of the National Trust, which acquired the 454 acre (184ha) estate in 1970, have noted that some of the rocks. Names have been changed with the passage of time. Old local names, such as the Great and Little Cannon, have also changed, with the Little Cannon now being known as the Smartie Tube! More modern personas have been given to others, such as Donald Duck and General de Gaulle, and of course, contemporary visitors, especially children, will delight in exercising their own imaginations on naming the strange features of this weird and wonderful playground.

By 1836 though, the new science of geology was beginning to controvert the fairy tale of Druidic construction. As the pioneer Yorkshire geologist Prof John Phillips in his *Illustrations of the Geology of Yorkshire* explained: 'The wasting power of the atmosphere is very conspicuous in these rocks; searching out their secret lamination; working perpendicular furrows and horizontal cavities; wearing away the bases, and thus bringing slow but sure destruction on the whole of the exposed masses.

The 200-ton Druid's Idol precariously perched on its 12in (30.5cm) pedestal

Those that remain of the rocks of Brimham are but perishing memorials of what have been destroyed'.

The National Trust's more modern explanation of the formation of Brimham Rocks starts around 335 million years ago, when what is now Britain was located close to the Equator where warm, tropical seas dominated. About 15 million years later, erosion from a great mountain range in the north transported silt, sand and pebbles by fast-flowing, powerful rivers, periodically flooding this tropical world. The grit from the rivers included crystals of steel-hard quartz and softer crystals of feldspar, which can still be seen shining out from the rocks at Brimham. The riverine deposits were then compressed and hardened over time to form the Millstone Grit from which Brimham Rocks were formed.

As the grit and sand was deposited, each event formed layers called bedding planes. Bedding planes represent a period of time and, depending on the angle they were laid down, show the direction in which the primeval river was flowing. In some places the bedding planes run diagonally as well as horizontally, showing where huge underwater sand dunes once existed. Depending on compaction and the type of grains deposited, different bedding planes have different degrees of hardness. Rain, frost, wind and sun have worn away the softer layers, causing these odd shapes in the rocks.

Brimham is a truly great place to take the kids, and they will love the ambush opportunities presented by the sandy

Tempting paths lead through the rocks

paths that wind in and out of the rocks, birches, heather and delicious purple bilberries. I recall a wonderful picnic we had with our children when we were on holiday at Summerbridge some years ago. We all clambered up to a suitably flat, table-topped rock and enjoyed conveniently locally picked juicy bilberries and ice cream while enjoying a fantastic view to the northern bounds of Nidderdale.

It is still a mystery to many why Nidderdale wasn't included as part of the Yorkshire Dales National Park when it was designated in 1954. It wasn't even included when the park was enlarged by nearly a quarter in the north-west, to include all of the Howgill Fells, in 2016. The original reason given for its exclusion was that the three now attractive and natural-looking reservoirs that flood its upper reaches had spoiled the 'natural' environment, and the interests of the water industry prevailed.

The Walk

Our walk starts from the extensive National Trust car park to the south of the rocks themselves. A broad, sandy ride leads directly through the rocks towards the Grade II listed Brimham House, originally built as a shooting lodge for Lord Grantley in 1792 but used to provide refreshments for visitors for the last hundred years. In addition to the usual aromatic National Trust gift shop and a café in some outbuildings, there is an interesting exhibition in the house, which attempts to answer the most common question asked at Brimham: 'How on earth were these extraordinary rocks formed?'

As explained in more detail above, in simple terms they are the result of aeons

Factbox

Location: Brimham Rocks is 8 miles (12.9km) north-west of Harrogate, and 3 miles (4.8km) east of Pateley Bridge, off the B6165 Ripley–Pateley Bridge road. The rocks are reached by taking the signposted minor road north from Summerbridge

Postcode: HG3 4DW

Length: As long as you like, but you should allow at least a couple of hours to fully explore the rocks

Terrain: The paths cover fairly easy terrain, but suitable footwear should be worn, especially if you are doing a bit of 'bouldering'

Map: OS 1:25,000 Explorer OL298, Nidderdale. There is a larger scale map in the National Trust's leaflet, which will show you where to find the featured formations

Refreshments: A convenient pub is The Half Moon, Fellbeck, Harrogate HG3 5ET

T 01423 711560
W half-moon.co.uk

For first-class real Yorkshire ham, egg and chips in various combinations, try The Firs Tea Rooms, Main Street, Summerbridge, Harrogate HG3 4JF

T 01423 781715
W thefirssummerbridge.co.uk

Sunburst on Brimham Rocks

Layers of time at Brimham

of natural erosion by wind, frost and rain, which first exposed and then gradually worked on the weaker joints and bedding plains of the Millstone Grit rocks to create the amazing shapes we see today. Comparison with the monumental sculptural works of Henry Moore is often made, and it is known that he gained inspiration from viewing bizarre Pennine tors such as these.

The panorama from the balcony of Brimham House is justly famous, extending from the comical shape of the Flowerpot past the Turtle and Eagle, round to Crown Rocks and the Cannon, and pointing menacingly out across Nidderdale.

There are literally hundreds of paths to explore around the many rock features of Brimham, but be sure you don't miss the beaked Turtle, which seems to be standing improbably on its hind feet in front and to the east of the House, or the Druid's Idol, an extraordinary example of natural balance which surely one day is doomed to topple. The astonishing Idol stands behind the House on the northern edge of the moor, close to the Druid's Writing Desk.

And almost inevitably, hidden away among the fallen boulders and lacy birches under the rocky escarpment beneath the moor's western edge, were once the Druids' Caves, which included their Parlour and Bedroom, but they have long since been obliterated by a rock fall. Maybe it is the fate of all idols one day to fall?

24.

Crossing the 'Wet Sahara'
Morecambe Bay, Lancashire

BELOW 'The Moses of Morecambe Bay' Cedric Robinson
RIGHT The vast expanse of Morecambe Bay

Cedric Robinson was truly the Moses of Morecambe Bay. Although the cold waters of the Rivers Kent and Winster, which empty out into the Bay, didn't exactly part for him as they did for the tribes of Israel crossing the Red Sea, only a fool would attempt the 8 mile (12.9km) crossing without the King's Guide to the Sands to safely shepherd them.

'There's only two people you can put your faith in when crossing these sands', Cedric, who died aged 88 in 2021, once emphatically told me, 'God and the Sand Pilot'. The same advice applies equally to new Sand Pilot Michael Wilson, a fisherman from Flookburgh, who took over from Cedric in 2019. In a moving tribute to his friend and mentor, Michael said it was time for Cedric to 'rest his sandy feet'.

Morecambe Bay's 120 square miles (311 sq km) of swirling currents and constantly shifting sands, which include some of the most treacherous quicksands in Britain, have been dubbed Britain's 'wet Sahara'. When the old coach route from Lancaster to Kendal used to take this perilous shortcut, as once famously painted by JMW Turner, several coaches and their horses were either overwhelmed by the quaking sands or overtaken by the

incoming tide. It rushes in at the proverbial speed of a galloping horse and can rise to 20 feet (6m) in height. A memorial in Cartmel churchyard to 140 victims starkly testifies to the dangers of underestimating these treacherous sands. More recently, in February 2004, at least 21 Chinese immigrant labourers employed to pick cockles at Warton Sands, near Hest Bank, were drowned by an incoming tide.

Morecambe Bay is vast; the Lake District and Arnside and Silverdale Area of Outstanding Natural Beauty (AONB) tumble down into its marvellous mudflats and the bay is recognised as one of the most important places for birds in Europe and for that reason has also been designated as a Special Protection Area (SPA). The Bay's glutinous mud is estimated to attract over a quarter of a million birds every year, for whom, according to the RSPB, it is nothing more than a vast restaurant or feeding station. The mud is packed full of cockles, shrimps, lugworms and mussels, which provide tasty morsels to feed a huge variety of birdlife. Curlews, dunlins, black-tailed godwits, redshanks, swirling flocks of knot and the distinctive piping oystercatchers all gather to feed on the estuary. Their different beak lengths and shapes allow them to find particular types of food within the layers of mud.

The rocky shore of Morecambe Bay

Cedric, a former fluke and flounder fisherman, had been the proud holder of the title of the Queen's Guide to the Sands for 56 years when he retired in 2019. It is an ancient honour that goes back to the 14th century when the Prior of Cartmel first instituted the office of Guide over the Kent Sands.

Cedric became the 25th royally appointed Guide by the Duchy of Lancaster in 1963. He looked back on his years of guiding everyone from royalty – he assisted the late Duke of Edinburgh over in a horse and carriage in 1985 – to countless charity walkers, giggling school parties and hikers keen to undertake one of the most unusual walks in Britain. When he retired it was estimated that Cedric had cheerfully taken over half a million people across the bay.

And in all those years, his salary as Queen's Guide remained constant at a modest £15 a year, although he lived rent-free with his late wife, Olive, at the Guide's Farm, Grange-over-Sands. He was awarded an MBE for his services on his first ever visit to London in 1999. 'I was more nervous at the investiture than if I'd been out in the middle of the bay on a foggy day', he admitted to me when I presented him with the Outdoor Writers' Guild's Golden Eagle award in 2003.

Much careful preparation goes into making each crossing completely safe, sometimes involving as many as 400 people. The guide goes out the day before, testing the sands, checking the tides and marking the safest, zig-zag route between Arnside and Grange with his previously prepared 'brobs'. These are laurel branch markers planted firmly in the sands at strategic crossing places in the shifting channels.

Even so, walkers attempting the route should expect to get rather more than their feet wet. It involves the crossing of the course of the River Kent, whose icy-cold waters can come up to thigh level, as well as splashing through a number of shallower dykes.

Cedric Robinson (second from the left) leads a party of walkers

Note: All crossings of Morecambe Bay must be made in the company of the King's Guide through the Guide Over Sands Trust

Ⓦ guideoversands.co.uk/contact-us

The crossing season usually runs from April to October but is entirely dependent on the weather and the state of the sands.

The Walk

The 8 mile (12.9km) walk usually starts from the esplanade in front of The Albion public house in the charmingly unspoilt and old-fashioned Victorian seaside resort of Arnside, on the Lancashire shore 2 miles (3.2km) north of Carnforth.

The usual route, although it can change from day-to-day, starts by heading south-west across the flat, wave-worn limestone rocks of the foreshore to the shingle bay of White Creek. This is where the party usually removes shoes and socks ready for the actual crossing. Your destination of Kent's Bank, south of Grange-over-Sands on the Cumbrian shore, is clearly visible, a mere 2 miles (3.2km) away as the oystercatcher (known locally as a 'sea-a-pie') flies. But your route can be up to four times as long, as it winds between the sand banks and gullies to safely cross the sands.

If you are lucky, the sun will be shining and the sands, whose texture constantly

Factbox

Location: Arnside is on the B5282, 22 miles (35.4km) south of Kendal, 16 miles (25.7km) north of Lancaster and 14 miles (22.5km) east of Grange-over-Sands. There is a car park on The Promenade at Arnside

Postcode: LA5 0HF

Length: The 8 mile (12.9km) route takes about 3½ hours

Terrain: It is easy, if soggy, walking, so don't be surprised to get your feet wet. Most people either use old trainers or simply remove their shoes and socks for the river crossings

Map: OS 1:25,000 Explorer OL07, The English Lakes: South-eastern area

Refreshments: Good local food is served at The Pheasant Inn, Flookburgh Road, Allithwaite LA11 7RQ

Ⓣ 01539 532239
Ⓦ thepheasantinnallithwaite.co.uk

For something a little grander, try the Hazelwood Restaurant or the Jacobean Bar, Cumbria Grand Hotel, Lindale Road, Grange-over-Sands LA11 6EN

Ⓣ 01539 532239
Ⓦ strathmorehotels-cumbriagrand.com

The former iron works chimney at Jenny Brown's Point

the route eventually turns west towards the highlight of the trip – the crossing of the Kent channel. On my first trip across the bay, which was early in the season, Cedric had warned us that it would be cold, and we found that the ochre-coloured river water that reached up to mid-thigh simply took our breath away. That was literally the case for one asthma-suffering member of our party, who succumbed to the bitter cold of the water and had to be carried across the river as we created a fireman's lift for him.

But the crossing is soon over, and you will wade triumphantly out onto the firmer, rippled sands on the Cumbrian side. The notorious Morecambe Bay quicksands form in the gullies where the water saturates the sands, and before we left, Cedric demonstrated the dangers to us by stepping out onto an apparently innocuous area, which wobbled and quaked like a jelly under his feet, threatening to suck him under at every step. He explained: 'The rule is, if it bends, it'll bear; but if it breaks, get out!' We needed no invitation to try out Cedric's theory, nor to linger too long at this sinister spot.

changes from hard ripples to the softer, wetter areas, will shimmer and live up to that 'wet Sahara' metaphor. This is how Cedric liked it. Leaning on his trusty staff like his Biblical nickname, he looked north towards the Lake District fells that feed the estuary and remarked: 'The bay has its own climate, y'know. You can sometimes see the weather rolling in up the coast, but it often seems to break before it reaches us and goes round towards the Lake District fells. It's a magical place, and I just couldn't imagine living anywhere else'.

After some time walking almost due south, apparently straight out into the Irish Sea and away from your destination,

It is now a few hundred yards to dry land, and you make your landfall near to Kent's Bank Station, on Network Rail's excellent and beautiful Cumbrian Coast service, which runs between Carlisle and Barrow-in-Furness. Unless you have a car waiting for you, a superb, scenic and sustainable way back is to catch the eastbound train, which crosses the 552 yards (505m) and 51 spans of the spectacular Arnside Viaduct, constructed in 1856, to return to your starting point at Arnside.

25.

'Out on the wily, windy moors':*
Brontë Moors, West Yorkshire
*Lyrics taken from 'Wuthering Heights', Kate Bush (1978)

The approach to 'Wuthering Heights'

'Wuthering' or 'withering' is a traditional North Country dialect adjective that comes from the Old Norse and means roaring like the wind on a stormy day. And according to Nelly Dean, Heathcliff's loyal servant in Emily Brontë's classic romantic novel *Wuthering Heights*, it fitted perfectly the 'atmospheric tumult' that often surrounded the bleak moorland hilltop on which the house was built.

'Pure, bracing ventilation they must have up there at all times, indeed; one may guess the power of the north wind blowing over the edge, by the excessive slant of the few stunted firs at the end of the house; and by a range of gaunt thorns all stretching their limbs one way, as if craving alms of the sun', as Nelly explained.

'Happily', she added, 'the architect had foresight to build it strong; the narrow windows are deeply set in the wall, and the corners defended with large, jutting stones'. Most authorities place the fictional Wuthering Heights at Top Withins, a roofless, ruined farmstead sheltered today not by firs but by two gnarled sycamores, on the wild moors

A view down Haworth's cobbled main street

to the west of the pretty West Yorkshire former mill town of Haworth, which is now the centre of what must be called the Brontë industry. And if proof was needed of the international interest in the writings of this strange and intensely self-centred family, you'll find some of the footpath signs we pass on the walk are in Japanese script.

Astonishingly, Kate Bush wrote her international chart-topping single 'Wuthering Heights' at the tender age of 18, becoming the first UK female artist to achieve a number one single with a self-composed song. She was inspired after seeing the last ten minutes of the 1967 BBC2 Hugh Leonard adaptation of the novel, which starred Ian McShane

as Heathcliff and Angela Scoular as Catherine Earnshaw. Bush then read the book, and coincidentally discovered that she shared her birthday (30 July) with Emily Brontë, 140 years later. She apparently recorded the vocal for the song – which if you relate it to the novel, Cathy is actually dead and therefore a ghost – in one take.

The grey cobbled hilltop town of Haworth in the Worth valley was where the Rev Patrick Brontë brought his family of Charlotte, Emily, Anne and Branwell, in 1809, when he took up the curacy of the parish church. He could never have guessed that Haworth's setting, on the edge of the grim, forbidding moors of the South Pennines, would have resulted in the extraordinary flowering of literary talent that it did.

There is no doubt that the moors were to play a big part in the lives of the Brontës, particularly those of the three talented sisters. They often took long walks from their home at the Parsonage, sometimes accompanied by their often drunken brother Branwell, up the steep valley of the Sladen and South Dean Beck, across the cloughs and dikes to the brooding, windswept moors above.

Charlotte's good friend Ellen Nussey sometimes accompanied them on these moorland walks, and she later described the experience: 'One long ramble made in these early days was far away over the moors to a spot familiar to Emily and Anne, which they called "The Meeting of the Waters". It was a small oasis of emerald green turf, broken here and there by small clear springs: a few large stones served as resting places; seated here, we were hidden from all the world, nothing appearing in view but miles and miles of heather, a glorious blue sky, and brightening sun'.

Of all the sisters, it appears it was Emily who was the most affected by the elemental wildness of the moors, and it certainly shows in *Wuthering Heights*, her only published novel. It is a towering masterpiece of human emotion, which perfectly captures the wild and untamed character of the moors. In her preface to the 1847 edition, published under the nom de plume of Ellis Bell (publishers did not think female novelists would sell in those unenlightened days), her sister Charlotte tried to explain the influence

the moors had on Emily: 'Ellis Bell did not describe as one whose eye and taste alone found pleasure in the prospect; her native hills were far more to her than a spectacle; they were what she lived in, and by, as much as the wild birds, their tenants, or as the heather, their produce'. Charlotte also wrote later: 'My sister Emily loved the moors...She found in the bleak solitude many and dear delights; and not the least and best-loved was – liberty'.

That's certainly a sentiment shared by generations of northern ramblers, and our walk follows in the footsteps of the Brontë sisters, visiting both the Meeting of the Waters, now known as the Brontë Falls, and the reputed site of Wuthering Heights, returning by the ridge-top village of Stanbury.

Such is the popularity of the Brontës in the Far East, some of the footpath signs are in Japanese

Factbox

Location: Haworth is just off the A6033, about 2 miles (3.2km) south of Keighley. There's a car park at the museum

Postcode: BD22 8DU

Length: About 7.5 miles (12km) and involves about 500 feet (152m) of gradual ascent

Terrain: Mainly on well-defined moorland paths, some of which are paved. However, boots and waterproofs are recommended

Map: OS 1:25,000 Explorer OL21, The South Pennines

Refreshments: Stanbury is blessed with a couple of excellent pubs at a convenient point on the walk, the award-winning Old Silent Inn, Hob Lane, Keighley BD22 0HW, where the food is claimed to be among the best in Yorkshire

T 01535 647437
W theoldsilent.co.uk

And the Wuthering Heights Inn, Main Street, Stanbury, Keighley BD22 0HB

T 01535 643332
W thewutheringheights.co.uk

There are also a number of restaurants and hostelries in Haworth

The Walk

We start from the Brontë Parsonage Museum car park, going through the gateposts opposite the museum and turning right. The lane soon becomes a paved field path, which leads up to West Lane. Turn left along the road and after about 80 yards (73m), take a left fork, on the lane signposted to Penistone Hill.

When you reach the junction with Moor Side Lane, take the stone-walled track straight ahead, signposted the Brontë Way and Top Withins. This track, which can be boggy in places, contours across The Slack with the Lower Laithe Reservoir below and passes several deserted farmsteads as it gradually descends to South Dean Beck.

This is crossed by the ancient Brontë Bridge, of slabbed clapper construction, while upstream to the left are the pretty Brontë Falls – Emily's 'Meeting of the Waters'. A natural gritstone boulder shaped like a chair near here is surely one of Ellen Nussey's 'resting places' and is inevitably now known as the Brontë Seat.

Take the path that leads steeply uphill, signposted 'Top Withins' and following the South Dean Beck over Sandy Hill and past deserted, circular sheepfolds until the dark, truncated shape of Top Withins, guarded by its windswept trees, comes into view. Crossing the beck and passing two more deserted farms (incidentally also called Withins) you eventually meet the Pennine Way 'motorway', coming in from the right.

The Brontë Bridge, on the way to Top Withins

Top Withins stands at nearly 1,400 feet (427m) above sea level and there can be little doubt, especially in winter, that it merits that northern epithet 'wuthering'. A plaque erected by the Brontë Society in 1964 honestly states that the buildings, even when complete, bore little resemblance to the house Emily described in the novel, 'but the situation may have been in her mind when she wrote of the moorland setting of the Heights'.

The former farmhouse achieved its ruinous state after it was struck by lightning during a thunderstorm in 1893. The roof was partially blown off, holes were made in the walls and windows were smashed. It was reported that in the kitchen, the blade of a knife was fused by the heat of the strike. The then residents, a Mrs Sunderland and her dog and cat, wisely fled the building in fear and trepidation. Maybe it was Cathy's revenge?

Turn right and follow the now-paved Pennine Way north, down over Scar and Flaight Hill, past the white-painted Upper Heights Farm. Bear left here, still on the Pennine Way, past Lower Heights Farm, and where the Way veers left after about 500 yards (457m), go straight ahead on the track signposted to Stanbury and Haworth.

As you enter Stanbury, which appears ahead, bear right and then take the first road on the right, signed to Oxenhope, to cross the dam of the Lower Laithe Reservoir. Immediately beyond the dam, turn left on a road which turns into a track as it climbs up to meet the road by Haworth Cemetery. You now retrace your steps into Haworth by walking left along the road, and across the stile to follow the paved field path back into the town.

Let's leave the last words to Kate Bush, in her wailing, wuthering classic:

Too long I roam in the night
I'm coming back to his side, to put it right
I'm coming home to wuthering, wuthering
Wuthering Heights

26.

Yorkshire's ghost village:
Wharram Percy, Yorkshire Wolds

BELOW Nineteenth-century cottages at Wharram Percy
RIGHT The roofless ruin of St Martin's Church

There's a chilling loneliness and indescribable melancholy about places in the countryside where people used to live, but which have, for whatever reason, been deserted. It somehow makes them even more bleak and desolate than the uninhabited wildernesses of mountain and moorland.

You can feel it in the sad remains of the ruined crofts left behind in the Scottish Highlands by the infamous Highland Clearances of the 18th and 19th centuries, or in the abandoned farms and villages of the West of Ireland, like the village of Slievemore on Achill Island in County Mayo, abandoned during the Great Potato Famine of the mid-19th century. I remember once on a walking trip to Connemara coming across one

such roofless, abandoned farmstead, a wizened elder tree now its only resident. In what was once the kitchen I found a large circular iron cooking pot, still lying half buried in the soil. I concluded the desperate fleeing family simply didn't have enough time or the strength to take it with them.

In England alone, there are estimated to be more than 3,000 deserted medieval

Sunk are thy bowers, in shapeless ruin all,
And the long grass o'ertops the mouldering wall;
And trembling, shrinking from the spoiler's hand,
Far, far away, thy children leave the land.
Ill fares the land, to hastening ills a prey,
Where wealth accumulates, and men decay:

Oliver Goldsmith, 'The Deserted Village' (1770)

villages, and the most common reason given for their abandonment is the Black Death or bubonic plague of the 14th century. But that's all too often an over-simplification, and there were many complex reasons for their desertion, as we will see on this walk.

Tucked away in a fold of the Yorkshire Wolds, the pinnacled tower and roofless aisle of an isolated ruined church stands close by a mill pond surrounded by mysterious bumps and hollows. Most people will never have heard of Wharram Percy, but to archaeologists, it's the most famous Deserted Medieval Village (DMV) in the country, some would say in Europe.

The Midlands and North of England are littered with such DMVs, marked on the map by the Gothic lettering the Ordnance Survey uses to record a non-Roman historic site. And Wharram Percy, near Malton in North Yorkshire, is the most thoroughly studied of any of them, with a continuous programme of research and excavation taking place for three weeks every July for over 40 years, led by a historian and an archaeologist – Maurice Beresford and John Hurst, joint founders of the Deserted Medieval Village Research Group.

But there are still many unanswered questions about Wharram Percy. As they conclude in their 1990 English Heritage book on the subject: 'The lesson for archaeology in general is that while on a moated or castle site, which is limited in area, it is practical to obtain the main story from a major excavation, a deserted medieval village, which may cover up to 40 acres (16ha), is so complex that the six per cent sample excavated at Wharram Percy is not sufficient to give a full and final explanation of the development of the site'. Their four decades of excavations, mainly carried out by hundreds of volunteers supervised by Beresford (usually accompanied by his dogs Lulu or Sheba) and Hurst, proved that the story of Wharram Percy extended well over the centuries back to the Bronze Age and included evidence of Roman, Anglo-Saxon, Viking and Norman, as well as medieval, settlement.

Although the Black Death must undoubtedly have taken its grim toll on the villagers of Wharram Percy, as it did in most communities in a national death toll that may have topped two million, there is no record of its effects here. But Beresford and Hurst proved beyond doubt that the final abandonment of the village in around 1500 had nothing to do with the Black Death. It happened when local landowners began to convert the landscape from its former arable use to more profitable sheep pasture, to provide wool for the burgeoning Pennine cloth-making industry in places like Leeds and Bradford. The final four families living in Wharram Percy were evicted and their houses demolished in 1500 to make way for sheep – a chilling precursor to the better-known Highland Clearances three centuries later.

On the way to Wharram Percy

The Walk

Our walk starts from the English Heritage car park off the B1248 to the south of Malton, just past Bella Farm. Follow the waymarked signs for the Yorkshire Wolds and Centenary Ways on an ancient holloway, which leads you gently downhill off Wharram Percy Wold towards the village in the valley.

When you reach a former line of the Malton and Driffield Railway in the valley bottom, head straight across to reach the first faint outlines of the crofts (houses) and tofts (fields) of the medieval village away to your right. The first you reach are the earthworks of the 12th or 13th-century North Manor, home to the medieval lords of the manor of Wharram Percy. It was probably built by Peter Percy (d.1266 or 1267), who became lord of the manor in 1254, and who was also possibly the man who gave his name to the village. Clustered around a courtyard at the highest point of the settlement, the probably two-storey building would have commanded a fine view down towards the crofts of the rest of the village, which at that time had a likely population of around 200 people.

The outlines of later medieval peasant houses and their strip fields visible on the slope above to the right lead on towards the site of what is known as the South Manor, which was unexpectedly found beneath them in 1955. Finds dating from the 8th–11th centuries prove that this part of the village was the site of an even earlier important residence, in Viking and Anglo-Saxon times.

The humps and bumps of the deserted village

Factbox

Location: Wharram Percy is 6 miles (9.7km) south-east of Malton on a minor road off the B1248, 0.5 miles (0.8km) south of Wharram-le-Street. The English Heritage car park is just to the south of Bella Farm

Postcode: YO17 9TD

Length: About 1 mile (1.6km), there and back, but allow at least a couple of hours to properly explore the site

Terrain: Uneven track, steep in places, but nothing too strenuous

Map: OS 1:25,000 Explorer OL300, Howardian Hills & Malton

Refreshments: The Royal Oak, 26 Market Place, Malton YO17 7LX

☎ 01653 692122
🌐 facebook.com/profile.php?id=100083329361954

Aerial view of Wharram Percy

We are now nearing the centre of the village, and the one remaining pantile-roofed 19th-century former farm workers' cottage (private) stands on the site of an earlier 18th-century building and farmyard. Beyond the cottage and just before you reach the church are the foundations of the 18th-century vicarage, overshadowed by the looming presence of St Martin's Church.

The first timber church on this site was built in the late 10th century and was possibly constructed by tenants on what was formerly the village green. An 11th-century Anglo-Saxon grave slab has been found in the church. This first church was gradually replaced and enlarged by the present stone building between the 12th and 16th centuries by the successive lords of the manor, the Percys and the Hiltons. It is amusing to surmise that the carved

The tower of St Martin's dominates the scene

or painted corbels in the eaves and at the ends of window mouldings in the church may represent the not-always-flattering faces of some former villagers, or their masters.

St Martin's also served the parishes of Thixendale, Burdale, Raisthorpe and Towthorpe, but when Thixendale built its own church in 1870 and the population of Wharram Percy had dwindled to a single household, it effectively became redundant. The last marriage took place there in 1928, and within 40 years, the church was in ruins.

The churchyard to the south contains headstones of the late 18th and 19th century, bearing surnames of families which are still found locally. Nearly 700 skeletons in 600 graves were excavated by Beresford and Hurst in the northern half of the graveyard, revealing many early deaths and signs of malnourishment. In 2017, a disturbing Historic England study of bones found in three pits between houses in the village discovered that many had been mutilated or burnt, apparently in order in ensure their spirits stayed in their graves. A skeletal biologist at Historic England concluded that it was a graphic reminder of how different the medieval view of the world was from our own.

Water is a valuable commodity in the chalk Wolds, where streams often disappear underground in summer. The vital stream at Wharram, which is simply known as The Beck, is fed by springs a little further south at the confluence of Deep Dale and Drue Dale at the southern end of the village. It has been dammed

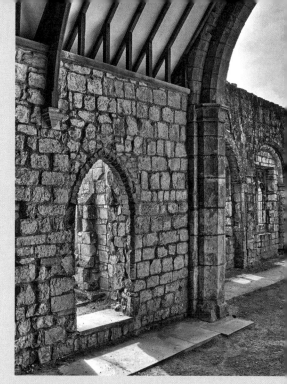

Interior of St Martin's Church

to create the mill pond, just beyond the church, since at least the 9th century. It would have been the focal point of the village, where sheep, cattle and horses would be taken to drink and where people could come to get water for cooking and washing, and no doubt share the latest village gossip. The mill would have ground corn to make bread for the villagers, but it was abandoned in the 12th or 13th centuries and the pond was stocked with fish during the later Middle Ages by the monks of Haltemprice Priory, near Hull.

Perhaps the last word on Wharram Percy should be left to Beresford and Hurst, the men who did so much to uncover its mysteries. 'The work there has helped to transform our knowledge of the different forms that human settlement in the English countryside has taken at various times, making the history of the English village one of continual change'.

27.

The bloodiest battle:
Towton, Yorkshire

BELOW St Mary's Chapel, Lead
RIGHT Looking into the now peaceful valley of the Cock Beck

Even the most amateur historian has heard of the Battle of Hastings, the last successful invasion of Britain on the date that schoolchildren remember. Or maybe the Battle of Bosworth Field in the English Midlands, which brought the Tudors to the English throne, or the battles for Scottish independence at Bannockburn or for the Jacobite cause at Flodden.

But few people, except perhaps ardent students of the Wars of the Roses, have heard of the largest, longest and bloodiest battle ever to be fought on English soil. It happened on a bitterly cold, snow and sleet-swept Palm Sunday, 29 March 1461, on a bleak plateau between the villages of Towton and Saxton, near Tadcaster in North Yorkshire. The combined numbers of the opposing forces of York and Lancaster have been estimated at over 50,000 and in the brutal bloodbath that followed, they fought hand-to-hand for at least three hours in the freezing wind and driving sleet and snow of that unseasonal spring Sunday.

The estimated death toll of 28,000, from the battle and the previous skirmishes

O pity, pity, gentle heaven, pity!
The red rose and the white are on his face,
The fatal colours of our striving houses:
The one his purple blood right well resembles;
The other his pale cheeks, methinks, presenteth:
Wither one rose, and let the other flourish;
If you contend, a thousand lives must wither.

William Shakespeare, *Henry VI, Part Three* (1591)

at Dintingdale and Ferrybridge, far exceeds what is usually claimed as the single most disastrous day in the nation's military history – the 19,000 killed in the carnage of the first day of the Battle of the Somme, during the First World War. It should be noted that this later, none-the-less horrendous, loss was from a British population of over 36 million in 1916, compared to only about three million in 1461.

Prof Charles Ross, an eminent historian of the period, has estimated that of all those eligible to fight (ie those aged between 16 and 60), a tenth found themselves on the Towton battlefield that fateful day. 'It was,' according to its most recent chronicler, historian George Goodwin, 'not merely a military engagement – it was a national catastrophe'.

Few people have heard of the Battle of Towton, though because of its sheer scale and significance, it surely deserves to be on the curriculum for every history student. Not only was it the bloodiest battle, Towton also fundamentally changed the course of English history. A direct result was that later that year, Edward IV replaced Henry VI and established the House of York as successors to the English throne, consigning Henry, the House of Lancaster and its supporters to history.

According to Goodwin, one of the main reasons Towton was allowed to fade from history was that Tudor propaganda insisted that Bosworth Field in 1485 was the key battle that ended the Wars of the Roses and put Henry Tudor on the throne. But tradition has it that it is always the victors who write the history, and because Towton was a Yorkist victory, it wasn't seen as favourable to the Tudor cause and therefore should be forgotten.

The signposted 3 mile (4.8km) Towton Battlefield Trail, created by the enterprising Towton Battlefield Society, explores the site of the battle on footpaths and roadside paths, with useful information boards along the way explaining the key points, its combat equipment and archaeology.

New light on the scale and severity of the slaughter in the battle was shed by an archaeological find at Towton Hall in 1996. Workmen discovered a mass grave containing about 50 male skeletons, ranging in height from 5.4-6 feet (1.6-1.8m). These were believed to be the remains of men who were slain during or after the battle, 535 years before. Further bodies were later recovered

Dacre Cross overlooking the battlefield

The Rockingham Arms, Towton

from beneath the dining room of Towton Hall, which is also believed to include what remains of the commemorative chantry chapel started by Edward IV and completed by his youngest brother Richard III after the battle in 1483.

There can be little doubt that Towton Hall was squarely in the path of the retreating Lancastrians, so it seems a safe bet to conclude that this mass grave was made as the Lancastrian army broke up and fled the field after the battle.

Osteoarchaeologists and archaeologists from Bradford and York universities conducted a detailed forensic study of the remains, and radiocarbon dating showed that the men, whose ages ranged from 17 to 50, were interred precisely at the time of the battle, in the mid-15th century. The skeletons exhibited a horrifying catalogue of multiple injuries, 'far in excess of those necessary to cause disability and death', with severe damage to their upper torsos, and many arms and skulls fractured or shattered. They also exhibited clear evidence of fierce hand-to-hand combat, with numerous arm and hand injuries resulting from attempts to parry blows.

Bioarchaeologist Shannon Novak of Bradford university concluded the remains revealed scenes of 'frenzied killing that involved numerous blows to the head often after (the victims) were incapacitated and unable to defend themselves'. The well-built man known as Towton 16, for example, had a total of eight blunt and puncture wounds to his skull delivered from both the front and back, indicating that he may have been summarily executed after the battle.

You can find out more about the bloody Battle of Towton from the regular walks and evening talks run by the Towton Battlefield Society (Web: towton.org.uk) throughout the year at Saxton village hall. The society was formed in the mid-1990s with the objectives of the preservation, protection and promotion of the sadly forgotten battlefield of Towton.

The Walk

We start the walk at the Rockingham Arms in Towton and head south through the village along the B1217 to meet up with the Towton Battlefield Trail on the right, just past the walled 17th-century Towton Hall (private), where many bodies from the battle were unearthed in 1996 (see below).

This broad fenced path leads gradually up alongside the B1217 to reach the 5 foot (1.5m)-high York stone Dacre Cross that appears on the skyline, the original of which was possibly erected soon after the battle. It was restored with the shaft inserted into a concrete plinth in 1929, and when I last visited, it was poignantly adorned with a solitary bunch of withered white Yorkist roses.

The cross was named after the Lancastrian leader Ralph, Lord Dacre of Gilsland, who died in the battle after being struck by a crossbow bolt having removed the gorget protecting his throat to take a sip of wine. Unusually for an aristocrat, Dacre was buried in what is now a 17th-century railed, tabletop tomb in the common graveyard of All Saints Church, Saxton. Dacre's horse

Factbox

Location: Towton is on the A162, about 4 miles (6.4km) south of Tadcaster

Postcode: LS24 9PB

Length: The walk is approximately 3 miles (4.8km) and should take about 1½ hours to complete

Terrain: Ascending alongside a quiet road and then an undulating grassy farm track. Stout footwear is recommended as the trail can be muddy

Map: OS 1:25,000 Explorer OL290, York

Refreshments: The Rockingham Arms, Main Street, Towton, Tadcaster LS24 9PB, is a family-run village pub offering hearty dishes and beer in a cosy atmosphere

☎ 01937 530948
🌐 therockinghamarms.pub

The redbrick Crooked Billet Inn, Saxton, Tadcaster LS24 9QN, is well-known for its gigantic Yorkshire puddings

☎ 01937 557389
🌐 crooked-billet.co.uk

Battlefield Trail sign

was allegedly buried with him, and sure enough in 1861 the skull of a horse was unearthed close by the tomb. There is also a modern white pyramidical sculpture in memory of the soldiers who died at Towton near Dacre's tomb in the churchyard.

The battle actually started in the broad plateau of arable fields known as North Acres, across the road from the cross. The battle lines were drawn as Lancastrian forces assembled to the north and the Yorkists to the south, facing each other 300 yards (274m) apart. It began with a hail of Yorkist arrows flying with the icy force of the blizzard behind them into the massed Lancastrian ranks.

In the words of Edward Hall's *Chronicle*, first published in 1548, 'This battayl was sore foughtĕ, for hope of life was set on euery parte and takynge of prisoners was proclaymed as a great offence, by reason whereof euery man determined, either to conquere or to dye in the felde. This deadly battayle and bloudy conflicte, continued. x. houres in doubtfull victorie'.

The action gradually moved west into the gruesome killing field of Bloody Meadow, which we visit next by turning right at the cross. This farm track leads to the edge of the escarpment and a viewing platform with an interpretive board overlooking the meadow, with the scattered trees of Renshaw Woods appearing in the deep valley below.

Scene of 'the bloodiest battle'

Interior of Lead Chapel

The appropriately named Bloody Meadow is now a flat pasture field on the western bank of Cock Beck. This open meadow, today peacefully grazed by sheep, was where many of the retreating and by now panicking Lancastrian forces led by Henry Beaufort, the 23-year-old Duke of Somerset, were ruthlessly slaughtered by the Yorkist army, which included Edward and was commanded by William Neville, Lord Fauconberg.

As the retreating Lancastrians struggled down and across the steep-sided Cock Beck, a stream then swollen by snow into a roaring torrent, they slid down its banks and many drowned, weighed down by their heavy plate armour. The beck was said to run red with the blood of the dead as the victorious Yorkists hacked at them with bill, spear and sword, and ruthlessly pursued the survivors – leaving a blood-stained 6 mile (9.7km)-long trail northwards across the snow. George Neville, Bishop of Exeter and cousin of Edward, wrote, 'one might have seen the bodies of these unfortunate men lying unburied over a space of nearly 6 miles (9.7km) in length and three or four furlongs (0.5 miles/0.8km) broad'.

A sign now leads right onto a broad, undulating grassy farm track running north through glorious countryside for about 1 mile (1.6km) along the edge of the eastern escarpment formed by the Cock Beck. We were accompanied by an elegant soaring red kite when I last did this walk.

When you reach the junction with the Old London Road, another sign indicates the sinisterly but aptly named Bridge of Bodies, which lies out of sight to the north-west. This was where the retreating Lancastrians, having destroyed the original bridge over the rushing Cock Beck to protect their rear, created a gory bridge of their own with the dead and dying bodies of their comrades, trapped and drowned in the headlong melee.

The track now leads easily back into Towton as you re-enter the village by the side of the Rockingham Arms.

28.

Chasing the Lambton Worm:
Penshaw Monument, Tyne & Wear

Penshaw Monument, 'a blackened northern Parthenon'

Standing like a blackened northern Parthenon in the middle of what was once the Durham coalfield and echoing the classical Greek Temple of Theseus in Athens, the Penshaw Monument is surely one of the most curious memorials in Britain.

The mock temple folly, near Houghton le Spring in Tyne & Wear, was erected in 1844 in memory of John George Lambton, the 1st Earl of Durham and a former Governor General and High Commissioner of British North America (now Canada), whose family seat was at Lambton Park in the valley of the Wear.

Lord Durham was known as 'Radical Jack' because in 1830, as Lord Privy Seal in Earl Grey's Whig government,

he was one of the four proposers of the long-awaited Reform Bill, which abolished the long-standing anomaly of the 'rotten boroughs'. Previously, a remote rural constituency was able to elect a Member of Parliament despite having very few voters, and the choice of the MP was typically in the hands of a member of the landed gentry. Lambton's time as Governor General of Canada was equally momentous because it was his version of a constitution, written in 1839,

Penshaw stands proudly on its hill overlooking the former Durham coalfield

which formed the basis of many of the dominion's modern laws.

The extraordinary 70 foot (21m)-high roofless Doric temple on Penshaw Hill is a worthy reminder of the great reformer, whose affectionate local nickname was 'King Jog' or 'Jog Along Jack'. This came from when he was asked in 1821 what he considered an adequate income for an English gentleman. He replied: 'A man might jog along comfortably enough on £40,000 a year' – which is equivalent to a staggering £4 million plus today. The monument was erected by public subscription – an indication of his popularity – and it was designed by John and Benjamin Green of Newcastle. When the foundation stone was laid in 1844, the ceremony was attended by Freemasons from all over the world, led by the Grand Master, the Earl of Zetland.

Lord Durham was married twice. Radical from an early age, he fell in love with Harriet, the illegitimate and under-age daughter of the Earl of Cholmondeley. When he was refused permission by his guardians to marry her, he wed her anyway in a runaway romance at Gretna Green in 1812. The marriage was confirmed later that year in an Anglican ceremony on her father's estate in Malpas, Cheshire. After Harriet's death three years later, he married Lady Louisa Grey in 1816, eldest surviving daughter of Charles Grey, the 2nd Earl Grey, future Prime Minister and leader of the Reform Movement.

The Penshaw Monument is a landmark for miles around, and still seems a strangely surrealistic sight in the midst of the former coalfield, towering above the villages of Fatfield, Philadelphia and Shiney Row, the residents of which use it as a popular place for a picnic.

Either Penshaw or more likely nearby Worm Hill was also the reputed home of a monster linked to one of Radical Jack's ancestors who lived at Lambton Castle during the Middle Ages. As a youngster this earlier John Lambton caught a strange-looking worm while fishing in the River Wear. He was about to throw the worm back when an old man appeared. He warned him he must not throw it back or he would suffer a terrible fate, so on his way home he tossed it into a well near the castle.

When he grew up, John joined a crusade to the Holy Land, completely forgetting about the worm, which grew to an enormous size and began terrorising the neighbourhood. At night it would sleep coiled nine times around a hill thereafter known as Worm Hill. It demanded a daily levy of the milk of nine cows, in default of which it would lay waste to the local countryside. Attempts to kill it proved fruitless, for each time it was cut in two, the halves merely joined together again.

When John Lambton returned to England, he was horrified to learn what had happened and consulted a local witch or wise woman to ascertain the best way of disposing of the monster. She advised him to stud his armour with knife blades in order to kill the worm but imposed the condition that he must kill the first living thing he met after his victory.

Lambton duly kitted himself out with a suit of bristling armour, and when the worm coiled itself around him in the ensuing battle, it literally cut itself to pieces, which were swept away in the River Wear before they could join up again. The sequel to the story is that hearing his son's bugle call, which heralded his victory over the hated worm, his father, who was supposed to have released his son's favourite greyhound when he heard the call, could not contain his joy and ran with open arms to be the first to congratulate him.

Lambton Castle

Young Lambton immediately appealed to the witch to lift the dreadful condition she had imposed on him and she relented, insisting instead that no Lambton chief would die in his bed for the next seven (or nine according to some accounts) generations. In the bloodthirsty days of almost constant warfare which existed in medieval England, that was probably a price worth paying.

The story of the Lambton Worm formed the basis of Ken Russell's 1988 cult horror movie, *The Lair of the White Worm* (see the Thor's Cave walk on page 130). In the same year the Lambton Worm came back to life in a sinuous 300 yard (274m)-long, work of art by Andy Goldsworthy who used spoil from a local pit at South Pelaw on the former Consett to Sunderland railway, which is now part of the 140 mile (225km) Sea-to-Sea Cycle Route. This work has recently been restored.

The view from the Penshaw Monument is truly stupendous. The River Wear, graveyard of the legendary worm, winds itself around the foot of the hill, with the East Coast mainline railway beyond. The tower blocks of Gateshead and Newcastle fill the northern skyline, while closer directly to the east is Sunderland, birthplace of so much of Britain's former maritime greatness. To the south, the triple towers of Durham Cathedral can just be made out, marking the ancient seat of the Prince Bishops of Durham, who ruled this land for so many centuries.

But the panoramic view also reveals a slowly healing landscape, once torn apart by the needs of industry and now almost recovered to its former beauty. The many polluting collieries of the past are long gone, regretfully many of their thriving communities with them, leaving Penshaw to revert to its ancient name, which simply means 'wooded hill'.

An aerial view of the Penshaw Monument

The Walk

We start our walk, which visits some of the places mentioned in the legend, from the car park at the foot of Penshaw Hill. You might just be able to make out the top of Lambton Park, ancestral home of the Lambtons, sticking out above the trees to the east.

Turn left on a track and then right across fields until you reach the Coxgreen Road at a crossroads. Go straight across then immediately right on a path, which leads past Low Lambton Wood on your right and down to the banks of the River Wear.

Turn right and walk along the riverbank and you soon come to the stone-arched well, where John Lambton allegedly dropped his worm with such disastrous effects. Past the small hamlet of Cox Green keep to the riverside path until you reach the place locally named The Worm's Lair; fortunately there was no sign of it when I passed.

When a path leads off right into Ayton's Wood, leave the river and follow the path passing Wood House Farm on your left. Continue along the access road to the farm until you see a footpath sign leading right into Pawson's Plantation, which according to the National Trust could have been the home of the witch who advised John Lambton about his spiked suit of armour.

The Penshaw Monument now appears again up ahead as you leave the trees of Penshaw Wood and make the steady climb back up to the monument for another chance to admire the wonderful views from the summit. Return downhill to the car park and your starting point.

Factbox

Location: The Penshaw Hill car park is on the A183 Chester Road, Penshaw, near Houghton-le-Spring, about 1 mile (1.6km) from the A19

Postcode: DH4 7NJ

Length: About 2.5 miles (4km), but allow at least 1½ hours

Terrain: Easy going on field and riverside paths

Map: OS 1:25,000 Explorer OL308, Durham & Sunderland

Refreshments: The Grey Horse, Penshaw Lane, Houghton-le-Spring DH4 7ER

☎ 01915 126080
Ⓦ greyhorsepenshaw.co.uk

Or the Shoulder of Mutton Inn, 1 Penshaw Place, Penshaw, Houghton-le-Spring DH4 7DY. Both are village pubs offering good food.

☎ 01913 852366

Is this the Worm's Lair?

29.

Kinder surprise:
Kinder Scout, Derbyshire

BELOW A walker on one of Kinder's edges
RIGHT A sunset view towards Kinder Reservoir from the top of
Kinder Downfall

Like many walkers before me and certainly many more since, I'll never forget my first encounter with Kinder Scout. It was the early 1970s, and I had escaped the choking confines of strike-torn Coventry with a fellow journalist for a day's walking in the Peak.

I remember the paper's somewhat supercilious drama critic asking us, in all innocence, who was this more benevolent member of the popular boys' youth movement we were meeting up with in Derbyshire?

Apart from knowing how to pronounce the name correctly (it's 'Kin-der'), we didn't know much more about the highest point in the Peak District than

him at the time. Neither of us had been there before, but I'd read up what looked like an interesting route delineated by Walter (WA) Poucher in that scratchy white pen, which was my introduction to the hills in the days long before I could read a map (*The Peak and Pennines*, 1966).

We set off from the neat National Trust hamlet of Barber Booth and into the

gradually narrowing ravine of Crowden Brook. There was, and still is, the feel of a Highland glen in the grand interlocking spurs of this approach to Kinder, and it remains one of my favourite routes to reach the plateau. Graceful rowans wept over tumbling waterfalls as the path soon gave way to rough gritstone boulders and we walked up into the silent, beating heart of the hills, watched over all the time by the looming buttress of Crowden Tower. Occasional light showers of rain did not deter us, for there was the promise of sun to come. An exciting little scramble near the infamous Keyhole Rock eventually brought us breathlessly out onto the summit plateau.

What a sight greeted our unbelieving eyes! We had never seen anything remotely like this before, and we were simply not prepared for it. Simultaneously, we both reflected we could have been on the Moon. A vast, rippling sea of peat hags and groughs stretched to the far horizon, with not a sign of vegetation nor life of any kind. Paradoxically, we felt on top of the world but at the same time as if we were looking at an ocean of chocolate-coloured breakers of peat.

Then, as the promised watery sun broke through the clouds, thin wisps of steam began to rise gently from the endless banks of peat. Kinder really looked like 'a vast heap of dinosaur droppings', as John Hillaby had so memorably described it in his classic *Journey Through Britain* (1968). The only sound to break the oppressive, primeval silence of this soggy wilderness was the now familiar, 'go back, go back' warning cackle of a brace of red grouse, and the faint cheep of meadow pipits sounding, again as Hillaby put it, 'like the last ticks of a clock that has almost run down'. It was, he concluded: '... an example of land at the end of its tether'.

Things have substantially changed on Kinder since then, thanks to the sterling work of the National Trust, its owners since 1982, and the award-winning Moors for the Future partnership. A ten-year programme of gulley-blocking, re-wetting and re-planting and, most importantly, the removal of an astonishing 38,000 over-grazing 'bandit' sheep, has seen Kinder bloom again. There is more vegetation now - heather, cotton grass and bilberry and associated wildlife - than I have seen in 50 years.

We continued round to reach the extraordinary natural sculpture park known as The Woolpacks, also known as The Mushroom Garden and even Whipsnade, from their weirdly animalistic shapes. This is a group of eroded gritstone rocks on the southern edge of the plateau which have been shaped into fantastic shapes by aeons of wind, rain, snow and frost. Among the many named formations, which are said to have inspired sculptor Henry Moore, are The Mother and Child or The Moat Stones, The Snail, and The Watcher. Nearby are also Pym Chair and The Pagoda.

I remember taking my good friend the respected mountain photographer John Cleare to see The Woolpacks one misty autumnal day. Even as a renowned Himalayan and Alpine climber himself, he confessed he was astonished by the weird rock formations and, not least, the endless photographic opportunities.

Of course, I've been back many, many times since, and old Kinder has never let me down. It's always the same, yet somehow always different. Unfailingly big, moody and magnificent, Kinder is truly more of a spirit than a mountain.

Kinder Scout, at 2,088 feet (636m) the highest point of the Peak District, is probably the most walked-upon mountain in Britain. But it is still a place of constant surprises - 15 square miles (39 sq km) of blanket peat bog with no easily perceivable summit, yet a place of kaleidoscopic and ever-changing beauty with a social and political history that is unmatched in British hills.

Some of the weird rock formations on Kinder's edges

Kinder Downfall

Edale, on its south side, is famed among hairy-kneed backpackers as the southern terminus of Tom Stephenson's 268 mile (431km) Pennine Way marathon. It was the scene over 90 years ago of 'the Battle of Kinder Scout'   the most infamous incident in the century-old battle for the cherished right to roam on our mountains and moorlands. In a carefully orchestrated and well-publicised assault on the grouse-shooting landlords' selfish embargo, about 400 ramblers, led by Benny Rothman of the Young Communist-inspired British Workers' Sports Federation, deliberately and spectacularly called their bluff. The ensuing scuffles with the waiting gamekeepers resulted in five young ramblers, including Rothman, being convicted and imprisoned for 'riotous assembly', merely for exercising what they believed to be their freedom to roam. It was a momentous and iconic milestone in the long campaign for access to the countryside, still celebrated annually by our Spirit of Kinder event.

The plaque commemorating the Mass Trespass at Bowden Bridge

The Walk

Our walk follows in the footsteps of the trespassers and shows some of the finest features of the once-forbidden mountain without actually stepping on the sacred slopes of Kinder. You can still appreciate its stern grandeur from this 'Trespass Trail', which was created by the Hayfield Kinder Trespass Group.

From the village centre, walk up the cobbled path by the side of the Royal Hotel to reach Kinder Road. You may recognise some of these locations, as they formed the backdrop to the 2013/14 Peter Moffatt BBC TV drama *The Village*, which starred Maxine Peake and John Simm.

After about 300 yards (274m), look out for the venerable cast-iron Peak & Northern Counties Footpath Society sign No 30, dated 29 May 1897, on your left, which commemorates the society's first major victory in securing this right of way crossing a shoulder of Kinder Scout from Hayfield to the Snake Inn in the Woodlands Valley.

Follow this path gently uphill on a holloway, which leads past a touching memorial to local lad 15-year-old Charlie Craig, a promising young cyclist who died in his sleep of heart failure in 2018. You pass through a couple of kissing gates to the wind-tossed copse of sycamores locally known as Twenty Trees (although there are now only 19). There are outstanding views from here, back towards Hayfield village and across to Chinley Churn and South Head.

The path from The Woolpacks towards Pym Chair

At the kissing gate with an information board, turn right to continue the main path through the heather of Middle Moor. In the distance you will see a prominent, white-walled former Shooting Cabin, once used by grouse shooters after the 'glorious Twelfth'.

Keeping the cabin to your left, you come across the PNCFS sign (registering 1,109 feet (338m), and which ironically warns 'Do Not Trespass') to Glossop, with views of the western aspect of Kinder Scout, the broken crags of Sandy Heys forming the edge, now opening up in front of you.

When the blue waters of the Kinder Reservoir come into view, keep to the higher path which leads round White and Nab Brows before descending on a very rocky and steep path towards the gash of William Clough and a wooden footbridge. To the left is the path up William Clough where the 1932 trespassers dared to leave the ancient right of way.

To return to Hayfield, take the often muddy lower path, which leads round the edge of the reservoir with views opening up to the south-west aspect of Kinder, marked by the 100 foot (30.5m) Kinder Downfall in its steep ravine. Kinder Downfall is famed for its extraordinary habit of flowing uphill when the prevailing westerly wind funnels up the valley to throw the falling water back on itself. If you see it as a dancing, shifting white cloud from here, you'll know it's going to be windy on top.

The path leads on, eventually reaching a stone-pitched, cobbled section that leads steeply down to the tree-lined waterworks road by the infant River Kinder, then down the metalled Kinder Road to the car park at Bowden Bridge.

Bowden Bridge quarry was the starting point of the 1932 trespass, and the weathered bronze plaque on the quarry face was unveiled by Benny Rothman on the 50th anniversary in 1982 to commemorate the fact. Cross the road and walk down to the Hayfield Camping and Caravanning site and follow the pleasant riverside path back into Hayfield.

Lord Roy Hattersley once described the Kinder Mass Trespass as 'the most

successful example of direct action in British history', and it was certainly the most iconic event in the century-old battle to regain access to our countryside. As Dame Fiona Reynolds, former Director General of the National Trust, wrote on the 90th anniversary in 2022: '... the freedom to walk there, with the joy it brings, remains one of the powerful reasons why Kinder Scout has such meaning and value to people today'.

Factbox

Location: Hayfield village is bypassed by the A624 Buxton-Glossop road, and there is a large car park to the west of the main road

Postcode: SK22 2JG

Length: About 5.5 miles (8.9km)

Terrain: Some moorland walking requiring boots, waterproofs, map and compass

Map: OS 1:25,000 Explorer OL1, The Peak District – Dark Peak Area

Refreshments: The Sportsman Inn, 135 Kinder Road, Hayfield SK22 2LE

☎ 01663 741565
Ⓦ thesportsmaninn.co.uk

Millie's Hayfield Tearoom and Chocolatier, 7 Church Street, Hayfield High Peak SK22 2JE

☎ 01663 741584
Ⓦ millieshayfield.co.uk

30.

Castles in the air:
Alport Castles, Derbyshire

BELOW Looking down on Alport Castles Farm
RIGHT Alport Castles, with The Tower centre left

It was a balmy midsummer's evening in the heart of the Dark Peak. I had taken a journalist friend of mine to see the tottering towers and eroded rock faces of Alport Castles, said to be the largest inland landslip in Britain, under the shadow of Bleaklow in the remote Alport Valley.

Suddenly, we became aware of a piercing 'kek, kek, kek' cry filling the air above us. To our delight we looked up to see a pair of peregrine falcons with their brood of three youngsters trailing in their wake, joyfully cavorting in the thermals rising from the rock face, which was by now glowing a warm gold in the westering evening sun. I knew that peregrines, the ultimate masters of the sky, had returned to their closely guarded nest site on the

Castles that year, after an absence of over three decades. To be lucky enough to see these dashing raptors revelling in the peace and solitude of that splendid setting, and in that golden evening light, became a precious memory which will always stay with me.

Unfortunately, peregrines have not been seen at Alport Castles recently, and they still suffer from inexcusable and illegal

persecution by the grouse shooting fraternity. But nationally, there has been an encouraging increase in their numbers, especially in the human-made canyons created by city centre spires and tower blocks.

Alport Castles is undoubtedly one of the geological and scenic highlights of the 555 square mile (1,437 sq km) Peak District National Park, but it is rarely visited because of its wild remoteness. Geologically speaking, the Alport Valley is made up of weak Carboniferous shales overlain by the harder Millstone Grit. Alport Castles formed when the 300 million-year-old Namurian sandstones

and shales of the Birchin Hat escarpment slipped away from the rock face, leaving a chaotic landscape of teetering towers and fallen boulders.

But what caused this enormous, half-mile (0.8km)-long landslip? It's thought that water seeping between the cracks and shale must have weakened the shale and caused it to slip away. The gritstone is naturally full of joints, so it breaks into blocks when the shale below becomes unstable. Frost and ice during the last Ice Age would have accelerated this process, and glacial erosion could have also over-steepened the side of the valley, causing it to slip away as the glacier receded.

Alport Mere

We start our walk from the Fairholmes Visitor Centre, in the shadow of the castellated Derwent Dam in the Upper Derwent Valley. Many valleys in the Dark Peak were flooded in the early years of the last century to create a series of reservoirs. Mercifully, Alport Dale escaped this fate.

The triple chain of the Howden, Derwent and Ladybower Reservoirs which trap and fill the Upper Derwent represent the largest area of water in the Peak and has been dubbed the Peak District's Lake District. The Derwent Dams were constructed by the Derwent Valley Water Board (now Severn Trent Water) to supply fresh, clean water to the fast-expanding industrial populations of Sheffield, Derby, Nottingham and Leicester.

The first two massive masonry dams constructed were the Howden and Derwent, between 1902 and 1916. During their construction, a temporary village, locally known as Tin Town because of its corrugated iron walls and roofs, housed the 1,000 navvies (labourers) and their families.

The larger Ladybower earthen dam and its two-armed reservoir downstream followed in 1943 and it took two years to finally fill with water.

The villages of Derwent and Ashopton were demolished to accommodate the reservoir, and their residents were re-housed at nearby Bamford. In times of drought, such as the summer of 2022, the foundations of some of the buildings of Derwent village, including the hall that was one of the first youth hostels in the Peak, can be seen rising from the water.

During the Second World War, the Howden and Derwent dams and reservoirs were used for practice flights and the dropping of the famous 'bouncing bombs' by the Avro Lancasters of 617 Squadron – forever after known as 'the Dam Busters'. They were chosen because they closely matched the target dams in the Ruhr Valley in Nazi Germany. The Derwent Dams were also later used as the backdrop to the 1955 film The Dam Busters, starring Richard Todd and Michael Redgrave.

The Walk

The walk starts from the car park at the Visitor Centre, by crossing the entrance lane and entering the dark coniferous forestry plantation opposite via a wooden gate. Cross a culvert bridge and follow the footpath left to meet a stone track, which you should follow up a short rise to a gate into a field. Passing Lockerbrook Farm (now an outdoor centre) you come to a junction of paths at the edge of a wood. Turn right here to a ladder stile, which leads up past Bellhag and Pasture Tor and across Lockerbrook Heights. After about a mile (1.6km) of steady moorland walking, this leads to the escarpment of Birchin Hat, with the Alport Valley to your left and Alport Castles below.

As you look down from the lip of the escarpment, you see how great blocks, such as the substantial one known as Little Moor, have broken away from the main cliff face and slid down the side of the valley. It has created a landscape of narrow chasms littered with angular boulders of grit. With a little imagination, they can resemble castles – hence that rather fanciful name – or even the buttes and mesas of far off Utah in the American West. This is especially the case with the most impressive feature, named The Tower, which is an isolated rock pinnacle that looks for all the world like a ruined medieval fortress. Beneath The Tower lies one of the Peak's only true mountain tarns, the reed-fringed pool known as Alport Mere, which supports no less than six species of dragonfly.

A 70-year-old Peak & Northern footpath sign to Alport Castles

Factbox

Location: The Upper Derwent Visitor Centre is located at Fairholmes, in the Upper Derwent Valley, about 2 miles (3.2km) up Derwent Lane, a minor road off the A57 near the western end of the Ashopton Viaduct

Postcode: S33 0AQ

Length: Just over 7 miles (11.3km); allow 4–5 hours

Terrain: There is some serious moorland walking on this route, so you need to be well equipped with boots and waterproofs

Map: OS 1:25,000 Explorer OL1, The Peak District – Dark Peak Area

Refreshments: There is a refreshment kiosk at the Upper Derwent Visitor Centre, Fairholmes, Bamford, Hope Valley S33 0AQ

☏ 01629 816527
🌐 peakdistrict.gov.uk/visiting/visitor-centres/derwent

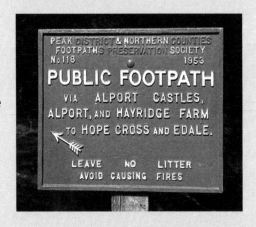

The track to Alport Castles Farm

After you've had a thorough exploration of the spectacular landslip, follow the faint footpath, which leads steeply down to a crossing of the Alport River near Alport Castles Farm. This remote farmstead was one of the secluded places where John Wesley, the founder of Methodism, preached his non-conformist doctrine in the 18th century. Every July it is still the scene of an obscure Methodist celebration known as the Love Feast. Instead of the usual communion wine and wafers, the congregation share fruitcake and water from a two-handled Loving Cup, to commemorate their proud non-conformist tradition.

Alport Castles Farm is also where the socialist and suffragette Hannah Mitchell was born and brought up. Mitchell, who received only two weeks' formal education by walking across the moors to Glossop every day, ran away from home and a domineering mother and worked in a Manchester clothing sweatshop. She eventually became a city councillor and magistrate. Mitchell was also a member of the Independent Labour Party and a prominent speaker alongside Emmeline Pankhurst in the cause of women's suffrage, which was not achieved until 1928.

From the farm, follow the unmetalled, hawthorn-hedged track, which leads down the valley for about a mile (0.8km) towards the A57 Snake Road. The Snake Pass, between the western arm of the Ladybower Reservoir at Ashopton and Glossop, is the most scenic route linking Sheffield and Greater Manchester. It reaches the dizzy height of 1,680 feet (512m) at the Snake Summit, where the Pennine Way crosses it. The road is perhaps best known from winter weather broadcasts – when it snows it is always one of the first roads to close and one of the last to reopen.

Despite what many people might assume from its winding nature, the pass actually takes its name from the serpent-headed coat of arms of the Dukes of Devonshire. The Dukes of Devonshire and Norfolk, both prominent local landowners, contributed towards the cost of the Sheffield to Glossop Turnpike road when it was constructed between 1818 and 1821.

About 2 miles (3.2km) to the west of here is The Snake Pass Inn, originally known as Lady Clough House. It was built in 1821 by the 6th Duke of Devonshire of Chatsworth and the Cavendish family's coat of arms formerly welcomed visitors over the inn's front door. The Inn is now closed.

Take great care when crossing the busy A57 and descend to the infant River Ashop to take the track signposted 'Upper Derwent' towards Rowlee Bridge. In woodland now, cross the water conduit and follow the footpath, which leads down to cross the A57 again, opposite Hagg Farm, an outdoor education centre run by Nottinghamshire County Council.

Passing through a couple of gates to the right of the farm, you will soon meet a bridleway junction. This is signposted and leads (right) through forestry plantations back down to your starting point at Fairholmes.

Alport Dale shows how the Upper Derwent used to look before the water engineers cast their greedy eyes on its water supply possibilities. And the amazing, spectacular landscape of Alport Castles shows the immense power of natural erosion in one of the Peak's most remote and least visited valleys.

Looking down on The Tower (left) with Kinder Scout in the background

31.

First settlers in Settle:
Attermire Caves, Yorkshire Dales

BELOW The entrance to Victoria Cave
RIGHT The rolling, drystone walled landscape of the Yorkshire Dales

One day in 1837, a local tinsmith named Michael Horner was out rabbiting with his dogs along the limestone escarpment of Attermire Scar, a couple of miles (3–4km) east of the ancient market town of Settle on the edge of the Yorkshire Dales.

Suddenly one of his dogs spotted a fox and chased it down into a narrow crevice in the crag. When the dog failed to return, Horner dug into the soil, removing the small boulders the blocked the crevice entrance and crawled inside to try to find his missing pet. But to his astonishment, instead he found fossilised bones, metal objects and some ancient coins in the undisturbed topsoil of the cave floor.

After he'd recovered his missing dog and crawled back out of the cave, Horner immediately told his boss, Joseph Jackson, who had a keen amateur interest in archaeology, of his unexpected find. But it was a year later, on 28 June 1838, the day 19-year-old Princess Victoria's coronation in Westminster Abbey, before Jackson actually crawled inside to investigate the cave for himself, which he patriotically named in honour of the new young queen.

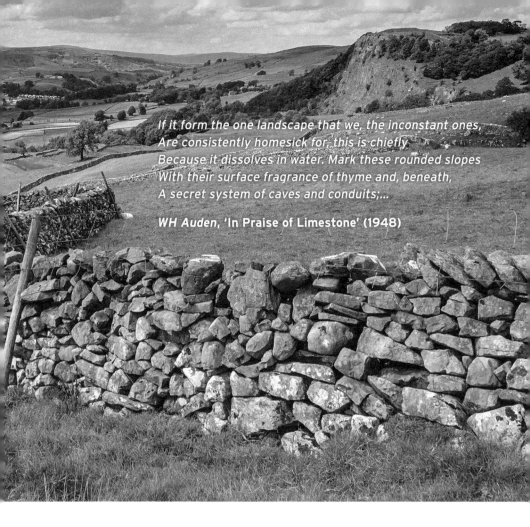

If it form the one landscape that we, the inconstant ones,
Are consistently homesick for, this is chiefly
Because it dissolves in water. Mark these rounded slopes
With their surface fragrance of thyme and, beneath,
A secret system of caves and conduits;...

WH Auden, 'In Praise of Limestone' (1948)

Jackson was the first person to excavate the cave, and he also became the founder of the Settle Cave Exploration Committee. In addition to the Romano British coins found by Horner, Jackson also recovered from the cave the fossilised bones of hippopotamus, rhinoceros, mammoth, brown bear and reindeer dating back over 130,000 years; a barbed harpoon point made from a deer antler; an antler rod and a possible lance point, proving that human occupation of the cave went back over 10,000 years.

The first full-scale excavation of Victoria Cave took place in the 1870s when Jackson was assisted by the respected geologist, cave explorer and antiquarian William Boyd Dawkins. They uncovered many more spectacular finds, including Roman and Bronze Age artefacts, brooches and more coins. Many of these finds are now housed in Craven Museum and Gallery at Skipton, which has an exhibition of items found in the cave, including the skull of a bear.

More recent and perhaps more scientific archaeology has shown that many of the fossilised bones could have been dragged into the cave by scavenging hyenas, and also that prehistoric people may have been hunting reindeer in the Dales as

Looking out from Victoria Cave

long ago as 12,500 BC, just after the glaciers of the Ice Age retreated.

The scene of this totally unexpected yet revelatory glimpse into the prehistory of the Dales is the objective of our walk, which also takes in some of the fascinating Carboniferous karst limestone scenery of Ribblesdale, including the strange outcrop of Warrendale Knotts.

The pearly-white limestone of the Yorkshire Dales was laid down in a shallow tropical sea during the Carboniferous period, around 350 million years ago, in conditions much like we see today in the Caribbean Sea or Great Barrier Reef of Australia. At that time, Yorkshire and most of what is now the British Isles were situated a few degrees north of the Equator, and the temperature was many degrees higher than it is today. Millions and millions of tiny sea creatures lived and died in these shallow tropical waters, and as

they died, they drifted in a constant cloud to the bottom of the primeval sea, eventually being covered and pressured by overlaying material to be petrified and turn into the fossil-rich limestone we see today.

For many visitors, the ancient market town of Settle is the gateway to the Yorkshire Dales. But while lots of peak-baggers may use Settle as a base to explore the higher Three Peaks country of Ribblesdale, they miss the delights of its classic karst limestone country, and evidence of the homes of the earliest settlers in these wild uplands in the crags and caves of Attermire, right on Settle's doorstep.

The 'karst' name for this type of scenery, characterised by underground drainage systems, sinkholes and caves formed by the dissolution of soluble rocks like limestone, comes from the Karst (or Kras) region, north-east of the Gulf of Trieste in Slovenia.

The Walk

From Settle Market Square, which is overshadowed by its own limestone crag known as Castleberg, the summit of which was laid out as a giant sundial in the 18th century, walk up the steep Constitution Hill, which rises to the left of The Shambles. When the road turns left, take the cobbled Banks Lane. Just beyond a small plantation, follow the track signposted Pennine Bridleway, which leads left.

The 205 mile (330km)-long Pennine Bridleway, which was fully opened in 2012 and was specifically designed for horse riders but is also suitable for mountain bikers and walkers, runs up the Pennines between Derbyshire and Cumbria. The southern terminus is either at Hartington Station on the Tissington Trail or at Middleton Top on the High Peak Trail in the Peak District, and the northern one the village of Ravenstonedale, below Wild Boar Fell near Kirkby Stephen in Cumbria.

Follow the bridleway as it climbs steadily across open fields and passes through a number of gates. At this point, the distant peaks of Ingleborough and, closer at hand, the distinctive, stepped lion couchant profile of Pen-y-ghent, come into view.

Climbing the Yorkshire Three Peaks of Pen-y-Ghent (2,277 feet/694m), Whernside (2,415 feet/736m) and Ingleborough (2,372 feet/723m) is a classic one-day marathon undertaken by thousands of walkers every year. The route, which covers 24 miles (39km) and involves 5,200 feet (1,585m) of

Factbox

Location: Settle is on the B6480, off the A65 Skipton-Kirkby Lonsdale road. Park at Market Place

Postcode: BD24 9EF

Length: A circular walk of about 4 miles (6.4km)

Terrain: Some steep slopes on uneven ground and tracks. Stout footwear is recommended

Map: OS 1:25,000 Explorer OL2, The Yorkshire Dales

Refreshments: The quaintly named Ye Olde Naked Man Café, 2 Market Place, Settle BD24 9ED, specialise in homemade produce with a bakery, sandwich bar and café

☎ 01729 823230
🌐 yeoldenakedmancafe.com/

The Talbot Arms, High Street, Settle BD24 9EX

☎ 01729 823924
🌐 talbotsettle.co.uk

The Golden Lion, Duke Street, Settle BD24 9DU

☎ 01729 822203
🌐 goldenlionsettle.co.uk

The Royal Oak, Market Place, Settle BD24 9ED

☎ 01729 822561
🌐 vixen-pubs.co.uk/royal-oak-hotel-pub-settle

A distant view of Attermire Scar

ascent, usually starts from Horton-in-Ribblesdale and should be completed within 12 hours if you are to qualify for the Three Peaks certificate. I did it many years ago, and it remains one of the toughest, yet most satisfying, walking marathons I have ever done.

Still following the Pennine Bridleway, when you reach the metalled Langcliffe Lane, turn right along the stony track, through two gates, and at the second, turn immediately right to down a narrow path, signposted Victoria Cave, alongside a wall. The serried battlements of Attermire Scar are now prominent in the view ahead.

The first significant cave you come to is the shallow Jubilee Cave, which was named in honour of the Silver Jubilee of King George V in 1935. It was first explored by local amateur archaeologist Thomas 'Tot' Lord, who found a bone bead and toggle, providing further evidence of early human occupation here.

An indistinct track heads beneath the crag towards the obvious gaping mouth of Victoria Cave, where there is a useful information board. Although you are advised not to venture into the cave, it's perhaps worth taking a sneaky peek just to get the view our prehistoric ancestors might have had 10,000 years ago, across the broad valley of the River Ribble towards Ingleborough and Three Peak country to the north-west.

Archaeology has revealed that the series of caves along the Langcliffe and Attermire Scars all originally existed at river level and were once considerably longer. They are the remains of former underground water passages which have been truncated by millions of years of erosion and successive glaciations during the Ice Ages.

Head back down to the path and continue along the base of the large limestone cliff known as Attermire Scar to your left. Turning right, ahead lie the weirdly shaped limestone outcrops of Warrendale Knotts, which also contain some shallow caves. Pass through the Knotts with the conical reef knoll of Sugar Loaf Hill on your left. These weathered limestone mesas and buttes can make this seem more like a scene in Arizona than Yorkshire.

When you reach a crossroads in the footpaths, turn left and follow the obvious grassy path that heads across open fields before dropping down to re-join Banks Lane. It's now just a question of retracing your steps into the Market Square in Settle.

Another view of the cave-haunted scar

32.

Cumbria's Grand Canyon:
High Cup Nick, Cumbria

BELOW Maize Beck tips into the chasm of High Cup Nick
RIGHT The dramatic view from High Cup Nick

Nothing quite prepares you for the jaw-dropping moment as you follow Maize Beck and cross the flat limestone outcrops and shake holes of High Cup Plain on Tom Stephenson's marathon masterpiece, the Pennine Way.

After you have crossed the Tees above the 600 foot (183m) tumbling cataract of Cauldron Snout and left County Durham behind to enter Cumbria, you suddenly find yourself teetering on the edge of a yawning abyss, with a whole new world at your feet.

For many people this is the greatest spectacle and most memorable moment on the entire 268 mile (431km) Way. High Cup Nick - the name really only applies

to the apex of the gorge on which you are standing - has with some justification been dubbed the Grand Canyon of the Pennines. This huge bite out of the western scarp of the range has also been named as the most glorious landscape feature in the whole of northern England.

The result of grinding glacial action during the last Ice Age, the vast amphitheatre drops away beneath your feet, with the tiny silver thread of High

Cup Gill winding through the valley hundreds of feet below. The views to the west extend far out across the misty Vale of Eden and the distant blue outline of the Lakeland hills. What a moment, and one which will make you forget those 158 thigh-aching, toe-blistering, bog-trotting miles (254km) you have endured to reach this magical point. It is, according to Alfred Wainwright, the respected fell-wanderer and author of *Pennine Way Companion* (1968), 'a great moment on the journey'.

The estranged but adopted Yorkshireman WH Auden, exiled in New York during the Second World War, regarded this spot as 'one of the sacred places of the earth' and he described it in his 1940 poem, 'New Year Letter':

> *There where the Eden leisures through*
> *Its sandstone valley, is my view*
> *Of green and civil life that dwells*
> *Below a cliff of savage fells...*

The 'cliff of savage fells', which mark the rim of the ravine, are columns of the steely-grey dolerite of the Whin Sill, which create the grandstand palisade of High Cup Nick. They include the sometimes hard-to-find rocky finger known as Nichol's Chair or Last, which is about 20 yards (18m) off the main path. It was

The elusive Nichol's Chair

named after a brave but more likely foolhardy Dufton cobbler who had the audacity - or sheer nerve - to climb to its airy summit and sole and heel a pair of boots while sitting on the tiny platform. Apparently, it was done for a bet and was not, like so many of these tales, a load of old cobblers...

The Pennine Way then descends on a pleasant path into a walled bridleway, which leads into the charming red sandstone village of Dufton, pleasingly grouped around its village green. As the ever-pragmatic Wainwright pointed out, it's slightly galling to note that your long-term objective of Kirk Yetholm is actually further away at the end of this glorious day than it was at the beginning. Thanks AW, but it was worth it.

The Walk

Reversing the usual south-north route of the Pennine Way, we start our walk to the highlight of High Cup Nick from the village green in Dufton. Dufton, an attractive collection of cottages some of which date from the 17th century, was a centre for lead mining during the 18th and 19th centuries. The Quaker-owned and community-conscious London Lead Company developed the village through the building of houses, a school, a library and the installation of piped water. The company also built the sandstone ball-topped fountain and circular water trough on the green, which forms the centrepiece of the village. Roughly translated from the Latin, the inscription on the fountain reads:

*There is a clear pool, whose waters
gleam like silver. It is not tainted by
shepherds, or by their she-goats grazing
on the mountain. Nor is it muddied by
cattle, or by birds or wild animals,
or by a branch fallen from a tree.*

Follow the country lane east from the village and at the charmingly named Billysbeck Bridge, you will meet the walled bridleway known as Narrow Gate on the left, which leads past Bow Hall Farm and unerringly uphill for a steady 4 miles (6.4km) to the top of High Cup Nick, passing the attractive Pennine outliers of Dodd Hill and Peeping Hill on the way.

This is a former lead miners' track, which follows a line of marker stones and cairns and passes an abandoned sandstone quarry with a lime kiln perched away to your left. The rough track runs along

Factbox

Location: Dufton is signposted on a minor road off the A66 near Appleby-in-Westmorland

Postcode: CA16 6DB

Length: About 8 miles (12.9km), there and back, but you should allow a full day

Terrain: This is a serious fell walk into high moorland country, and although on easy paths, good boots, waterproofs and a map should be used

Map: OS 1:25,000 Explorer OL19, Howgill Fells & Upper Eden Valley

Refreshments: The red sandstone-walled Stag Inn, Dufton, Appleby-in-Westmorland CA16 6DB, which overlooks the village green, was built in 1703 and is a CAMRA-listed, walker friendly pub that serves good wholesome food

☎ 01768 351608
Ⓦ thestagdufton.co.uk

Dufton village green with Dufton Pike in the background

'The Grand Canyon of the Pennines'

a broad shelf in the hillside, with steep, scree-covered slopes to the left and a sheer drop down to the stream of High Cup Gill to the right. It eventually leads around Blackstone Edge past a spring under a boulder called Hannah's Well towards the head of the gorge at Narrowgate Beacon, topping out at the not inconsiderable Pennine height of 1,936 feet (590m).

The great gorge of High Cup Nick has sometimes been compared to the glacial trenches of the Cairngorms, and it looks totally impossible that the tiny High Cup Gill could have carved out this dramatic chasm. And of course, it didn't. It was the grinding power of the glaciers of the last Ice Age some 10,000 years ago which were the agents responsible for this over-deepened valley. The dramatic cliffs around its edges are an outcropping of the igneous Great Whin Sill, exposed by

the passage of the ice, and the boulders which litter the valley floor are the relics of the collapsed sill wall.

The Whin Sill is quite literally an outstanding landscape feature of this part of northern England. High Cup Nick is virtually the westernmost exposure of this volcanic rock, forced up as magma

View from inside the lime kiln

through weaknesses in the overlying sedimentary sandstone and limestone during the Carboniferous period some 300 million years ago. The Whin Sill forms the foundation of the spectacular Caldron Snout and High Force waterfalls, met earlier on the Pennine Way to the south, which crash over other exposures of this hard, erosion-resistant rock.

It was also used by the Roman Emperor Hadrian as a natural defence against the barbarian Picts and Scots to the north when he constructed his famous and eponymous 73 mile (117km)-long Wall linking the North Sea to the Irish Sea in AD 22. He perched this great northern barrier of the Roman Empire on the Whin Sill escarpment, and it is still perhaps best seen at places like Sewingshields Crag, near the excavated fort at Housesteads, or towering above the lake at Crag Lough. The Whin Sill continues south-eastwards until it reaches the North Sea and the crags on which the splendid castles on the Holy Island of Lindisfarne and at Bambrough were constructed, and then out to the seal and seabird-haunted, jagged rock islands of the Farnes, anchored off the Northumberland coast.

Returning to High Cup Nick, when the wind comes strongly from the west, you might be treated to the unusual sight of a waterfall flowing uphill, a phenomenon the Nick shares with Kinder Downfall in the Peak District. If the wind is strong enough, the stream that flows into the nick can sometimes be seen hanging in the air and even actually flowing backwards from whence it came. On a wet day, you can literally get soaked, as I have, from above and beneath at the same time!

View from the trail looking towards Dufton Pike

The cliffs of High Cup Nick have in recent years seen the welcome return of peregrine falcons, and those superb fliers can sometimes be seen floating on the updraughts from the Whin Sill crags as they hunt for their prey. The hoarse croaks of an 'unkindness' of ravens have also been heard recently echoing from the crags.

Reversing our outward route and heading back downhill on Narrow Gate, a great panorama unfolds before you to the west, taking in the eastern Lake District Fells, with the smoothly rounded Howgill Fells to the north and the western Pennines to the south. Immediately to the north is the shapely pyramid of Dufton Pike (1,578 foot/481m), which is another popular walk from its eponymous village, with great views to the west.

Eventually the track becomes metalled again, running gently downhill under the shade of oak, ash and sycamore trees. Arriving at the unclassified road, turn right and head back into Dufton.

33.

A curious encounter with Wainwright: Cautley Spout, Howgill Fells, Cumbria

BELOW The view up the valley of Cautley Holme Beck towards the Spout
RIGHT A distant view of Cautley Spout

The silver-haired old man sitting by the tumbling waterfall in his battered anorak and puffing his trusty briar seemed to be alone with his thoughts. Despite the apparently unwelcome attention of the television film crew buzzing around him, it was obvious his mind and spirit were elsewhere.

His bespectacled eyes constantly drifted away from the camera up the gorge, where the water cascaded steeply down between weeping rowans, or to the wild green coombe across the valley which had been scooped out by an Ice Age glacier.

There was a time, before pushy publishers insisted on putting his photograph on the dust jackets of his best-selling books, when he would have walked many a mile

to avoid such a situation. Those were the days when plain 'A Wainwright' was proud of his closely guarded anonymity, when he would deliberately hide behind a wall or rock as a school party approached or he found a summit was already occupied, simply to avoid what he regarded as idle conversation.

I got the strong impression on this, my first and only meeting with the legendary

fell wanderer Alfred Wainwright, that he was not enjoying the experience and would much rather be tramping the fells on his own, even though he was then in his 79th year.

I had been walking with my family up to the spectacular 650 foot (198m) cascade of Cautley Spout in the eastern Howgill Fells, in the far west of the Yorkshire Dales National Park. As we descended the path from the waterfall, we came across Wainwright perched by the side of the beck, surrounded by the film crew.

I immediately recognised the snowy white hair and mutton-chop whiskers

and, ever the opportunistic journalist, I waited until the crew had finished their filming with AW before grabbing the chance of a rare interview with the iconic and notoriously shy character myself.

As many others had found before me, I discovered that Wainwright was grumpy and non-committal with most of his answers. I remember that our conversation was interrupted as two RAF Phantom jets screamed down the valley of the Rawthey, apparently playing supersonic tag with one another. As their thunderous roar echoed back from the cliffs of Cautley Crag, we agreed that it was a shame the boundaries of the

The River Rawthey near Low Haygarth

National Park could not be extended skywards.

When the producer eventually indicated that my time was up, Wainwright's eyes once again drifted up the hills and he asked me how far I was going that day? His voice was full of the unspoken regret that he didn't have the day to himself and his beloved mountains. And as he was shepherded back to the waiting Land Rover which was parked in a green oasis at the end of the track just below our meeting place, I couldn't help thinking that it was a sad figure who shouldered his battered old rucksack and set off down the trail, alone with his memories once more.

Wainwright's seven classic and meticulously self-penned *Pictorial Guides to the Lakeland Fells* had guided me, and countless thousands of other fell wanderers, up the 214 summits of his beloved Lake District since the first one was published in 1955. They had become an unprecedented success story when they topped the best-seller lists, and they have now sold more than two million copies. All profits from their sales go to Animal Rescue Cumbria – Wainwright always professed he liked animals more than people.

His reluctance for self-promotion and publicity was as well-known as his books. When he was interviewed by Sue Lawley on BBC Radio 4's *Desert Island Discs* in 1988 (she had to travel up to Manchester to catch up with him), she asked him what kind of music he liked, he memorably replied: 'I prefer silence'.

Wainwright described the location of our suggested walk to Cautley Spout in his *Walks on the Howgill Fells* (1972) as '... the most impressive corner of the Howgills, with dramatic scenery and splendid views'. And the series of tumbling waterfalls of Cautley Spout as '... the finest in the Howgills and one of the highest in the country'.

The Walk

We start our walk at the famously teetotal Cross Keys Temperance Inn on the A683 at Cautley, where a quotation by William Blake carved on a lintel there might have been penned with Wainwright in mind:

Great things are done
when men and mountains meet:
These are not done by jostling
in the street.

Before it became an inn in the early 18th century, the Cross Keys was a farmhouse known as High Haygarth, the earliest recorded occupant being a Thomas Bland in 1619. The oldest part of the building is the parlour and the room above, but the property was extended in the mid-17th century and again in the early 18th and 19th centuries after it had become an inn. It was bequeathed to the National Trust in 1949 in the will of Mrs Edith Adelaide Bunney in memory of her sister, Mary Blanche Hewetson, on the condition that it remained an unlicensed inn, which it is to this day.

We start our walk from the inn, where just to the north of the buildings, you cross the footbridge over the River Rawthey, signposted to Cautley Spout. Turn left following the obvious path until you reach Cautley Holme Beck, which comes down from the right.

With the broken buttresses of Cautley Crag towering away to your left and the steep, broken ground of Yarlside to your right, follow this easy path gently up the bracken-strewn valley of Cautley Holme Beck towards the beckoning gash of Cautley Spout, which now appears in full view ahead. Cautley Holme Beck rises just below the contour in the upper slopes of The Calf (2,218 feet/676m), the highest point of the Howgill Fells.

Factbox

Location: The Cross Keys Inn at Cautley is on the A683 Sedbergh-Kirkby Stephen road, about 4 miles (6.4km) from Sedburgh

Postcode: LA10 5NE

Length: It's about 3 miles (4.8km) there and back to the falls from the Cross Keys. The extension to the Calf would extend the walk by 5.5-6 miles (8.9-9.7km)

Terrain: Boots and waterproofs are recommended, because you are in quite serious mountain country here and the paths could become quite rough and wet

Map: OS 1:25,000 Explorer OL19, Howgill Fells & Upper Eden Valley

Refreshments: The Cross Keys Temperance Inn, Cautley, Sedburgh LE10 5NE, has a pleasant restaurant, but don't expect to be served wine, unless you bring your own! The inn is run by the National Trust, and for bibliophiles, it has the added bonus of a book café

T 01539 620284
W cautleyspout.co.uk

The Cross Keys Inn

Not before time, the entire 40 square miles (104 sq km) of the Howgills were incorporated into the Yorkshire Dales National Park in 2016, after a reorganisation of its boundaries that linked the Dales to the Lake District National Park across the Lune Gorge and the snarling ribbon of the M6 motorway.

But the landscape of the Howgills is quite unlike that of their near neighbours, the craggy volcanic rocks of the Lake District and the limestone-dominated Yorkshire Dales. They are formed of a grey Silurian sandstone, which weathers to give a smooth, gently rolling landscape, usually uncrossed by drystone boundary walls and thus giving an unrivalled sense of freedom to the walker.

Wainwright, in an unusually lyrical mood, described them thus: 'They are sleek and smooth, looking from a distance like velvet curtains in sunlight, like silken drapes at sunset; they are steep-sided but gently domed, and beautiful in a way that few hilly areas are'.

Cautley Spout, which by now you have reached, is England's highest cascade-type waterfall that is entirely above ground. The broken, twisting, rowan-decked series of lace-like cascades, which form Cautley Spout, tumble down the steep-sided rocky ravine at the head of the wild glacial valley of Cautley Holme Beck. It is one of the most impressive, yet least visited, sights in the Yorkshire Dales National Park. Only Fell Beck on the southern slopes of Ingleborough, which falls an unbroken 340 feet (104m) into the open pothole of Gaping Gill, above Clapham, and Fossdale Beck, which leaps 100 feet (30m) at Hardraw Force into its hidden amphitheatre behind the former Green Dragon Inn near Hawes in Wensleydale, can compare.

When you reach the foot of the falls, crashing down to your left, you have a choice of paths. To get a really intimate view of the series of cascading waterfalls, you must scramble steeply up the north bank. But take care, this is a potentially dangerous path and not for anyone unsure on their feet or scared of heights.

An easier but longer option is to take the path north, which eventually leads to Bowderdale Head, between Bowderdale and Yarlside. And if you are feeling really fit and equipped for a mountain trek, from Bowderdale Head you can follow this path left (west), which rises easily to the reigning summit of The Calf, passing a tiny windswept tarn on the way. From the trig point on the summit of The Calf there are splendid views on a clear

View from the top of Cautley Spout down the valley of Cautley Holme Beck

day across to the distant Lakeland fells, extending to Coniston Old Man, the Scafells, Great Gable and Helvellyn to the north, while to the south-east, Yorkshire's renowned Three Peaks – Pen-y-Ghent, Whernside and Ingleborough – stand in proud isolation.

When you have had your fill of The Calf and the magical cascades of Cautley Spout, just make your way back down the valley of Cautley Holme Beck to the Cross Keys Inn at the foot of the valley.

Perhaps the last word on the beguiling Howgills should be left to Wainwright. In his day at least he said: 'One can walk all day here knowing full well that not another soul will be seen, and that one's footsteps may never again be trodden for years'.

34.

Monolithic maidens:
Long Meg and her Daughters, Cumbria

BELOW Long Meg
RIGHT Meg (right foreground) overlooks her daughters

Considerably less known and therefore less visited than the other Cumbrian stone circles such as Castlerigg and Swinside, Long Meg and her Daughters, near the village of Little Salkeld in the Eden Valley, is actually larger than Stonehenge and one of the earliest stone circles in the country.

William Wordsworth was so impressed by the 358 x 295 feet (109 x 90m) flattened circle of around 69 stones that he wrote: 'Next to Stonehenge, it is beyond dispute the most notable relick [sic] that this or probably any other country contains'.

The isolated towering megalith of Long Meg herself - 12 feet (3.7m) high and weighing over nine tons - was constructed from the local red

sandstone, while her daughters all consist of grey volcanic rhyolite almost certainly transported, possibly as glacial erratics, from the Lake District.

As might be expected, Long Meg and her Daughters have attracted their fair share of folklore. The most repeated legend, common to many other stone circles, is that they are a group of maidens (or witches) who were caught dancing on

Speak Thou, whose massy strength and stature scorn
The power of years, - pre-eminent, and placed
Apart, to overlook the circle vast, -
Speak, Giant-mother! Tell it to the Morn

William Wordsworth, 'The Monument' (1822)

the Sabbath and turned into stone. Another states that if you break off a piece of stone from the red sandstone monolith of Long Meg herself, the stone will bleed.

The earliest recorded account appears to be from the so-called 'wondrous wizard' Michael Scott (c. 1175–1230) of Kelso in Scotland, who practised astrology in Palermo, Sicily and was somehow magically transported to 17th-century Britain. There he not only 'cleft the Eildon Hills in twain' but also endowed Long Meg's stones with a magic power so that no one could count the stones in the circle and reach the same number twice.

If you were successful, the witches' coven would be brought back to life, or you would be turned to stone yourself. (Once again, this belief in uncountable stones is common in other British stone circles).

But there seems to be some sort of astrological thinking behind the construction of this massive yet little known stone circle. Aubrey Burl, the foremost authority on British stone circles, discovered that from the centre of the circle, the two portal stones in the south-west segment line up with Long Meg and the sunset over the distant Helvellyn in the Lakes at the midwinter solstice.

An aerial view of Long Meg (left) and her Daughters

More recent archaeological investigations by Paul Frodsham of Altogether Archaeology concluded that the Long Meg complex of monuments should be regarded as one of Britain's most important Neolithic sites. He also found that there may be a cultural connection between the pecked curvilinear rings and spirals discovered in the 19th century on the east face of Long Meg with Irish passage grave art, such as that found in the similarly dated Neolithic passage tombs of Newgrange and Knowth, in the Boyne Valley, County Meath. The concentric circles and at least one anti-clockwise spiral bear a strong resemblance to the Irish rock art and are very different in character to the more common cup-and-ring art found in the rest of Northern Britain. Frodsham also suggests that the motifs may originally have been pecked onto the surface of a river cliff, such as those near Lacy's Caves (which we will visit later on in our walk), which was later quarried and erected overlooking the pre-existing stone circle.

The Walk

We start our walk in the charming village of Little Salkeld, which lies in the shadow of Cross Fell, at 2,930 feet (893m), the highest point in the Pennines, in the peaceful Eden Valley. Little Salkeld's pink-walled 18th-century mill is Cumbria's only fully operational watermill, and still produces stone-ground organic flours.

Take the road north out of the village and you will soon come across a sign pointing the way to Long Meg and her Daughters. Following the signs, you'll reach Wordsworth's 'circle vast' in about 15 minutes. Grazing cattle allowing, take plenty of time to explore the stones and see how many you can count. But don't try it again or you may find yourself in a witches' coven – or even petrified!

It is thought that the circle was built on this wide sandstone terrace above the east bank of the River Eden in around 3300 BC, with maternal Long Meg herself being added slightly later. A line of mature oak trees now march across the circle, somehow adding to the sense of essential timelessness of the monument.

Leaving Long Meg and her Daughters, follow the path north along the edge of a plantation that leads to her diminutive cousin, Little Meg. Often obscured in summer by long grass, the ten or so stones of Little Meg were once thought to form another stone circle but are now considered to be the large kerb stones that surrounded a Bronze Age burial cairn. One of the stones carries carvings of a spiral and five concentric circles, but be warned, they are extremely difficult to see.

Factbox

Location: Park carefully in Little Salkeld, which is 1.5 miles (2.4km) north of Langwathby on the B6412, off the A686 Penrith-Brampton road

Postcode: CA10 1NW

Length: Just over 5 miles (8km); takes about 2½ hours

Terrain: Moderate; mostly on quiet lanes and fields, woodland and riverside paths involving a little ascent

Map: OS 1:25,000 Explorer OL5, The English Lakes: North-eastern area

Refreshments: The nearest pub that also serves food is The Highland Drove Inn, Great Salkeld, Penrith CA11 9NA

☎ 01768 870304
🌐 thehighlanddrove.co.uk/

Spiral rock art on Long Meg

Crossing a field, take the quiet lane which leads to the equally quiet village of Glassonby. The originally 13th-century red sandstone church of St Michael and All Angels, which stands a mile (1.6km) south of the village, is actually not the parish church of Glassonby but of the lost village of Addingham. Addingham was completely destroyed when the River Eden burst its banks sometime in the 14th century.

Take the road from Glassonby towards Kirkoswald and you soon arrive at Daleraven Bridge across the River Eden. Take the occasionally surfaced and gradually rising riverside path, which leads upstream and takes you up through the pleasant Tib Wood until you eventually reach the fabled Lacy's Caves. These are carved into the rich red sandstone cliffs, which according to archaeologists, could also have been the possible source of the stone of Long Meg herself.

Lacy's Caves consist of a series of five chambers named after Lieutenant Colonel Samuel Lacy of Salkeld Hall, who commissioned their construction, allegedly by an army deserter, in the 18th century. Lacy also installed a real-life hermit and is thought to have used the caves as a curiosity for the entertainment of his guests. The area was originally also planted with ornamental gardens including some blousy rhododendrons which still survive. Over the centuries, visitors have covered the roofs and walls of Lacy's Caves with a mass of graffiti carved into the living rock. Take care

Lacy's Caves overlook the River Eden

Inside Lacy's Caves

here because there are steep drops – but splendid views – down to the rushing River Eden below.

The eccentric Lacy once attempted to blow up the Long Meg circle, which was also on his land, presumably in the interests of agricultural improvement. But when the work was started by his labourers, 'such a storm of thunder and lightning, and such heavy rain and hail ensued as the fell-sides never before witnessed'. The labourers fled for their lives, vowing never to meddle with Long Meg again.

An alternative, less fanciful but perhaps more meteorologically sound theory is that the storm may have been the result of Britain's only named wind – the Helm Wind. The Helm still occasionally blows with some ferocity down from the slopes of Cross Fell – which perhaps not coincidentally was formerly known as 'Fiends Fell' and believed to be the haunt of evil spirits. The imminent coming of the wind is signalled by a cap or 'bar' formed by a standing wave of cloud over the escarpment and is created when a strong north-easterly strikes the south-western slopes of Cross Fell. It can sound like an approaching express train, and has been known to blow people over, uproot trees and destroy crops in the valley below.

Leaving the caves, the path now drops down to the river, which passes over a series of stepped outcrops near the weir of the disused Force Mill. Look out for dippers along the river here.

Passing through woodland you will notice that in places the path follows the metalwork and sleepers of a former railway line. The tracks lead to and eventually pass the site of the disused Long Meg gypsum mine, which operated between 1880 and 1976. The branch line linked the mine to the Settle-Carlisle Railway, where a now disused signal box still bears the name Long Meg Mine.

The path now leads onto the lane which brings you back to our starting point on the village green in Little Salkeld.

Little Salkeld watermill

35.

Land's End of Yorkshire:
Spurn Head, Humberside

BELOW Remains of groynes at Spurn Head
RIGHT An aerial view of Spurn Head's insubstantial spit

Spurn Head, the 3 mile (4.8km)-long spit of sand and gravel which curls around the mouth of the Humber in East Yorkshire like the tail of a reprimanded dog, is a truly otherworldly place, unlike anywhere else in Britain.

The feeling of exposure to the elements is overwhelming, as the sea closes in on either side, constantly eating away and threatening the permanence of this slender spit, which dwindles to a mere 50 yards (46m) at its narrowest point.

To the east, gigantic tankers float ghostly by on the tide, waiting their turn to enter the Humber, passing the grim, castellated outlines of the Second World War forts isolated out in the North Sea.

The latest addition to the skyline is the forest of white-painted towers and sails of the huge Humber Gateway wind farm, which harvests the wind to power more than 150,000 homes in East Yorkshire. The constant wind whispers mournfully through the spiky marram grass and the skeletal,seaweed and barnacle-encrusted groynes march out to the sea, as skeins of screaming seabirds seem to mock your very presence. It's Yorkshire's very own version of Land's End.

But beware, this walk is not without its perils. You must always be aware that there is a half mile (0.8km) 'wash over' section of soft sand, which is regularly taken back by the greedy sea at high tide. This effectively cuts off the end of the peninsula from the mainland – creating as it does Yorkshire's one and only true island.

The dynamic natural processes that created Spurn are still constantly modelling the landscape today. In December 2013, for example, Spurn became a permanent island again as a huge tidal surge flooded large areas of the spit and swept through 500 feet (150m) of the narrowest part of the peninsula, completely destroying the road that formerly led to the point.

This restlessly shifting peninsula was formed as sediment, sand and gravels were carried down from the rapidly eroding Holderness coast to the north by a process known as longshore drift. It's been estimated that more than 30 towns and villages have already been lost since Roman times on this, the fastest eroding coastline in Britain. Consequently, the position of the tip of the point has gradually lengthened or shortened and moved steadily westwards with the tides since then.

Spurn signpost

Despite its apparent impermanence, Spurn boasts a fascinating human history, leaving behind a legacy of lost towns, the remains of a railway, gun emplacements, derelict buildings and at least five lighthouses. In 2022, academics and archaeologists from the University of Hull became excited at the prospect of locating one of the most famous of these former settlements, the prosperous medieval port of Ravenser Odd.

At the height of its fortunes in the early years of the 14th century, Ravenser Odd - the name comes from the Old Norse *hrafn's eyr*, possibly meaning 'raven's tongue or point' - was a seaport of national importance. It achieved a Royal Charter and borough status in 1298/9, for which the then huge sum of £300 was paid. The thriving town contained more

than 100 houses, along with many busy warehouses and quays. It had its own market and an annual fair, a town mayor and customs officers, and sent no less than two MPs to the Model Parliaments of the time. More than 100 merchant ships a year called at Ravenser Odd, which was accused of stealing trade from Grimsby and Hull.

Ravenser Odd was also the site of the embarkation of the Norwegian army of King Harald Hardrada before his crushing defeat by King Harold Godwinson at the Battle of Stamford Bridge in 1066, just 19 days before the Battle of Hastings. In 1399, Henry Bolingbroke, later to become Henry IV, landed on the spit called Ravenser Spurn, and the Kilnsea Cross, which now stands in the private Holyrood House, Hedon, was reputed to have been erected to mark the spot.

The port was well enough known to be mentioned by William Shakespeare in no less than three of his histories, most notably in *Henry IV, Part One* when Henry Percy (nicknamed Hotspur), describes it as where his father, the Earl of Northumberland, landed 'Upon the naked shore of Ravenspurgh...' Edward IV also landed on the headland when he returned from exile in Holland to depose Henry VI in 1470.

But by the middle of the 14th century, regular flooding by the sea signalled the beginning of the end for Ravenser Odd, and the merchants started to move away. In 1355, the town's chapel was flooded, exposing the bones of corpses in its graveyard. And as the sandbanks gradually shifted, the town was slowly swept away, and storms over the winter of 1356–57 completely flooded it, leading to its abandonment.

The final chapter in the history of Ravenser Odd was written in January 1362, when a south-westerly storm surge, known as the Grote Mandrenke or Saint Marcellus' flood, combined with exceptionally high tides to submerge the last traces of Ravenser Odd into the cold grey waters of the North Sea.

The shifting sands of Spurn have always presented a danger to seafarers, and the first lighthouse was erected on the spit in 1427, when a hermit named William Reedbarrow was granted the right to claim dues from passing ships to build it. It was to take another two centuries before Justinian Angell, a London merchant, received a patent from Charles II in 1676 to 'continue, renew and maintain' the two lights which then existed at Spurn Head.

Angell's lighthouse lasted for a century until the respected lighthouse engineer John Smeaton, builder of the famous Eddystone Light off Plymouth, was commissioned by Trinity House Hull to build a new 'Low' Lighthouse in 1776. This operated until 1895 and its stunted, wave-worn tower still remains on the beach.

Smeaton's light was replaced by the present 128 foot (39m)-tall 'High'

Spurn High (centre) and Low (left) Lighthouses

lighthouse, actually the highest in the north of England, designed by Trinity House engineer Thomas Matthews. Modern electronics made this last black-and-white painted lighthouse redundant in 1985, but it is open most weekends and Bank Holidays for those wishing to get a grandstand view of the peninsula.

Spurn's varied wildlife was recognised when it was made a National Nature Reserve (NNR) in 1951, now managed by the Yorkshire Wildlife Trust. Its exposed position on the windswept east coast of Britain makes it one of the finest sites in Britain for birdwatchers wishing to 'tick-off' rare migrating birds. A sighting of a single wryneck, hoopoe, bee eater or shrike can attract flocks of twitchers from all over the country.

More common wildfowl such as mallard and shelduck find shelter in the mudflats beyond the shingle ridge in winter, while passage migrants include curlew, dunlin, knot, oystercatcher, redshank, tern and turnstone. Smaller songbirds include pied and spotted flycatcher, redstart, whinchat, wheatear, fieldfare and redwing, often in enormous numbers. A 'fall' of more than 15,000 swallows was noted on one day.

The North Sea off Spurn can deliver too, and you might even be lucky enough to catch sight of seals or a blowing humpback whale, which have also been seen.

Spurn High Lighthouse from the shore

The Walk

Our walk starts at the Yorkshire Wildlife Trust's excellent Spurn Discovery Centre, in Spurn Road, Kilnsea. It is important to check the tide times before you set out (Web: ywt.org.uk/nature-reserves/spurn-national-nature-reserve#tidetimes), unless you want to be cut off at Spurn Head. If you don't want to walk or get your feet wet, the YWT runs a seasonal Spurn Safari – a three-hour guided wildlife tour in a specially converted ex-military vehicle starting from the Discovery Centre.

It's a bracing 3 mile (4.8km) walk to the tip of the Head and its lighthouses, with plenty of opportunities, and no less than four hides, for you to stop and view the wildlife along the way. There is no access for other vehicles and dogs are not allowed. You will see traces in the road near the start of the walk of the single-track, standard gauge railway which was built during the First World War to service the gun batteries then stationed on the Head. The railway was fondly remembered by the community of lifeboatmen and lighthouse keepers and their families at Spurn Head, and only closed in 1951.

The buildings and legacy of the now-abandoned community at Spurn can still be traced – look out for the chalk football crowd drawn onto a wall where the local children used to play. The buildings are now used by the Royal National Lifeboat Institution (RNLI), whose crews live there when they are on shift. They are one of the only full-time paid lifeboat crews in the UK.

But Spurn Head remains as it always was, a truly wild, elemental place. Forever at the mercy of the weather and the voracious tides, no two days at Spurn can ever be the same, and a visit will stay long in the memory.

Factbox

Location: Take the A1033 from Hull to Patrington then the B1445 towards Easington and Kilnsea. Turn right at the T-junction in Easington towards Kilnsea and right again at the crossroads in Kilnsea to reach the Spurn Discovery Centre

Postcode: HU12 0UH

Length: It's about 3 miles (4.8km) to the tip of Spurn Head, making a round trip of 6 miles (9.7km)

Terrain: Starting on a metalled road, the route swiftly degenerates to an uneven sandy or gravel path, often littered with seaweed from the latest encroachment

Map: OS 1:25,000 Explorer OL292, Withernsea & Spurn Head

Refreshments: There is a takeaway café in the Yorkshire Wildlife Trust's Spurn Discovery Centre, Spurn Road, Kilnsea HU12 0UH

☏ 01964 650144
Ⓦ ywt.org.uk/spurn

36.

From industry to tranquillity: Lathkill Dale, Derbyshire

The village of Monyash

Lathkill Dale is a lovely Derbyshire dale with a Jekyll and Hyde nature. On the one hand, it is one of the most important parts of the beautiful Derbyshire Dales National Nature Reserve (NNR), famous for its crystal-clear limestone river and abundant wildlife. And on the other – although hard to believe today – it was the scene of intense industrial activity during the 18th and 19th centuries.

We start our journey exploring the two contrasting sides of the character of Lathkill Dale from the pretty White Peak village of Monyash, whose name is thought to come from Old English and means 'many ash trees'. Monyash was granted its right to hold a market in 1340, and the ancient market cross still stands on the village green.

The reason for its settlement high on the fast-draining White Peak limestone plateau, where a water supply was rare and essential, were its five 'meres' (clay-lined ponds), of which only Fere Mere now survives. Two hundred years ago, however, it was an important lead mining centre, when most of the inhabitants were engaged in the dual economies of farming and mining.

The Walk

From the car park, walk down to the village green, passing the Market Cross, and turn left past the Bull's Head pub, now thankfully returned to its original traditional name after some years going under the unfortunate and totally inappropriate name of The Hobbit.

Cross the road to enter the churchyard. The elegant spire of St Leonard's Church, Monyash has recently commemorated the 900th year of its foundation in around 1100. Extensively restored in 1887, the building retains its Decorated style transepts, aisles and nave arcades, reflecting the tiny village's former importance as a market township. A path leads south through the churchyard and a series of squeezer stiles into a walled farm lane, which is signposted the Limestone Way. Follow this lane until it ends at Fern Dale, a small, dry tributary of Lathkill Dale, which is crossed by three stiles. At a gate, you join another farm track leading directly in about half a mile (0.8km) to One Ash Grange.

The name 'grange' almost always indicates an outlying farmstead, which in medieval times belonged to a monastery or abbey, and One Ash Grange is no exception. There are estimated to be at least 45 granges in the Peak District. This compact little settlement perched on the brink of Cales Dale was owned by Roche Abbey in South Yorkshire. Once the site of a Peak District National Park camping barn, it is now more famous for its beautifully preserved stone pig sties.

St Leonard's Church, Monyash

Factbox

Location: Car park in Chapel Street, Monyash

Postcode: DE45 1JJ

Length: 4.5 miles (7.2km); allow 2–3 hours

Terrain: Many squeezer stiles at start, then fairly easy dale walking with a rocky scramble towards the end

Map: OS 1:25,000 Explorer OL24, The Peak District – The White Peak Area

Refreshments: The Old Smithy Tearooms and Restaurant, Church Street, Monyash, Bakewell DE45 1JH

☎ 01629 810190
🌐 oldsmithymonyash.com

The Bulls Head, Church Street, Monyash, Bakewell DE45 1JH, on Monyash's village green

☎ 01629 812372
🌐 thebullsheadmonyash.co.uk

Looking down on a frosty Upper Lathkill Dale from Parson's Tor

Follow the track to the left of the first barn to a stile at the end of the Dutch barn. The path now descends steeply into the rocky defile of Cales Dale, which is followed (left) beneath imposing, fern-clad limestone crags to reach Lathkill Dale and cross the infant Lathkill by a wooden footbridge.

The River Lathkill exhibits that strange feature of streams that run for all or part of their course across Carboniferous limestone, as in summer, when the water level is low, it can disappear completely to run for most of its course underground. This situation has been exacerbated by centuries of lead mining in the area, after large-scale drainage of the workings – usually by tunnels known as 'soughs' – led to a significant lowering of the water table.

Charles Cotton, joint author with Izaak Walton of *The Compleat Angler* (first published in 1653 and never out of print since), described the 'Lathkin' (the Lathkill) in the 17th century as 'by many degrees, the purest, and most transparent stream I ever yet saw, either at home or abroad, and breeds, 'tis said, the reddest and the best trouts in England'.

Downstream from the junction with Cales Dale, the broad path alongside the Lathkill enters the semi-mature woodland Palmerston Wood, where the ruins of the engine house of the Mandale Lead Mine, looking like an Aztec temple emerging from the trees, can be visited. The Mandale Mining Company began here in 1797, keen to work the Mandale Sough lead vein, which they knew was below the level of the River Lathkill. It took 23 years to excavate this sough. A 35 foot (11m)-diameter waterwheel was installed in 1840 to pump water out of the mine and when this was found to be inadequate it was replaced in 1847 by a 165hp Cornish-type steam engine. The mine closed in 1852, having lost the not inconsiderable sum of £36,000. Further up the dale are the remaining pillars of the aqueduct which fed the original waterwheel at the Mandale Mine.

This part of the dale is probably the richest for wildlife, and you may see dipper, kingfisher and grey wagtail hunting in the clear waters of the river; white-clawed crayfish, bullhead and lamprey thrive in the river, and nuthatch and woodpeckers in the woodland.

Turn left over the footbridge from Cales Dale and follow the path that leads westwards up the dale passing, after the first stile, the partly hidden adit (entrance) to the Holmes Groove lead mine, which is across the river to the left.

The bold limestone crag high up on the right, where another dry valley enters, is known as Parson's Tor. Called Fox Tor until 1776, its name was changed to commemorate the tragic death of the Rev Robert Lomas, rector of Monyash, who fell to his death from the tor when returning home from Bakewell on horseback one stormy night. He is buried in Monyash churchyard.

Continue up the increasingly impressive dale, now open and treeless, with many upstanding limestone crags frowning down on the path. The more open dale sides are famous for their herb-rich flora where over 50 different species of plants have been identified per square metre. This in turn supports butterflies such as the orange-tip and northern brown argus.

The dam at Carter's Mill

A peep inside a Lathkill Dale adit

Many years ago, I remember taking this path with a farmer friend of mine from Warwickshire who was a keen lepidopterist. Spotting the brilliant yellow flowers of rockrose growing among the rocky screes, he said: 'That's the food plant of the brown argus'. Right on cue, a northern brown argus fluttered down to take its fill from the tiny flowers.

After a few more yards, to your left the gaping maw of Lathkill Head Cave yawns. Lathkill Head Cave is what is known as a 'resurgence' cave, where the River Lathkill emerges from the hillside in spectacular fashion during the winter months when the water level is high. To see the Lathkill gushing forth from its birthplace under the limestone crag to rush downstream to join the Bradford at Alport is one of the little known and seldom seen wonders of the Peak. Cavers have explored about 200 feet (61m) into the hillside, but this kind of activity is only for the experts, and non-cavers should not be tempted to enter too far.

Continue up the dale, where the limestone walls now start to crowd in onto the path, and in summer you may be lucky enough to see some fine stands of the rare purple-flowered and yellow stamened Jacob's Ladder blooming in the dale bottom. It gets its name from the ladder-like appearance of its pointed leaflets. The path is now confined to a rocky scramble over and around some large boulders, improved after work by volunteers.

The scree of broken stones coming down from the right is from the now-disused Ricklow Quarry, where 'figured marble' was extracted in Victorian times. This was a highly fashionable polished grey limestone in which there were a large number of decorative crinoid fossils. Crinoids are often mistakenly called sea lilies, but were actually a marine animal with feathery pinnules, related to modern starfish, brittle stars, sea urchins and sea cucumbers. Because of the regular cross-section of their stems, these fossils are sometimes locally known as 'Derbyshire screws'. You can see excellent examples of crinoids in the polished doorstep as you enter the Bull's Head pub in Monyash.

The dale now opens up again and you cross a series of stiles where in summer you could well be ticked-off, as I often have been, by the resident pair of wheatears, which nest in the broken down drystone walls in this part of the dale.

Eventually you emerge onto the B5055 Bakewell road by a stile and a water treatment plant. Turn left and cross the road to enter Bagshaw Dale, a shallow dry valley which is an extension of Lathkill Dale. Crossing a series of stiles and gates, you emerge through drystone walls onto the Taddington road, where you turn left into Chapel Street to return to the car park and village centre.

37.

Finding Cuddy's Cave:
St Cuthbert's Cave, Northumberland

Pine-crowned Cuthbert's Cave

If you have ever taken Billy Shiel's boat out from Seahouses on a bird-watching trip to the Farne Islands off the Northumbrian coast, you may well have encountered some of 'Cuddy's Ducks'. That's the affectionate local name given to eider ducks, nearly 500 of which still breed annually on the rocky outcrop of Inner Farne.

These charming birds, once the local source of comfy eiderdown, are named after Northumbria's patron saint, Cuthbert, who once lived in great austerity as a hermit on Inner Farne, alongside his beloved feathered friends.

The eider is the largest of our diving ducks with the drake's upper feathers snowy white, a sage-green nape, and a jet-black crown and lower feathers. If you get close enough, you'll hear their unique, 'ooo-oo' or 'ooo-er' call, which always reminds me of the 'oo-er, missus' catchphrase of comedian Frankie Howerd.

Cuthbert is said to have so entered the confidence of the eiders that he allowed them to nest anywhere they wanted, even next to the chapel altar. He was also alleged to have placed the ducks under his personal protection, ruling that no-one should eat or disturb them.

About 500 years after Cuthbert's death, a Durham monk named Reginald recorded: 'In the Island of Farne there are certain creatures which since the days of the blessed Cuthbert have been hand-tame... These birds have been named after the blessed Cuthbert himself... They are so tame that they nest inside dwelling houses, where they come to the table, and construct their nests under your bed, yes, and even under the bed coverings...'. Perhaps that's how eiderdown first became popular?

The Venerable Bede (c. 673-735) related another story concerning Cuthbert and his St Francis-like love of animals. When he was visiting another monastery, the monks noticed that he went out in the middle of the night and didn't return until morning. Curious to find out what he did, one night a fellow monk followed him. He discovered that Cuthbert waded out into the sea up to his neck and stayed there until morning when he returned, knelt on the beach, and prayed. When he did so, the monk watched in astonishment as: '...two otters bounded out of the water, stretched themselves out before him, warmed his feet with their breath, and tried to dry him with their fur. They finished, received his blessing, and slipped back to their watery home'.

The summit of Greensheen Hill, looking toward the distant Cheviots

Cuthbert is believed to have been born into a noble family in Dunbar, near the mouth of the River Forth in Scotland, in the mid-630s. This was about a decade after the conversion of King Edwin of Northumbria to Christianity in AD 627. Bishop Paulinus of York had baptised Edwin at his palace at Ad Gefrin, in the shadow of the spectacular Iron Age hillfort of Yeavering Bell near Kirknewton in what is now the Northumberland National Park.

It is believed that Cuthbert was fostered as a child to a family near Melrose, later joining the monastery there. One night while still a boy and employed as a shepherd, he had a vision of the soul of St Aidan being carried to heaven by angels, and he later discovered that Aidan, who was to have such an influence on Cuthbert's young life, had died that night.

In around AD 635, Paulinus' successor Oswald invited Irish monks from Iona, including Aidan, to found the monastery at Lindisfarne, where Cuthbert was eventually to spend much of his life. Cuthbert was known for his charm and generosity to the poor, and for his reputation of the gift of healing and insight, which led many people to consult him, gaining him the nickname of the 'Wonder Worker of Britain'.

He retired from monastic life in AD 676, guided by his desire for a peaceful, more contemplative life. With his abbot's permission, he went to a place that Archbishop Eyre identified as tiny St Cuthbert's Island off Lindisfarne, but which other authorities claim was the location now known as St Cuthbert's Cave,

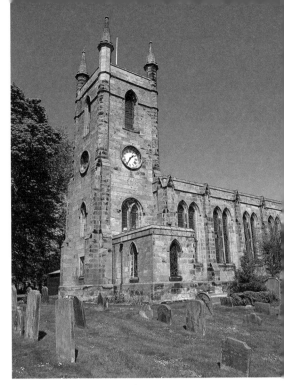

Belford's Parish Church of St Mary

in the Kyloe Hills near Belford, which we will visit on our walk. Shortly afterwards, however, Cuthbert moved to the Inner Farne island off the Northumberland coast, where he again committed himself to a life of austerity and isolation. Persuaded by King Ecgfrith, he was reluctantly consecrated as Bishop of Lindisfarne in 685. But shortly after Christmas 686 he returned to his cell on Inner Farne, where he died in 687, and was buried at Lindisfarne.

After Cuthbert's death, many miracles were attributed to him, and he became the lasting symbol of the identity of Northumbria. Prior to the death of Thomas à Becket at Canterbury in 1170, he was described as probably the most popular saint in England.

When the Vikings embarked on their initial, infamous raid on the holy abbey of

The view from Greensheen Hill

Lindisfarne in AD 875, according to *The Anglo-Saxon Chronicle*, Eardulf, Bishop of Lindisfarne, and Abbot Eadred had the body of St Cuthbert disinterred and his followers 'wandered about' for seven years with his coffin, while trying to avoid the Vikings.

It eventually found a resting place at St Cuthbert's church in Chester-le-Street until 995, when another Danish invasion led to its removal to Ripon. But the wagon carrying his coffin became stuck in the mud on the road, and guided by what they thought was Cuthbert's wishes, his followers took him to Durham, where a new stone church had been built on a peninsula of the River Wear. Known as the White Church, this was the Saxon predecessor of the present magnificent Norman cathedral, the centrepiece of the modern Durham World Heritage Site. In 999, Cuthbert's relics were reburied in the new church, along with the book known as the St Cuthbert Gospel, claimed to be the oldest Western book to have retained its finely decorated leather binding.

Cuthbert's ornate shrine in Durham Cathedral was destroyed during the Dissolution of the Monasteries by Henry VIII in the 16th century, but his relics survived and are still kept there. When his tomb was opened in the 19th century, his intricately carved Anglo-Saxon wooden coffin and various other relics were recovered, including a Saxon square cross of gold, embellished with garnets, which became the heraldic symbol of St Cuthbert in the arms of both Durham and Newcastle universities.

Ancient graffiti in Cuthbert's Cave

The Walk

As mentioned earlier, one of the places in which Cuthbert supposedly hid himself, and where the monks may have taken shelter with their holy relic while on the run from the Vikings, was Cuthbert's Cave near Belford, which we visit on this walk.

From the village, look out for a wooden St Cuthbert's Cave sign and follow the narrow lane to the free National Trust car park at Holburn Grange Farm.

From the car park, follow the wide, grassy path through the Holburn Moss nature reserve up to the top of Greensheen Hill (672 feet/205m) where you will be greeted by some truly spectacular views. These extend to the lofty Cheviots to the west, and to the east, the glorious Northumberland Coast, including the fine castles at Bamburgh to the south and Lindisfarne to the north. The other scattered Farne Islands and the Longshore Lighthouse can be seen anchored out in the North Sea beyond Bamburgh.

Go through the gate at the top of the hill and turn right, following the sign on a gate which announces that St Cuthbert's Cave is only a quarter of a mile (0.4km) away. The land where the cave is situated was formerly owned by the Leather family, who consecrated it in 1936 to use for family interments. The cave and surrounding 13 acre (5ha) site on which it stands were gifted to the National Trust in 1981.

Follow the path that eventually leads through a plantation of mature conifers until you turn left to continue uphill, and you soon come to Cuthbert's Cave. Topped by a crown of conifers, the shallow but quite extensive cave was formed beneath a huge, overhanging sandstone rock and is supported by a single natural stone pillar. Some of the graffiti carved on its walls date back to the 18th century: one I saw was dated 1752. The cave is surrounded by other huge, flat sandstone boulders shrouded in bracken and watched over by stately foxgloves.

Factbox

Location: The National Trust car park, free to visitors to the cave, is located just outside Belford village. Belford is a 5-10 minute drive from the A1 on the B1649 road towards Wooler

Postcode: TD15 2UJ

Length: About 3 miles (4.8km), there and back

Terrain: Easy going on field and woodland paths

Map: OS 1:25,000 Explorer OL340, Holy Island & Bamburgh

Refreshments: The Black Swan, 1 Market Place, Belford NE0 7ND, is recommended

☎ 01668 213473
ⓦ theblackswanhotel.
yourwebsitespace.com/

WALES

Looking down on Lyn y Fan Fach
from Bannau Sir Gaer

38	39	40
Town of Giants: Tre'r Ceiri, Llŷn, North Wales	To the 'Roman' Steps: Rhinog Mountains, Snowdonia	Skomer's seabird city: Skomer, Pembrokeshire Coast
4 miles/6.4km	**4 or 6 miles/6.4 or 9.7km**	**4 miles/6.4km**
41	42	43
The legend of the Lady of the Lake: Lyn y Fan Fach, Brecon Beacons	'The Cure of all Diseases': St Govan's Chapel, Pembrokeshire Coast	Source of Stonehenge's bluestones: Preseli Hills, Pembrokeshire
2.5 miles/4km	**1.5 miles/2.4km**	**15 miles/24.1km**

38.

Town of Giants: Tre'r Ceiri, Llŷn, North Wales

BELOW A gateway to the hillfort
RIGHT The view from Tre'r Ceiri extends across Caernarfon Bay towards the cloud-covered peaks of Snowdonia

The 30 mile (48.3km) long Llŷn Peninsula is where the mountain heights of Snowdonia poke a rocky finger out westwards towards the shimmering blue waters of the Irish Sea.

The triple summits of Yr Eifl, near Llanaelhaearn at the base of the peninsula in Gwynedd, is often Anglicised to The Rivals. But it actually means 'the fork' in Welsh and is a name which perfectly fits the three-pronged summits of Tre'r Ceiri (1,591 feet/485m), Garn Ganol (1,850 feet/564m) and Garn Fôr (1,457 feet/444m).

The all-encompassing views from the reigning summits of Yr Eifl can extend for nearly 100 miles (161km), southwards across the shining waters of Cardigan Bay to Mynydd Preseli, the possible source of the Stonehenge blue-stones, and to the dim blue outlines of Ireland's Wicklow Hills across the Irish Sea to the west. To the north, the Isle of Man can sometimes be seen, with the Lake District fells beyond. Nearer at hand, the serrated skyline of Snowdonia's peaks is ranged along the eastern horizon with Yr Wyddfa

prominent, and the west coast of the holy island of Anglesey is also visible.

It's humbling to think that exactly the same view could have been enjoyed some 2,000 years ago by the residents of the 5 acre (2ha) Iron Age hillfort that encircles Tre'r Ceiri, the isolated easternmost summit of Yr Eifl.

Many archaeologists have been unconvinced with the term 'hillfort' for the mighty earthworks which encircle so many of our British hills. For them it conjures up entirely the wrong kind of image, of Asterix and Obelix-type Ancient Britons holding out against the armoured

might of Rome, whereas in most cases there is no evidence of conflict. Tre'r Ceiri is a good example, which seems to have enjoyed a long and peaceful life as an airy township commanding some of the finest views in Wales.

But why would the Celtic tribesmen of what is now Gwynedd want to live in such an apparently inhospitable place over 1,500 feet (457m) above the sea, when there was plenty of opportunity for easier settlement in the lush valleys of Llŷn beneath? Current thinking is that apart from the obvious military significance of such a commanding hilltop, the township may only have been used during the

A panoramic aerial view, showing the extent of the five-acre (2ha) Tre'r Ceiri hillfort, enclosed by its drystone wall

summer, as a seasonal outlook for the community's herds of grazing livestock. But no one really knows.

Tre'r Ceiri was first brought to popular attention by Thomas Pennant, the Welsh naturalist, traveller, writer and antiquarian, in his *A Tour of Wales*, first published in 1773. On arriving at Tre'r Ceiri, Pennant expressed himself astonished: 'On the Eifl is the most perfect and magnificent, as well as the most artfully constructed, British post I ever beheld', he breathlessly wrote.

He described the construction of the huts as being 'of various forms; round, oval, oblong, square'. This is now regarded as evidence for the different

phases of occupation, with the later, more rectangular enclosures dating from Romano-British times being developed from subdivisions of the original circular Iron Age huts.

Dr AHA Hogg, the acknowledged expert on British hillforts, was in no doubt as to the importance of Tre'r Ceiri, where he did so much of his research. He wrote in his *Hill-forts of Britain* (1975): 'It is probably the best preserved of all the hill towns of southern Britain, and certainly can give a better idea than any other of the original appearance of a place of this kind'.

The first construction on Tre'r Ceiri was a summit cairn dating from the Bronze Age, which was badly damaged by treasure-

seeking Victorian antiquarians. It was followed by the spectacular building, probably by the local Ordovices tribe during the Iron Age, perhaps 2,000 years ago, of the still-impressive drystone ramparts of the hillfort, some of which still stand 15 feet (4.6m) high.

The hillfort has a long and narrow oval shape as it encircles the summit, and its fine stone ditchless ramparts have ramps leading up to a walkway, which is protected by a parapet. There are two large and four minor gateways, which give entry to the fort. Inside these formidable fortifications, the foundations of about 150 circular huts have been traced beneath the thick bracken, heather and bilberries, and many are still plainly visible to the modern visitor.

Archaeologists have estimated that this lofty hilltop could have supported a population of up to 400 people.

Tre'r Ceiri was probably continuously occupied and re-occupied over many hundreds of years, as buildings seem to have been re-used and sub-divided, as Pennant observed 250 years ago, to create some 'semi-detached' dwellings, all of which would have been roofed with turves or thatched with heather.

The Welsh name of Tre'r Ceiri means 'the Town of the Giants', from cewri, plural of cawr (meaning 'giants'). Massive structures such as this were thought to be well beyond the ambitions of the local population, and it was assumed they must have been the work of a race of giants.

Factbox

Location: Tre'r Ceiri is reached from the small car park off the B4417 Llithfaen road, 1 mile (1.6km) south of Llanaelhaearn on the A499 in Gwynedd, North Wales

Postcode: LL53 6NU

Length: About 4 miles (6.4km), there and back

Terrain: It is a strenuous climb to reach the hillfort, and if you wish to visit the other summits of Yr Eifl, you will need some hill-walking experience and the proper clothing and equipment

Map: OS 1:25,000 Explorer OL253, Lleyn Peninsula West

Refreshments: The nearest places for refreshment are the Caffi Meinir Nant Gwrtheyrn, Llithfaen, Pwllheli LL53 6NL

☎ 01758 750442
🌐 nantgwrtheyrn.org/cafe-and-restaurant

Or the pub run by the community at Tafarn y Fic, Llithfaen, Pwllheli LL53 6PA

☎ 01758 750473
🌐 tafarnyfic.com

The Walk

It's an easy, if steep, 2 mile (3.2km) walk to reach the hillfort from the small car park on the B4417 Llithfaen road, a mile (1.6km) south of Llanaelhaearn. As you approach the still-impressive western ramparts of the hillfort, its entrances and staggered gateways are clearly visible.

If you are still feeling fit after your exploration of the hillfort, it's worth dropping down west to the col of Bwlch yr Eifl to climb up to the other summits of Yr Eifl, from which the views are equally splendid.

It's a stiff and rocky climb to the central summit of Garn Ganol, the highest point on Llŷn, which has an ancient cairn and a trig point crowning the top. The northernmost summit of Garn Fôr, also known as Mynydd y Gwaith, has a cliff face that drops sheer into the Irish Sea at Trwyn y Gorlech, and has an ugly radio relay station on top. Some of the granite quarries on Garn Fôr produced rocks for curling stones, some of which were used in the 2006 Winter Olympics in Turin.

The last word should perhaps be left to AHA Hogg, who spent so much of his working life as an archaeologist at Tre'r Ceiri and recognised the tremendous continuity of history that the site offered. 'Tre'r Ceiri... though often cited as a 'typical' hillfort, is unique in Britain, for although occupation continued into that period, and later elsewhere, only at this site is the complete plan of a native town of the Roman period exposed to view'.

39.

To the 'Roman' Steps:
Rhinog Mountains, Snowdonia

'The rock of the arrows' – Carreg-y-Saeth, Cwm Bychan

The boulder-strewn, heather covered summits of the Rhinog range in the west of Snowdonia are said to provide some of the roughest, toughest walking in Wales.

But these wild Celtic Badlands also provided the perfect hideaway for a notorious band of medieval outlaws who terrorised the coastal plain of Ardudwy, which lies between the Rhinogs and the sea. The rustlers would steal cattle, goods and slaves before returning with their booty to their virtually inaccessible secret mountain hideout.

A persistent local legend says that on one raid into Clwyd they kidnapped several young women from a village, who apparently quickly settled down and made their home with the Rhinog rustlers. But a posse of angry local men from the Clwyd village was formed and they pursued the bandits, who had stolen their wives and girlfriends, into the hills. Eventually finding their way to the outlaws' lair via the remote pass of Bwlch Tyddiad, they surprised and slaughtered many of them before seizing the women to take them down the pass back home.

Evidently the women had fallen in love with their captors and, distraught by the killing of their new-found partners, rather than return to lowland Clwyd they all threw themselves into a lake close to the pass and drowned. Before you dismiss this as an old wives' tale, the isolated lake just to the north of the summit of Bwlch Tyddiad is still known today as Llyn Morwynion – which translates as 'the lake of the maidens' – although in view of their perfidiousness, to call them 'maidens' could be a trifle generous.

The rustlers and their pursuers would have used the famous so-called Roman Steps to reach Bwlch Tyddiad, the 1,294 foot (94m)-high pass that separates the 2,360 foot (719m) summit of Rhinog Fawr

to the south and the craggy fastnesses of Craig Wion to the north.

These ancient engineered steps into the hills are still named as if they had been built by the Romans, and to be fair, the remains of a small Roman auxiliary fort have been discovered at Cefn Caer at Pennal, a few miles to the south. A local legend says a ghostly troop of Roman soldiers with pack mules can sometimes be seen trudging up the Roman Steps, and that anyone who follows them will be led to a secret hoard of gold.

But judging from their size and construction, the steps are much more likely to be medieval in origin and probably formed part of a packhorse

A frosty road to Rhinog Fawr and Rhinog Fach

Nearing the summit of the Roman Steps

Cwm Bychan, which is one of the sources of the Afon Artro, are watched over by the frowning, serried terraces of 1,483 foot (452m) Carreg-y-Saeth. The English translation of this name is 'the rock of the arrow', which may be another reminder of the area's turbulent history.

Because of their rare untouched upland habitat, the Rhinogs are a National Nature Reserve (NNR), a Site of Special Scientific Interest (SSSI) and a Special Area of Conservation (SAC). In addition to all these national classifications, the Rhinog NNR is also the only Biogenetic Reserve in Wales. This is a designation made by the Council of Europe and brings the Rhinogs into a network of special habitats across the Continent, which are set aside because of their importance in preserving the genetic variety of European wildlife.

trail linking Trawsfynydd in the east and Harlech on the coastal plain of Cardigan Bay. Another story claims that there is a secret tunnel from the steps which surfaces at Harlech Castle. A more plausible theory is that they were cut by workers at the long-disused quarry near the summit to get to their place of work. There are probably about 2,000 steps in all (don't try counting them!) and some are missing but many are in as good condition as the day they were laid – whenever that might have been.

Our walk follows in the footsteps of the Romans (possibly), the Ardudwy brigands (maybe) and the packhorses (most likely) through the beautiful, secluded vale of Cwm Bychan. This is one of the least-known but loveliest corners of the Snowdonia National Park. The peaceful, ancient oak embowered waters of Llyn

Among the rare and endangered species that make the Rhinogs their home and which you might come across on our walk are the guttural croak of the ravens, which nest in the crags of Carreg-y-Saeth and the higher Rhinog summits. Ring ousels, also known as the mountain blackbird, nest in some of the crags and mountain streams higher up on our route, and northern wheatears – whose ancient name meant 'white-arse' – and pied flycatchers are among the many migrant visitors that come here during the summer. In some of the wetter parts of the Rhinog moorlands there are important areas of internationally rare blanket bog, formed by decaying lime-green sphagnum moss, and here the yellow catkin-like flowers of bog myrtle can sometimes be seen fringing the edges.

Factbox

Location: Cwm Bychan is reached by a narrow country lane with passing places leading 5 miles (8km) east from the B4573 at Harlech. There is a small car park and campsite

Postcode: LL45 2PH

Length: Depending on how far you want to go, the summit of Bwlch Tyddiad is about 4 miles (6.4km), there and back, but add another 2 miles (3.2km) if you go to the summit of Rhinog Fawr

Terrain: Easy going until you reach the Steps, but then some quite steep climbing up to over 1,000 feet (305m), so sturdy boots and waterproofs are required, especially if you continue to the summit of Rhinog Fawr

Map: OS 1:25,000 Explorer OL18, Harlech, Porthmadog & Y Bala

Refreshments: The Victoria Inn, Llanbedr LL45 2LD, is a traditional village pub on the bank of the River Artro in Llanbedr

☎ 01341 241213
🌐 robinsonsbrewery.com/pubs/victoria-inn-llanbedr

The Walk

We start our walk from Cwm Bychan by passing through an iron gate in a massive stone wall, which is signposted to the Roman Steps, and follow the clear path that beckons towards Bwlch Tyddiad. The path skirts the lovely flower-rich meadows at the head of the lake before entering more beautiful, centuries-old oak woodland, which is alive with birdsong in spring and summer, such as that of the migrant black-and-white pied flycatcher.

Climbing over a stile you enter the heather moorland of the rugged Rhinogs, then across a lovely little stone-arched footbridge over a small stream. You'll soon reach the foot of the famous stone steps, cleverly pitched and graded to make the climbing easier. The venerable stone staircase leads steadily upwards, passing through burgeoning banks of heather, which add a glorious touch of colour to the grey rocks if you are there in late summer. There are also low bushes of bilberry which, again in summer, can provide a tasty passing snack as you continue the remorseless climb up the steps.

At last the gradient eases, and you arrive at the large cairn that marks the top of Bwlch Tyddiad, which is a good place to stop and enjoy the view of the remote hills of Snowdonia to the north. Bleak moorland and blocks of dark green bottle-brush coniferous forests take up the immediate view on the eastern side of the pass, but the views of the distant hills to the north including the Arans, Arenig Fawr, Moel Siabod, and the reigning pyramid of Snowdon itself offer wonderful compensation.

The wild summit of Bwlch Tyddiad, looking towards the Arans

If you are feeling really fit and properly equipped for a genuine mountain climb you might want to attempt the summit of Rhinog Fawr, from which the views are even better. You'll need to descend slightly from Bwlch Tyddiad to take the rough, bouldery path by a wall through the heather on the left. The path climbs steeply towards Llyn Du ('black lake'), a desolate small tarn cradled in the northern hillside of Rhinog Fawr, surrounded by the bristling crags that lead up to the summit. One huge, smoothly polished slab of rock plunges directly into the depths of the still waters of the lake. It's a spectacular scene of mountain wilderness, which makes the arduous ascent through some of the Rhinog's roughest territory seem well worth the effort.

You'll need to scale the rocky ridge at the western corner of the tarn to reach the two cairns that mark the summit of Rhinog Fawr, with its extensive views of the Snowdon massif and even as far as The Rivals beyond the blue of Tremadoc Bay and the long line of cliffs marking Cadair Idris to the south. Nearer to hand the views across Bwlch Drws Ardudwy to the mural precipices of Rhinog Fach (2,333 feet/711m) and Y Llether are even more spectacular. (In case you were wondering, the Welsh word *fawr* means 'large' and *fach* means 'small').

In this desolate wilderness, you might even come across   and if you are downwind of them you'll probably smell them first – the herd of feral goats that also inhabit the Rhinogs.

Retrace your steps for the return route via Bwlch Tyddiad and down the Roman Steps, over the footbridge and through the woodland green meadows around the head of Llyn Cwm Buchan to regain your starting point.

40.

Skomer's seabird city:
Skomer, Pembrokeshire Coast

BELOW An aerial view across Midland Island and The Neck looking east towards a distant Skomer
RIGHT Skomer Island and the Mew Stone in the distance (left) from the Deer Park

Pembrokeshire thrusts its rock-clawed fingers out into the storm-wracked Celtic Sea as the last windswept western outpost of Wales. Conversely, it was also the first landfall for many invaders throughout its history, such as the Vikings who named so many of its physical features.

These include the scattering of five islands around its scalloped coastline – Ramsey, Caldey, Skokholm, Grassholm and our destination on this walk, the naturalist's paradise of Skomer.

The salty tang of the sea is always present in the Pembrokeshire Coast National Park, because nowhere within its boundaries is more than 10 miles (16km) from the ocean - and most places

are only a couple of miles (3-4km) away. That wonderful coastline, surely one of the most beautiful in Europe, is followed by the 186 mile (299km) Pembrokeshire Coast National Trail, which now forms part of the 870 mile (1,400km) Wales Coast Path. This was the first of its kind in Europe and is a fine way to explore Britain's only predominately coastal National Park, which celebrated its 70th birthday in 2022.

But we leave the mainland behind for our walk around Skomer, a 720 acre (291ha) island, which has been described by TV naturalist Iolo Williams as 'the diamond in the crown jewels of Welsh wildlife'. Skomer is a National Nature Reserve (NNR) managed by the Wildlife Trust of South and West Wales, a Site of Special Scientific Interest (SSSI), a Special Protection Area (SPA), and it is surrounded by a Marine Nature Reserve (MNR). Williams has said if he could choose one Welsh nature reserve that could hold its own against any in the world, it would be Skomer.

We had quite a start to my last trip to the island. As we waited to board the

The *Island Princess* arrives at North Haven

Looking across to High Cliff

tiny *Island Princess* at the remote rocky cove of Martin's Haven on the Wooltack Point peninsula, a mercurial peregrine falcon flung itself from the cliffs above and swooped down in furious pursuit of a collared dove.

'Wow! That'll take some beating when we get to the island,' commented one excited and highly professional-looking birder, telescope, camera and tripod draped around his neck. 'Maybe we should stay here!'

I'm glad we didn't, because despite a grey, mainly sunless day shrouded by sea-frets, Skomer was still at its very best. As we stepped off the boat at North Haven after the choppy but mercifully short 15 minute trip, clouds of clown-like puffins were zipping in and out of their burrows around the harbour or floating around in communal 'rafts' out at sea. Walking up the steep path from the harbour, we found ourselves being showered by earth as puffins were excavating their nesting burrows in the slopes above.

The Walk

An inquisitive grey seal popped up off the rocky shore of The Neck opposite to welcome us as we set off on the easy 4 mile (6.4km)-stroll around the island. It's a steady climb up from North Harbour, crossing the remains of ancient cultivation terraces, to reach the isolated 5 foot (1.5m)-tall menhir known as the Harold Stone, a monument possibly erected during the Bronze Age.

Turn left to follow the broad coast path, which leads down towards the grey-roofed, timber-framed Warden's House that was constructed in 2005 and overlooks North Haven. It guards the narrow entrance to the projecting headland known as The Neck. The South Castle or Neck camp is a promontory fort bounded by a still visible 300 foot (91m)-long rampart on the southern side, which probably dates from the Iron Age. The fort is best seen from the oddly named Captain Kite's rock, which is also a good place to spot seals in the appropriately named Seal Hole cave on the western side of The Neck.

The path now heads south along what is known as the Welsh Way, where noisy lesser black-backed and herring gulls roost. Ahead, High Cliff supports colonies of kittiwakes, razorbills and guillemots on the narrow ledges overlooking South Haven. Beyond the South Plateau straight ahead is the magnificent sea stack of the Mew Stone, where cormorants nest every year.

Back on the main path again and the shrill cries of a cacophony of seabirds fill

Factbox

Location: The ferry at Martin's Haven is near Marloes, signposted off the B4327. You'll need to book your passage with Pembrokeshire Islands Boat Trip.

☎ 01646 603123
🌐 pembrokeshire-islands.co.uk

Skomer can be visited from April to September; for full details go to welshwildlife.org/day-trips-skomer-island

Postcode: SA62 3BJ

Length: The round-island route is about 4 miles (6.4km)

Terrain: On easy, but sometimes rocky paths

Map: OS 1:25,000 Explorer OL36, South Pembrokeshire

Refreshments: Nothing on the island, but The Lobster Pot Inn at Marloes, Haverfordwest SA62 3AZ does excellent food

☎ 01646 636233
🌐 thelobsterpotmarloes.co.uk

Or the Runwayskiln Café at Marloe Sands SA62 3BH

☎ 01646 636545
🌐 runwayskiln.co.uk

the air to warn that you are approaching one of the most unforgettable and spectacular ornithological sights in Britain - Skomer's seabird city, which is known as The Wick. This quarter mile (0.4km)-long, precipitous chasm in the coastline is the guano-streaked home to tens of thousands of seabirds, which occupy strictly segregated levels according to their species. The onomatopoeic, diminutive but noisy kittiwakes occupy the ground floor, roosting on the lowest ledges, while razorbills, with their black plumage and distinctively striped broad beak, nest in niches and crevices higher above the sea. The chocolate-brown guillemots, on the other hand, jostle together on the more open ledges, where they lay their single pear-shaped egg on the bare rock. Above all these in the 'penthouses' of the easternmost upper cliff nest are our closest relatives to the wandering albatross - the so-called 'grey gliders of the Atlantic', the elegant grey-winged fulmar. These magnificent petrels soar and wheel effortlessly on stiff, outspread wings across the crowded scene on the updraughts caused by the vertical cliff face.

As if that wasn't enough to feast your eyes upon, puffins nest almost literally under your feet on the path above The Wick. We had to pause to allow a 'puffin crossing' across the path as the comical 'parrots of the sea' scuttled back and forth. Some carried neatly stacked rows of glistening silver sand eels in their gaudy, multi-coloured beaks, and emitted

Puffins congregate opposite The Wick

their growling, deep-throated 'arr-r-r-r', sounding like a West Country yokel, as they went.

Skomer is home to about half of the world's population of the rare Manx shearwater (150,000 birds), which also nest on these slopes, but you'll only see them if you are here after dark. This elegant, scythe-winged shearwater nests in burrows like the puffins but spends all day fishing out at sea, only returning to its burrows under cover of darkness. These dusky globetrotters spend their winters an incredible 7,000 miles (11,265km) away, off the coasts of Argentina and Brazil.

Following the path west, you soon come to the sheltered bay known as Tom's House, with cushions of pink thrift and spikes of golden gorse decorating the clifftops. The scree slope and boulder beach here is a favoured breeding site for tiny storm petrels – otherwise known as Mother Carey's Chickens – which spend their winters off the coasts of South Africa and Namibia. Far out to sea you may just be able to see the white-capped outer island of Grassholm, with a cloud of birds hovering above it. The white is not snow but the guano left by the 40,000 pairs of gannets – around 10 per cent of the entire world population – that nest on the uninhabited rock.

Turning north now and passing the rocks of the Pigstone and Pigstone Bay, you might spot more seals basking on the rocky beaches. But the best place to see grey seals is on the extreme northern point of Skomer, around the roaring currents that separate the rocky island

The Garland Stone

of the Garland Stone from the island mainland. At low water, they often haul out on the skerries to bask, and quite often to quarrel and fight with one another. The nearby cliffs are favoured sites for members of the crow family, with ravens and red-beaked choughs joyfully soaring and tumbling in the updraughts.

Turning inland up the iris-starred North Stream Valley, I felt like I had entered a child's paint-by-numbers landscape. The interior of the island seemed to be swathed in a colourful carpet of bluebells, and red and white campions. It was an unforgettable sight and truly a feast for the senses.

It's just a short step now to reach The Farm, which stands at the centre and

The trig point on Gorse Hill above The Farm, the highest point on the island (259 feet/79m)

highest point of Skomer. Built in the early years of the 19th century, the farm and former cowsheds are now used for accommodation for visitors and volunteers working on the island and must be a welcome shelter on Skomer's frequent stormy days.

Walking due east you pass through the habitat of yet another of Skomer's unique wildlife treasures. These now bracken-covered fields are home to the Skomer vole, which is a distinct island race of the mainland bank vole. Like many island species, the Skomer vole is about half as big again as its mainland cousin and has a richer brown fur. It feeds on the abundant bluebell seeds and astonishingly on toxic bracken, a proven carcinogen.

The fields that lead back down past the Harold Stone and North Haven are heavily grazed by Skomer's large population of rabbits, which were introduced to the island in the Middle Ages. Their burrows are often re-used by puffins and shearwaters, and they are tolerated because their grazed 'lawns' keep scrub down, encourage flowering plants and increase botanical diversity.

As I regretfully left Skomer on the *Island Princess* again, I found myself agreeing with the anonymous 11th-century author of *The Mabinogion*, who described Pembrokeshire but could equally have been describing Skomer as *gwlad hud a lledrith* – 'the land of mystery and enchantment'.

41.

The legend of the Lady of the Lake:
Llyn y Fan Fach, Brecon Beacons

Looking down on Llyn y Fan Fach

Llyn y Fan Fach is a mysterious hidden lake cradled by the huge, sweeping precipices of Bannau Sir Gaer, one of the highest points of the Black Mountains (Mynydd Du), formerly known as the Carmarthen Fans, in the wild west of the Bannau Brycheiniog, formerly Brecon Beacons, National Park.

This is one of the secret places of Wales – rich in folklore and legend, some of which may go back as far as the Iron Age and are still vivid in the imagination of the local people who live in the shadow of these forbidding Devonian Age mountains.

The legend of the Lady of the Lake concerns a young farmer's son from the village of Myddfai in the valley to the

north who, apparently sometime in the 13th century, grazed his father's cattle in the upland pastures around the remote lake in the heart of the mountains.

One day, as he rested by the rocky lake shore, he was amazed to see a beautiful young girl emerge from the lake and proceed to comb her long, lustrous hair. He immediately fell in love with this vision of loveliness and vowed to marry

Swirling mist fills the cwm below the Black Mountain escarpment

the fairy princess, who, unknown to him, was a member of the Tylwyth Teg (the fairy folk). She tempted him by refusing his offer of newly baked bread on two occasions, but finally agreed to wedlock at his third attempt.

However, she warned the lad that if he struck her without cause on three occasions or touched her with cold iron after they were married, she would return to the lake, taking all her possessions with her. The princess' dowry included as many fairy sheep, cattle, goats and horses as she could count in a single breath, all of which magically emerged from the lake, just as she had done.

For many years, the marriage was a happy one for the couple who lived at

Esgair Llaethdy near Myddfai, and they were blessed with three fine sons. But one fateful day the farmer tapped his wife on the shoulder with an iron bridle, apparently to ask her to fetch a horse, and she tearfully reminded him of her warning of the consequences if he struck her three times.

Two years later, however, he patted her again, this time in an attempt to comfort her because, overcome by emotion, she was crying at a wedding. However, that innocent tap counted as the second blow.

The fateful third happened when the fairy princess was caught laughing at a funeral and the farmer's son touched her lightly on the arm in an innocent attempt to stop her.

The princess immediately returned to their farm on the hillside above Myddfai and she led all their cattle, sheep and goats back up the mountain to Llyn y Fan Fach, where they all disappeared under the black waters, leaving the distraught farmer alone on the shore.

However, she did not forget her sons, and returned to see them one day as they mourned their mother by the lakeside. She gave Rhiwallon, her eldest son, a leather bag that contained the healing secrets of the Otherworld, and showed them all the medicinal herbs that grew on the mountain and taught them how to use them to cure human ailments.

So the legend of the Physicians of Myddfai was born, and the three brothers became the most famous physicians in Wales, and were even appointed to the court of Rhys Gryg, of Dinefwr, the Prince of South Wales. Generations of the family inherited the gift of healing and are supposed to have continued to follow in the profession. Allegedly, the last-known descendant was still practising medicine in the late 19th century and became a physician to the royal court of Queen Victoria in England.

There may be some truth in the tale, because a gravestone in the porch of St Michael's Church, Myddfai, commemorates 'David Jones of Mothvey (Myddfai), surgeon who was an honest and skilful man', who died in 1719, and his eldest son John Jones, also a surgeon, who died in 1739. Local folklore identifies these two doctors as members of the renowned family of physicians in the direct male line. The last-known descendant, Dr C Rice Williams of Aberystwyth, died in 1842.

A number of other families in the Myddfai district later also claimed descent from Rhiwallon, the most notable being Morgan Owen, who was Bishop of Llandaff and who died in 1644. Bishop Owen certainly inherited much of the estate of the physicians in the area of Myddfai. Some of the brothers' remedies – a collection of treatise on humours, medicinal herbs and similar subjects attributed to Rhiwallon – were included in the 14th-century *Red Book of Hergest* under the heading 'Meddygon Myddfai'.

Some authorities have attributed the story of the Lady of the Lake to an ancient, dimly remembered folk tale, which may be a distant echo of the coming of foreign metal-working immigrants to Wales at the start of the Iron Age, some 2,000 years ago. The fairy princess' curse involved the farmer

A track between Trecastle and Llanddeusant

being warned from touching her with an object made from the newfangled, and to local people then apparently magical, metal. Of course, when the farmer accidentally touched his fairy bride with the bridle, it resulted in her disappearing with her dowry back under the dark, inky waters of Llyn y Fan Fach.

Red kites are fed at a nearby feeding station

In times past, local people used to gather on the lake shore on the first Sunday in August – Lammas Day, or the old Celtic festival of Lughnasadh – hoping to catch a glimpse of the romantic fairy and her cattle. And it was also said that anyone who bathed in the lake – which was thought to be bottomless – would be eternally beautiful.

The easiest approach to the secret lake is from the tiny village of Llanddeusant, where the former Old Red Lion Inn is now the youth hostel. Also close to the village is the Llanddeusant Red Kite Feeding

Station, opened in 2002 after fundraising by local people.

Here you can witness the results of one of the most successful conservation programmes in Britain. Thirty years ago, there were only a handful of red kites left breeding in the sheltered woodlands of Central Wales, and they were in grave danger of extinction. Today, however, the graceful, fork-tailed raptor is a common sight in most counties of Britain, and there are thought to be over 2,000 breeding pairs in the UK. Visitors to the centre can watch from a specially built hide as the elegant birds ferociously compete for the regularly provided food.

Llanddeusant Youth Hostel, formerly the 18th-century Old Red Lion Inn

The Walk

From the village car park take the track up the valley of the Afon Sawdde via the hamlet of Blaenau. This is now on waterworks roads and tracks but follows the possible route that would have been taken by the young Myddfai farmer when he first took his animals up to the hidden lake.

You soon pass a trout farm, with its associated weir and hatchery, and you should continue up the path until the looming glacial cirque that encloses Llyn y Fan Fach (the name means 'little lake of the mountain') comes into view. When you emerge at the lake, it is a little disappointing to find that it is now tamed, much enlarged and adapted for use as a reservoir. The dam was constructed during the First World War to create the reservoir and provide an additional water supply to the fast-expanding industrial town of Llanelli.

But the sight of the dam wall and pump house cannot detract from the grandeur of your surroundings. The mural chocolate layer-cake Old Red Sandstone precipices of Bannau Sir Gaer form an imposing backdrop and lead up to the reigning east-facing summit of Bannau Brycheiniog, at 2,631 feet (802m), the highest point of the Carmarthan Fans.

The shores of Llyn y Fan Fach make a great spot for a picnic, or you may just want to wait to see if you'll spot the mythical Lady of the Lake. But if you do, don't make the mistake of the farmer's son and marry her and subsequently be accused of any kind of domestic violence.

Factbox

Location: Llanddeusant is about 5 miles (8km) south-east of Llangadog on a minor road off the A4069 Llandovery-Gawun Cae Gurwen road

Postcode: SA19 9UL

Length: About 2.5 miles (4km), or can be extended

Terrain: Easy going, mainly on waterworks roads and tracks

Map: OS 1:25,000 Explorer OL12, Brecon Beacons National Park, Western Area

Refreshments: The Red Lion, Church Street, Llangadog SA19 9AA, is probably the nearest hostelry

☎ 01550 777228
Ⓦ facebook.com/TheRedLionLlangadock/

The Myddfai Community Hall and Visitor Centre, Myddfai, Llandovery SA20 0JD, has a cosy café serving local delicacies

☎ 01550 720449
Ⓦ myddfai.org/myddfai-cafe/

Return to Llanddeusant by the same route to complete the easy 2.5 mile (4km) round trip.

If you are feeling reasonably fit and equipped for a mountain hike, you

The dam and weir at the foot of Llyn y Fan Fach

could continue up the slopes of Tyle Gwyn to the right of the lake and follow the path that leads around the lip of this impressive escarpment to the airy summit of Bannau Brycheiniog to get a magnificent aerial view of the shimmering lake.

Or you could follow the ridge to the north, walking over Picws Du and Fan Brycheiniog until you see a path on the left heading down to the plateau below towards Llyn y Fan Fach's sister lake, which is called Llyn y Fan Fawr (in Welsh *fach* simply means 'small' and *fawr* means 'large'). Then follow the path along the lake's edge and the ridge

Looking upstream to Llyn y Fan Fach

until you can make your return to the shore of Llyn y Fan Fach and down to Llanddeusant again. But be warned: this would add an extra 8, quite tough mountainous miles to your walk.

42.

'The Cure of all Diseases': St Govan's Chapel, Pembrokeshire Coast

St Govan's Chapel is tucked away in a cleft in the cliffs

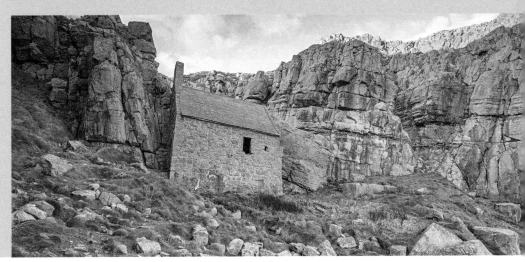

There are estimated to be no fewer than 700 holy wells in Wales, but undoubtedly the most romantically sited is that just below St Govan's Chapel, a tiny hermit's cell at the foot of St Govan's Head, near Bosherton, in the Pembrokeshire Coast National Park.

St Govan (*Gofan* in Welsh), who died in AD 586, was a hermit who apparently originally lived in a fissure in the steep limestone coastal cliffs. St Govan's Chapel was built under the cliffs sometime in the 13th century, below the bold headland that now bears his name.

Much mystery surrounds the identity of Govan himself. One tale claims he was an Irish monk who travelled to Wales to find people who knew the abbot who had trained him. That abbot has been variously identified as the nation's patron saint, David, who has obvious strong links with Wales' smallest cathedral at nearby St David's, or St Ailbe (or Elvis) of Emly in County Tipperary, Ireland, who allegedly fostered and baptised the saintly David.

Another story identifies Govan as Gawain, King Arthur's nephew and one of

Steps below the chapel lead down to the sea

magically opened up, leaving a fissure just big enough for him to hide in until the danger had passed. In gratitude, he decided to build his chapel and stay on under the cliff, maybe to warn local people of an impending attack by pirates if they were ever to return.

Govan survived by eating fish from the sea and drinking from the two clear springs that issued from the foot of the cliff. The chapel was close to one of these, and the other lower one, now enclosed in a corbel-roofed well house, became the holy well. But both springs are now dry.

Many legends surround St Govan and his sacred well, and bathing in its waters was supposed to cure scrofula, paralysis and dropsy among many other diseases, and it was considered especially efficacious in eye ailments and rheumatism. One of the first accounts of the holy well was by the renowned botanist John Ray. Following his visit in 1662, he wrote: 'Thence the same day to St Gobin's [sic] Well by the Sea Side, where, under the cliff, stands a little chapel, sacred to that Saint, and a little below it a Well, famous for the Cure of all Diseases'.

Another legend concerns Govan's silver bell, which he was said to have kept in the tower of the chapel – this is unlikely because the chapel probably wasn't built in his day. The bell allegedly had a perfect tone and clarity, which was probably what attracted those pesky pirates again, because they raided the chapel and stole it. But a greater power intervened, and a heavenly host of angels flew in and took it back from the pirates, returning it to the grateful hermit.

the Knights of the Round Table, and some versions of his legend claim he went into retreat in his later years and was buried in or near the chapel. Most likely though, this was simply an association made due to the similarity of their names.

Govan was possibly one of the Celtic Christian saints who arrived from Ireland in small wooden boats or coracles in the 6th century AD. Celtic saints often travelled the seas around Ireland, Brittany and Wales, either to spread the word of Christianity, or simply to lead lives of austerity in remote places, where they felt they could be closer to their God.

According to the legend, as Govan reached the coastline of South Wales, he was set upon by pirates, who came either from Ireland or Lundy Island in the Bristol Channel. He fled to the headland now known as Govan's Head, where the cliff

To prevent the pirates returning and stealing the bell again, the angels encased it in a huge stone, now found at the water's edge below the chapel and appropriately known as the Bell Rock. The legend claims that when St Govan 'rang' the stone thereafter, its peal had become a thousand times stronger – and surely offered an even greater invitation to the pirates!

Beneath the chapel, but accessible only to experienced cavers by abseiling down the cliff, is a huge cave system named Ogof Gofan ('the cave of Govan'), which apparently contains a 'cathedral-like structure'. The cave was rediscovered in 1966, but it had been used by people for thousands of years, when it was situated many miles from the sea. Exactly the same applied to Goat's Hole Cave at Paviland on the Gower Peninsula, where the 33,000-year-old Palaeolithic 'Red Lady' (who was actually a young man) was found in 1823.

Built into the base of the Carboniferous limestone cliff, St Govan's tiny two-chambered chapel measures only 20 x 12 feet (6 x 3.6m) and its walls are constructed from the local limestone. The majority of the chapel was built in the 13th century, although parts of it may date back further, to the 6th century, the time of St Govan. The slate roof is a much more modern addition.

Another legend suggests that St Govan lies buried underneath the chapel's altar, located at the east end of the building, and that his handprints are imprinted on the floor of his cave. The cave was once a popular place with local people for making wishes, some of which apparently would be granted by the saint.

The building is accessible from the clifftop by climbing down a set of 52 stone stairs, and there is a persistent legend – no doubt encouraged by the tourist business – that the number of steps is said to vary depending on whether you are ascending or descending. You can test the theory – if you have enough breath left, that is – after climbing back up the steps.

St Govan's Head and the chapel both fall within the NATO Castlemartin Firing Range and Military Training Area, so before you can take the walk, you must check if the range is open to the public. Whether military live firing should still be permitted in a National Park specifically set aside by the government for its 'quiet enjoyment' is another question.

Interior of St Govan's Chapel

Factbox

Location: Bosherton is off the B4319, about 4 miles (6.4km) south of Pembroke. From Bosherston, take the single-track road to the Castlemartin Training Area entrance, and follow the directions to the St Govan's car park

Postcode: SA71 5DR

Length: About 1.5 miles (2.4km)

Terrain: Easy walking on surfaced paths, but the 52 steps down to the chapel are quite steep and can be slippery when wet

Map: OS 1:25,000 Explorer OL36, South Pembrokeshire

Refreshments: The appropriately named St Govan's Country Inn, Bosherston, Pembroke SA71 5DN, actually features St Govan's Chapel as its pub sign

☎ 01646 661792
Ⓦ facebook.com/
StGovansInnBosherston

The Stackpole Inn, Jasons Corner, Stackpole, Pembroke SA71 5DF, a Welsh winner in the National Pub and Bar Awards, is also recommended

☎ 01646 672324
Ⓦ stackpoleinn.co.uk

The Walk

Leave the car park on the surfaced path next to the disabled parking bays and turn left onto the Pembrokeshire Coast Path. The coastal heath and unimproved grassland here provide an ideal habitat for the aerobatic red-legged coastal crow known as the chough, and it also supports many other birds such as wheatears, skylarks, meadow pipits, stonechats and various kinds of warbler.

After a short while the footpath reaches the edge of the cliff with wonderful views out to sea. From here you will see the steep 52 steps leading down a defile to the chapel in its beautiful, secluded cove tucked away under the cliffs.

After visiting St Govan's Chapel and climbing back up those apparently uncountable steps it's only a ten minute walk along the clifftop, following the 186 mile (299km) Pembrokeshire Coast Path, to reach St Govan's Head, with its magnificent ocean views. The cliffs here are home to many seabirds, including guillemots, razorbills and kittiwakes, so take your binoculars.

The Pembrokeshire Coast Path forms part of the 870 mile (1,400km) Wales Coast Path, which opened in 2012 as the first dedicated coastal path in the world to run around the entire length of a country's coastline. The path was developed by the Welsh Government in partnership with the former Countryside Council for Wales, 16 local authorities, and the Pembrokeshire Coast and Snowdonia National Parks, and took six years to complete.

Fifty-two steep steps lead down to the chapel

If you are feeling really fit, you could continue walking in either direction along the Coast Path to Barafundle Bay, or you could head back to Bosherston and spend some time wandering around the pretty Bosherston Lily Ponds, especially recommended in June when the water lilies are in bloom. You might also see otters, coot, moorhen, mute swans, herons and kingfishers, and the more than 20 species of dragonflies that have been recorded here.

Note: Before you do this walk you must contact the Pembroke Visitor Centre

☎ 01437 776499

The Castlemartin Training Area

☎ 01646 662367

Or check online to see if you are allowed on the range

Ⓦ gov.uk/government/publications/castlemartin-firing-notice--2

43.

Source of Stonehenge's bluestones:
Preseli Hills, Pembrokeshire

BELOW View from the summit of Foel Cwmcerwyn
RIGHT A distant view of the Preseli Hills

I'd heard the softly calling 'cuc-koo, cuc-koo' drifting up through the balmy, early summer air as I approached the splintered, rocky summit of Foel Cwmcerwyn, at 1,759 feet (536m) the highest point of the Preseli Hills and the Pembrokeshire Coast National Park.

As I wandered around the jagged doleritic outcrop, admiring the splendid panorama which extended out towards the Irish Sea, I took plenty of photographs. But it was only when I got home and inspected them more closely and enlarged one that I realised that the bird I had photographed sitting on the topmost stone was that elusive cuckoo.

It somehow seemed appropriate, as I knew that according to Celtic folklore cuckoos

were supposed to have the ability to travel between this and the underworld and were often associated with death and the afterlife. A cuckoo's call was even said to have the power to summon the dead.

And I was soon to realise that the 8 mile (12.9km)-long prehistoric ridgeway known as the Golden Road along the crest of the Preselis was studded with burial mounds and cairns. This was where the Bronze

Age people of what is now Pembrokeshire buried their high-status dead, where they could both be seen and could watch over their descendants. Maybe my cuckoo on Foel Cwmcerwyn was doing just that...

The Preselis are the only real hill country in the Pembrokeshire Coast National Park but are too often overlooked by visitors, who, quite understandably, usually come to admire its wonderful coastline and beaches (see Govan's Chapel, page 249). But the hills are perhaps best known among archaeologists as the source of the original bluestones that form the centrepiece of Britain's most impressive prehistoric monument at Stonehenge, 180 miles (290km) away on Salisbury Plain in Wiltshire.

It has long been known that the 42 spotted dolerite stones – so-called because the igneous, blueish tinged rock includes white spots – in Stonehenge's inner circle originated from the Preseli Hills. And for many years it was believed that the Stonehenge bluestones came from Carn Menyn, near to the eastern end of the Golden Road, and were transported down to the sea at Milford Haven for their long journey to Salisbury Plain.

But more recent research by a team of archaeologists and geologists led by

University College London has found that the dominant source of Stonehenge's bluestones was quarries on the outcrop of Craig Rhos-y-felin, on the northern slopes of the Preseli Hills, below Carn Menyn and the Golden Road. This quarry, which includes some unfinished bluestones, has been identified as the main source of the type of rhyolite that has been found at Stonehenge.

The mystery still remains as to why and how the stones were quarried in the Preselis and transported to Salisbury Plain some 5,000 years ago. One of the more fanciful theories has been their natural transportation as erratics by glaciers during the last Ice Age. But the latest findings seem to cast doubt on the most widely accepted theory that the bluestones were transported from the Preselis to Stonehenge by water taken south to Milford Haven, up the Bristol Channel and then along the River Avon towards Salisbury Plain. As these quarries are on the north side of the Preselis, the megaliths could just as easily have gone overland around the Bristol Channel to reach their destination.

Team leader Prof Mike Parker Pearson of UCL said: 'What's really exciting about these discoveries is that they take us a step closer to unlocking Stonehenge's greatest mystery – why its stones came from so far away. Every other Neolithic monument in Europe was built of megaliths brought from no more than 10 miles (16km) away'.

Parker Pearson added that they were now looking to find out just what had made the Preseli Hills so special 5,000 years ago, and whether there were any important stone circles there, maybe built as 'prototypes', before the bluestones were transported to Stonehenge.

The Golden Road on the Preselis

The Walk

As I walked up from the village of Rosebush (in Welsh: Rhos-y-bwlch, which means 'a gap or pass in the moor') and skirted the dark coniferous forest of Pantmaenog, the cuckoo had been a constant companion. Reaching the first cairn-topped summit of Foel Feddau on the famed Golden Road, the views behind opened up to reveal a splendid westward panorama towards Dinas Head, Fishguard and the glittering Irish Sea.

According to *The Mabinogion*, a 12th and 13th-century compilation of ancient oral Welsh legends, King Arthur and his knights fought a bloody battle with a terrible boar called Twrch Trwyth, down to the south-west of Foel Feddau in the grassy cwm below Foel Cwmcerwyn. We will meet Arthur again later on along our walk.

Once you've gained the necessary height, walking the Golden Road is a grand promenade taking you over some wild moorland along the very spine of the Preseli Hills, following a well-trodden path that is claimed to date back to the Neolithic period, some 5,000 years ago. It is thought to have been a main route for travellers to and from Ireland, part of a trade superhighway along which gold mined in the Wicklow Mountains in Ireland was carried south-east as far as Wessex. And it's not too much of a stretch of the imagination to think that this much frequented highway may even have been used by the Neolithic

Factbox

Location: Park carefully in Rosebush village

Postcode: SA66 7QU

Length: 7.5 miles (12km); 4 hours one way, but can be shortened at any point to return to Rosebush

Terrain: Mainly clear paths over grassy moorland, but not waymarked on the higher sections, which can be boggy, so boots, waterproofs and map and compass are essential

Map: OS 1:25,000 Explorer OL35 North Pembrokeshire

Refreshments: Rosebush's community-owned pub Tafarn Sinc (or the Zinc Tavern in English), Bryn Terrrace, Rosebush, Clynderwen SA66 7QU. Formerly the Precelly Hotel, it was built in 1876 with timbers and corrugated galvanised iron sheeting from the former railway station

📞 01437 532214
🌐 tafarnsinc.cymru/eng/index.php

The jagged summit rocks of Carn Menyn

Bedd Arthur stone circle

transporters of those Stonehenge bluestones.

The views are truly breathtaking and dotted all along the way on either side of the path are prehistoric remains under the windswept moor grass. Passing the minor top of Mynydd-bach you soon approach the rocky tor of Carn Bica, topped by its own Bronze Age burial cairn.

Close to Carn Bica, down the slope to the south, there is a stone circle known as Bedd Arthur ('Arthur's grave'). This

elliptical ring of stones is one of many places in Britain which is claimed to be the last resting place of the legendary 'Once and Future King'. Maybe Merlin, Arthur's wizard and mentor, who in some stories is supposed to have magically transported Stonehenge's massive sarsen stones from Ireland and persuaded giants to re-assemble them, may have passed this way after all?

The next landmark just to the south is the jagged summit rocks of Carn Menyn which, like all the Preseli tors, are the result of many thousands of years of

weathering by snow, ice, rain and wind on the tough 170-million-year-old dolerite. Before the recent discoveries at Craig Rhos-y-felin, Carn Menyn had traditionally been thought to be the source of the bluestones used to build the inner ring of Stonehenge.

If you have the energy – and remember, you have to make the return journey of up to 7 miles (11.3km) along the Golden Road back to Rosebush – it's worth the extra bit of effort to climb to the Iron Age hillfort that encircles the summit of Foeldrygarn, just off the path to the north. The Welsh name translates to 'the hill of the three cairns', and sure enough, within the confines of the fort there is a trio of Bronze Age burial cairns. They predate the fort by several thousand years and are claimed to be the last resting place of three kings named Mon, Maclen and Madog.

Broadcaster and author Wynford Vaughan-Thomas perfectly summed up his own experience of the Preselis: 'Everywhere you feel the presence of the megalithic tomb-builders, of the Iron Age warriors who piled the stones for the great hillforts and of kindly and absent-minded old Celtic saints'.

SCOTLAND

The Trotternish Ridge on the Isle of Skye

44

'Looking into the abyss of time': Siccar Point, Berwickshire

BELOW The ruins of St Helen's Church
RIGHT Descending towards Siccar Point

One bright summer's day in 1788, a small boat set out from the mouth of the Dunglass Burn on the estate of chemist Sir James Hall, heading for a trip along the Berwickshire coast. It was a voyage that would change our understanding of time forever, and what we think about the age of the Earth.

In the boat with Hall were John Playfair, a Church of Scotland minister and mathematician, and most notably 62-year-old James Hutton, a pioneering geologist and gentleman farmer, who has been dubbed 'the father of modern geology'.

Before that day, the generally accepted view of the age of the Earth was that promoted by Archbishop James Ussher, primate of all Ireland, in his *The Annals of* the World, published in 1658. Using the chronology of the Bible and linking it to established dates in world history, Ussher had calculated, with somewhat suspicious precision, that the world had begun at around six o'clock on the evening of Saturday, 22 October, 4004 BC.

Ussher's date had been accepted by Christians and scientists for 130 years, and even in the early 1700s, 50 years

after his death, it was still being included in the margins of the authorised King James Bible. Before Ussher published his calculation William Shakespeare, writing *As You Like It* in 1599, has Rosalind advising Orlando: 'The poor world is almost six thousand years old'.

Scientists of the Enlightenment, such as Comte de Buffon Georges-Louis Leclerc and Gottfried Wilhelm Leibniz, had questioned Ussher's spurious theory, and European missionaries had discovered that Chinese written history went back for many centuries before Noah's flood, which was alleged to have taken place around 2300 BC.

The little boatload of scientists who were to conclusively prove that the Earth had existed much further back into what is now known as Deep Time carried on south down the coast, passing Cove Harbour, Pease Bay and the clifftop ruins of St Helen's Church, until it came to the rocky, sea-washed promontory known as Siccar Point.

Here they found what Hutton later described as 'a beautiful picture of this junction washed bare by the sea'. The 'junction' he was looking for was what he called the 'unconformity' of two rock types from vastly different eras lying adjacent to one another. He found it in the horizontal layers of the younger dusky pink 280-million-year-old Old Red Sandstone lying on top of the nearly vertical strata of the much older light grey Silurian rock known as greywacke, which dated back 430 million years. Hutton's famous 'unconformity' was illustrated by the almost unimaginable time gap that existed between the two sets of strata. He later wrote of how he had 'rejoiced at my good fortune in stumbling upon an object so interesting in the natural history of the earth, and which I had been long looking for in vain'.

Playfair's description of how he experienced that mind-blowing moment is a classic of early scientific writing:

What clearer evidence could we have had of the different formation of these rocks, and of the long interval which separated their formation, had we actually seen them emerging from the bosom of the deep? We felt ourselves necessarily carried back to the time when the schistus (greywacke) on which we stood was yet at the bottom of the sea, and when the sandstone before us was only beginning to be deposited, in the shape of sand or mud, from the waters of a superincumbent ocean. An epocha still more remote presented itself, when even the most ancient of these rocks, instead of standing upright in vertical beds, lay in horizontal planes at the bottom of the sea, and was not yet disturbed by that immeasurable force which has burst asunder the solid pavement of the globe. Revolutions still more remote appeared in the distance of this extraordinary perspective. The mind seemed to grow giddy by looking so far into the abyss of time...

Thirty-six years later in 1824, Hall returned to Siccar Point with another young Scottish geologist named Charles Lyell, who was to become one of the most eminent and influential geologists in Britain in the 19th century. Lyell expanded, developed and made more

Hutton's Unconformity

The cliffs at Siccar Point

widely available Hutton's revolutionary theory in his *Principles of Geology* (1830), which became, and still is, a Bible in itself for budding geologists.

Hutton's Unconformity at Siccar Point has also become something of a Mecca for geologists, world famous as the most important site described by Hutton in support of his literally earth-shattering ideas on the origin and age of the planet. Some geologists visiting Siccar Point for the first time have been known to burst into tears.

With the eye of faith, the junction between the older, vertical layers of greywacke and the younger, lichen-spattered Old Red Sandstone can still clearly be seen, allowing you to appreciate the evidence for an ancient Earth where the action of uniform, continuous natural processes are still occurring today.

This principle, which is known as uniformitarianism, had a profound impact on the young science of geology and was summarised by the phrase: the present is the key to the past. Or as Hutton famously concluded his 1788 paper describing his discovery at Siccar Point to the Royal Society of Edinburgh: 'The result, therefore, of our present enquiry is that we find no vestige of a beginning – no prospect of an end'.

Thankfully, Siccar Point remains much as it was when Hutton visited in 1788. Standing on the clifftop overlooking the Point you can perhaps see why Hutton chose this place to make his monumental discovery because, as always, the landscape reflects its underlying rocks.

Looking south, the steep grey cliffs of greywacke, which also make up much of the sparsely populated Southern Uplands, rise to Fast Castle Head (the fictional setting for Walter Scott's 1819 novel *The Bride of Lammermuir*) before plunging into the North Sea, while to the north and west, the softer, younger sedimentary rocks, such as the Old Red Sandstone, create gently rolling, more populated farmland, before rising to the Lammermuir Hills.

One of the best approaches to Siccar Point is along the coastal path – part of the Southern Upland Way – from Cockburnspath to the north. Cockburnspath is the eastern terminus of the 212 mile (341km) Southern Upland Way, a long-distance footpath that links the west and east coasts of Scotland.

The parish of Cockburnspath was once part of the dowry in the so-called 'Marriage of the Thistle and the Rose', given by James IV of Scotland to Margaret Tudor, daughter of Henry VII of England, on their marriage in 1503. The 16th-century Market Cross in the centre of the village celebrates this momentous union of nations with carved emblems of a thistle on two of its faces and a rose on the other two.

The Walk

Follow the waymarked Coastal Path along the clifftops, with great views of the rocks exposed below on the seashore. The path meets a minor road and descends to the entrance to the Pease Bay Caravan Site. Just inland from here is the Scottish Wildlife Trust's Pease Dean Nature Reserve, a beautiful, ancient semi-natural woodland. (Dean is a North Country word for a valley). Ferns, mosses and liverworts thrive in these wet, sheltered conditions, and in spring and summer, the woodland floor is covered with bluebells, primroses and wood anemones.

From the caravan park and after crossing a ford, the road climbs steeply, and a set of steps to the left takes you back to the clifftop for a short while before you join the minor road that leads to the Drysdale vegetable processing site, which is located in the former Cambus Quarry. Follow this road to a parking area on the left about 100 yards (91m) before the entrance, where an interpretation board beside the gate gives information about Siccar Point.

Go through the gate and walk along the left, seaward, edge of the field, past the gable end and overgrown ruins of St Helen's Church, and follow the path alongside the fence. The church once served the former village of Old Cambus (from the Gaelic *Allt-camus*, meaning 'stream of the bay'), granted by Edgar to the monks of Durham in 1098. The Norman church dedicated to St Helen is thought to date from around this time.

Factbox

Location: Cockburnspath is located on the A1 about 35 miles (56km) east of Edinburgh. There is a small car park signposted for Siccar Point

Postcode: TD13 5YR

Length: About 4 miles (6.4km), there and back

Terrain: Easy field paths, but Siccar Point itself is at the foot of a steep, grassy slope and beware, the rocks can be slippery

Map: OS 1:25,000 Explorer OL346, Berwick-upon-Tweed

Refreshments: There are no pubs in Cockburnspath, but the Community Shop in the Village Hall TD13 5XY, is a great place to pick up some home-made lunch on your way to Siccar Point

☎ 07460 842845
🌐 shop.copathandcove.org/

Pease Bay Caravan Site

The path to Siccar Point

At the far corner of the second field, you'll see a kissing gate and another interpretation board. Go through the gate, and about 50 yards (46m) beyond this you get to the clifftop with the rocks of Siccar Point spread out beneath you. The key features as observed by Hutton can be seen from the top of the slope, but to get to the point itself, you'll have to negotiate a very steep, grassy incline, which can be treacherous, especially when wet, as I discovered.

But to put your hand between the two strata – what geologists call 'the contact' – is to feel the weight of over 50 million years of missing geological time, and to take a peep into Playfair's 'abyss of time'.

If you'd rather approach Hutton's Unconformity by sea as he did, Eyemouth Rib Trips run from Eyemouth along the coast passing Siccar Point:

T 07941 441995
W eyemouthribtrips.co.uk

45

Columba's tears:
St Columba's Bay, Iona

BELOW Breakers constantly polish the stones of St Columba's Bay
RIGHT St Mary's Abbey, Iona

Sadly, most peoples' experience of the sacred Celtic island of Iona is ruled by two sets of ferry times. For the vast majority of the island's 130,000 annual visitors, their time on Iona is limited to a swift dash up to the restored medieval abbey church of St Mary's and back again to catch the next ferry to Fionnphort on Mull.

This is usually followed by a drive across Mull's single-track road for the two-hourly ferry back to Oban from Craignure.

Even though their visit is necessarily curtailed by the need to catch those ferries, it would take the most insensitive of site-tickers to leave Iona without catching something of the intangible magic of what to most people is simply the most beautiful island in the Hebrides.

As that great connoisseur of the Scottish mountain scene WH 'Bill' Murray pointed out, Iona seems to have a purity of light and colour which somehow exceeds all the others. 'Tiree has equal clarity of air but not of colour, which in Iona invades even her seas', wrote Murray in *The Hebrides*.

'One's first and abiding impression is of greenness and fairness, and of a grace peculiar to the union in one small island of a multiplicity of minor excellences'.

Even those whistle-stop day-visitors see something of Iona's unsurpassed 'minor excellences' in the range of subtle colouring as they leave the salmon-pink granite rocks of Fionnphort on the short, mile-long (1.6km) crossing to the landing place on St Ronan's Bay. The dazzling white sands which greet them stretch out under the waters of the Sound of Iona and miraculously turn to almost Mediterranean shades of azure and aquamarine before reaching the deeper sea.

But the best way to appreciate the varied colours and the genuine wildness of Iona is to take the boggy paths across the Sliabh Siar, the rocky spine of unimaginably ancient Lewisian gneiss, which are among the oldest rocks anywhere in the world and which make up the south and east of the island, to reach Columba's Bay.

This is the historic spot where St Columba, or Colum Cille, landed on Iona in AD 563, fleeing from his native Ireland. Legend has it he had disgraced himself by copying the Book of Psalms and then refusing to hand the copy back, a petulant action for which he never

The sunlit cloisters of the abbey

forgave himself because it resulted in the bloody battle of Culdrevny where 3,000 men died. He vowed never to return to Ireland and headed north-east towards the then heathen Hebrides, to light the lamp of Christianity, which was eventually to illuminate the whole of pagan Europe. He landed in his skin-covered coracle, of the type still in use in the Aran Islands, on the stony beach known as Port a' Churaich, or the Port of the Coracle, near the south-eastern tip of the island.

Once ashore, Columba climbed to the nearest high point above the beach, the heather-covered hill known as Carn Cul ri Eirinn (the Cairn of the Back to Ireland) and cast his eyes westwards to see if he could still see his beloved homeland. He could not, but as Bill Murray has pointed out, it must have been a misty day, for the hills of Ireland are in fact just visible in good conditions from the summit cairn, 80 miles (129km) away beyond Islay and to its right. Carn Cul ri Eirinn (242 feet/74m) is still one of the finest and wildest viewpoints on Iona. I was last there on a hazy summer's day, when beyond the dazzling white strand of Camus Cul an t-Saimh (the Bay at the Back of the Ocean) the low hills of Tiree and Coll seemed to float above the Atlantic like the fabled Tir nan Og (the Land of the Ever-young).

I had just spent a pleasurable hour beachcombing among the kaleidoscope-coloured pebbles which shine like precious jewels when polished by the foaming surf on the twin beaches of Port a' Churaich and Port an Fhir-Bhreige (the Port of the False Man). And the most prized pebbles of all are those of the lime-green flecked Iona marble, evocatively known as Columba's tears.

The Walk

The easiest route to the southern end of Iona is by way of the east-west road – Bruthach na Ceapaich (the Ascent of the Tillage Plot), which rises over the fertile central plain of the island from the sandy bays of the east coast. Passing the rough hay meadow of Lagnagiogan (the Hollow of the Thistles) on a still summer evening, you may hear the unmistakeable grating call of the corncrake, a sound like passing your fingernail sharply over the teeth of a comb. This is one of the last British sites for this very rare and secretive rail, once common in our hay meadows and cornfields, and now actively encouraged to breed here by special RSPB and NatureScot management schemes.

Further on, just before you drop down to the dazzling white sands of the Bay at the Back of the Ocean across a broad, grassy sward of the machair - now partly occupied by the Iona Golf Course - you pass a small crag to your left. This is Cnoc nan Aingeal (the Hill of the Angels) where the saintly Columba was seen to commune with the heavenly host by

A number of Celtic crosses stand outside the abbey, including St John's Cross (foreground)

Factbox

Location: Iona is off the west coast of the Isle of Mull in the Hebrides. It is reached by catching the 40-minute Caledonian MacBrayne ferry from Oban to Craignure on Mull, and then driving across the island via Glen More and the Ross of Mull to Fionnphort for the short ferry trip to Iona

Postcode: PA76 6SL

Length: The walk to Columba's Bay is a round trip of about 6 miles (9.7km), starting and finishing at Iona village, or Am Baile Mor

Terrain: Moderate walking. You should allow at least 4 hours

Map: OS 1:25,000 Explorer OL373, Iona, Staffa & Ross of Mull. The Iona Community produces an excellent 1:10,000, about six inches to the mile, map of the island, which is the best for walking

Refreshments: There are two hotels in Iona village, the Argyll Hotel, Iona PA76 6SJ

☎ 01681 700334
🌐 argyllhoteliona.co.uk

The St Columba Hotel, Iona PA76 6SL

☎ 01681 700304
🌐 stcolumba-hotel.co.uk

Refreshments can also be obtained from the Abbey restaurant at PA76 6SQ

The cottages of Iona's main street are backed by Cnoc Mor ('Big Hill')

an eavesdropping monk from his newly established monastery.

The way south down to the pebble beach of Port a' Churaich from here is a real delight, passing the island's only remaining natural loch – Loch Staonaig – once the island's main source of drinking water. You thread your way through the rocky, heather-covered outcrops of grey gneiss down into grassy greensward of Lag Odhar (the Brown Hollow), which is often occupied by a herd of contented cattle. Here and there in the damper spots, patches of the bright yellow flag iris – another Ionan speciality – enliven the pastoral scene.

Difficult to find but well worth the effort is the secret pass of Liana an Tairbh, which leads off to the east of Lag Odhar and down past the elder-haunted ruins of Tobhta nan Sassunaich (the House of the Lowlanders (or Englishmen)). From here you turn right to pass the further ruins of Tigh nan Gall (House of the Strangers), and then steeply down a narrow defile into the strange, lost world of the Iona Marble Quarry.

This is yet another of Iona's many surprises, for here, tucked away in one of the wildest and most remote spots on the island, are the rusting remains of industry. The Duke of Argyll quarried and transported out by sea the prized, green-veined marble from the late 18th century until the final effort in the early 20th century. You can still see evidence of that last fruitless attempt in the remains of the Gloucester-made gas engine that powered the machinery, the water tanks and cutting frame, along with the cut blocks of the gleaming stone, which are scattered in great heaps below the glistening quarry face and in the surging waves of the Irish Sea.

You can never escape the spirit of Columba on Iona, and he is attributed with this often-quoted poem about his beloved island:

In Iona of my heart, Iona of my love,
Instead of monks' voices shall be the lowing of cattle,
But ere the world come to an end
Iona shall be as it was.

46.

Monarch of the glens:
Glencoe, Argyll, Highlands

Looking east down cloud-wreathed Glencoe

The brass sign in reception of the Clachaig Inn in the heart of wild Glencoe used to read: 'No Hawkers or Campbells'. The wry message, of course, was left more for the amusement of tourists than in any sense of lasting revenge for the infamous massacre of Macdonalds, which took place near here in 1692.

The effects of that heinous act of treachery, which seemed even worse to Highland minds because the Campbells ignored the traditional peace-pact granted by their hosts' hospitality, inevitably colours nearly every visitor's view of the glen. The Victorians, with their unrestrained taste for the melodramatic and with no regard at all for its true meaning, dubbed it the 'Glen of Weeping'.

Charles Dickens hated the place, and claimed its very recollection made him shudder. Glencoe was, he said: 'perfectly terrible', and 'an awful place... there are scores of glens, high up, which form such haunts as you might imagine yourself wandering in, in the very height and madness of a fever'. HV Morton waxed even more hysterical in his *In Search of Scotland*. 'Here is a landscape without mercy', he wrote. 'As far as Glen Coe is concerned, the first germ of life has never struggled from the warm slime'.

More recently, Glencoe was used in the *Harry Potter* film franchise for a number of shots in several of the movies, including the location of Hagrid's Hut in *Harry Potter and the Prisoner of Azkaban* (2004). Most of the filming was done across from Clachaig Inn in the impressive gash of the Clachaig Gulley, usually the final descent on the classic Aonach Eagach ('the notched ridge') scramble. In many of the scenes you can also see the surrounding hills, Signal Rock forest and Torren Lochan, and Glencoe was used for the bridge leading to Hogwarts.

It is without doubt the most majestic and the most dramatic of all Scotland's glens – a rich mix of brooding history, glistening rock, soaring buttresses, and towering peaks, which are usually hidden from view under constantly shifting veils of mist. Truly, as the distinguished Scottish nature writer Jim Crumley has written, Glencoe is the monarch of the glens.

For the traveller heading north for Fort William along the A82, Glencoe always comes as a bit of a shock after the gently undulating, lochan-spattered wilderness of Rannoch Moor. The first sign that something dramatic is about to happen is the astonishing sight of the great, gullied

Coire Gabhail 'the Lost Valley'

pyramid of rock that is Buachaille Etive Mor, the Great Herdsman of Etive, which stands sentinel to both the entrance to Glencoe and Glen Etive, leading off to the south-west.

The Buachaille, as it is affectionately known, always strikes me as the very epitome of mountain majesty, and I still have vivid memories of seeing it for the first time and being, quite literally, struck speechless. Being a native of East Anglia, I had never seen so much naked rock all in one place. Fortunately for me and my three pals from the village, discretion swiftly became the better part of valour in our foolhardy, headlong assault on the 3,351 foot (1,021m) summit, equipped only in our winkle-picker Chelsea boots and Pac-a-macs.

This walk visits one of those scores of 'high up' glens which so haunted the fevered mind of Dickens. Coire Gabhail (pronounced 'Corry Gale') is also known as the Lost Valley of Glencoe. It is situated between the first and second Sisters of the famed Three Sisters of Glencoe – the triple buttresses of Beinn Fhada, Gearr Aonach and Aonach Dubh – which hang menacingly over the A82 and thrust north from the 2,772 foot (845m) reigning summit of Bidean nam Bian like the knuckles of a clenched fist.

The guidebooks claim that Coire Gabhail (it means the coire, or hollow, of capture) was where the Macdonalds hid the cattle they had stolen from their neighbours, in the days when cattle-rustling was something of a croft industry in the Highlands. Certainly, the broad green sanctuary of Coire Gabhail is well hidden

The tumbling waters of Allt Coire Gabhail are followed upstream

from the old road that passes through the glen below. But, as we will see, it would take a very determined rustler to drive a herd of cattle up into this mountain fastness, although equally it would be very easy to defend it with a handful of claymore-wielding warriors.

There is some controversy over our route to Coire Gabhail. When WH Murray came here in 1939, as described in *Mountaineering in Scotland* (1947, and originally written on toilet paper in a PoW camp), he faced a knee-deep wade of 20 yards (18m) to cross the raging torrent of the River Coe, which at that time was 'sullied by no bridge'. In those days, according to Murray, 'a man might come here for a week and be alone. He might

Looking across Glencoe towards the Aonach Eagach ridge at sunrise

pitch a tent on that meadow and be as much out of sight and sound of civilisation as if he dwelt at the North Pole'.

Those days are long gone, and signposts, steps, stiles and bridge were erected by the National Trust for Scotland, which acquired the 5,680 acre (2,299ha) Glencoe and Dalness estate in 1935 and 1937 largely through the beneficence of Percy Unna, president of the Scottish Mountaineering Club. But Unna attached certain rules to the gift, including the provision that the Trust would maintain the estate in 'primitive' condition for all time. By 'primitive', Unna explained, he meant among other things that the hills should not be made easier or safer to climb, that paths should not be extended or improved, and that no signs or cairns should be erected.

The NTS ran into trouble from the Scottish wild land lobby for the way in which it had contravened the so-called 'Unna Rules', especially in Glencoe and specifically in opening up the Lost Valley. Its response was that Unna also wanted unrestricted access to the public, and safety factors had to be considered when large numbers of walkers had proved that they wanted to visit the Lost Valley. It did, however, bow to the pressure and removed all signposts to the valley from the road and also removed the former glaringly ugly visitor centre near the Clachaig Inn to a new eco-friendly centre near Ballachulish, well outside the pristine recesses of the glen. It has also recently built a replica of a 17th-century turf-roofed house at the abandoned clachan (small village) of Achtriachtan.

The Walk

As we will see, it is still a tough and difficult walk to reach Coire Gabhail, and this route should only be attempted by fit and experienced hillwalkers. We start from the roadside car park in Glencoe, following the obvious path down towards the river, close to the Meeting of Three Waters waterfall. A series of wooden steps now take you down into the narrow, rowan-hung gorge of the Coe, which is crossed by a footbridge, and up and out the other side.

The reconstructed path now winds steeply up through the rocks and heather, with fine views back across the glen to the serrated ridge of Aonach Eagach opposite. Eventually you reach the deer fence, which is crossed by a tall ladder stile, to start the climb around the side of the dramatic mass of Gearr Aonach towards the valley.

The path constricts and passes through the rare temperate rainforest of sparse woodland of birches and rowans high on the western bank of the Allt Coire Gabhail, which thunders beneath through a series of spectacular waterfalls. Take extra care here, for many people have

Factbox

Location: The A82 bisects Glencoe, which is 17 miles (27.4km) south of Fort William. The car park is on the left side of the road, about 2 miles (3.2km) before reaching the Clachaig Inn

Postcode: PH49 4HX

Length: The walk is about 5 miles (8km)

Terrain: The walk is extremely steep and rough and should only be attempted by experienced and well-equipped hillwalkers

Map: OS 1:25,000 Explorer OL384, Glen Coe & Glen Etive

Refreshments: There is a café at the National Trust for Scotland, Glencoe Visitor Centre, Glencoe, Ballachulish PH49 4HX

📞 01855 811307
🌐 nts.org.uk/visit/places/glencoe/highlights/visitor-centre

The 300-year-old Clachaig Inn, Old Village Road, Glencoe, Ballachulish PH49 4HX, is a popular haunt of climbers and offers a good pint or dram, and hotel and self-catering accommodation – whether you're a Campbell or not

📞 01855 811252
🌐 clachaig.com

A golden eagle

slipped on this narrow path, which is crossed by many exposed tree roots.

Keep to the path and river as close as you can, as the climb steepens towards the mouth of the coire above. This is difficult country, and a sure footing is needed to negotiate the many large boulders that have fallen down the screes from the ridge of Gearr Aonach above. After crossing the infant river and what seems a lifetime enclosed by rock and trees, you eventually emerge into the astonishing enclosed valley of Coire Gabhail by a huge, house-sized boulder, which partially blocks the entrance.

The scene that presents itself is truly breathtaking. At a height of about 1,200 feet (365m), the flat green meadow floor is completely enclosed by the precipitous walls of Gearr Aonach and Beinn Fhada, which sweep round to the great buttresses at the head of the valley and the pass of Bealach Dearg, which eventually leads up to the unseen summit of Bidean nam Bian to the right. If you are really lucky, as I was on my first visit, you'll be greeted by the magnificent sight of a golden eagle soaring effortlessly on fingered wings above the Bealach.

Walk up the valley as far as you wish, perhaps to the last rowan where the infant Allt Coire Gabhail sinks beneath the rocks, and then make your way back the way you came, carefully as before, down that steep, rocky staircase, over that controversial footbridge, and back to the car park.

The entrance to Coire Gabhail

47.

The fabled Table of Skye:
The Quiraing, Isle of Skye

The fabled Table at the heart of the Quiraing

The description of the Quiraing on the remote Trotternish peninsula in northern Skye in Walter (WA) Poucher's classic *The Scottish Peaks* (1965) was irresistible: '... on closer inspection it will be found not only to consist of the weirdest collection of perpendicular buttresses and pinnacles in Britain, but also to hide away in its uppermost recesses an oval Table covered with smooth, sheep-cropped grass of vivid hue, which might well make an excellent putting green situated in one of the most spectacular amphitheatres in the country'.

As his biographer, I thought it was typical of the golf-loving Poucher to see the potential for a putting green in such an inaccessible place, but I knew that on my first visit to Skye, I had to find that fabled Table. Legend has it that this was where local clans corralled their stolen cattle, safely hidden from the eyes of their owners, or maybe even to hide them away from Viking raiders.

A breathless scramble through that 'weirdest collection of perpendicular buttresses and pinnacles' of the Quiraing brought me to the southern end of the Table, and I stopped for my sandwich lunch with my feet dangling over the edge. I got chatting to a couple of other walkers, one of whom turned out to be a sound recordist for the BBC in London.

Our blather was suddenly interrupted by the sound of falling rocks from the vertical, 100 foot (30.5m) walls of 1,781 foot (543m) Meall nan Suiramach directly behind us. To our horror, we watched as a sheep fell directly from the top of the crag and, in full summer fleece, bounced once, twice, three times as it hit the Table before disappearing over the edge.

'Wow', gasped my new recordist friend, who obviously found it difficult to switch off work mode: 'A human body must sound just like that if it fell!'

The Quiraing (the name is thought to come from the Old Norse *Kví Rand*, which means 'round fold') forms part of the 20 mile (32.2km)-long Trotternish ridge, a massive landslip in the Jurassic sedimentary rocks, which are overlain by basalt lava flows, sills and dykes. Further south stands the similarly created 160 foot (49m) rock exclamation mark of the Old Man of Storr, visible in so many views across Loch Fada and Loch Leathan north of Portree. But because of the friable and loose nature of the rock, these pinnacles are generally considered unsuitable for rock climbing, although the Old Man was climbed by the renowned Manchester climber Don Whillans in 1955.

As might be expected in an island famed for its fairy tales, the ghostly spires of the Quiraing are no exception. A white cow was said to graze on the grassy Table in the heart of the Quiraing at dawn on

Looking south down on the Trotternish ridge

Midsummer's Day, but it would only give up its milk to a virgin. The magic milk was claimed to taste exactly like whatever the drinker might have wished, and it was believed to never turn sour. For many years, when the cow made its annual appearance, it was milked by the fairest lass drawn from the local villages.

Predictably, as in so many of these tales, it all ended badly when a Glaswegian tinker, who had heard the story in Portree, lay in wait one Midsummer night to claim the milk for himself. After ravishing the appointed maiden and leaving her for dead, he disguised himself with a wig and climbed up into the heights of the Quiraing to reach the Table. Sure enough, there was the mythical cow, but it obviously sussed him out because as he attempted to milk it, it tossed him on its horns and unceremoniously dunked him into Staffin Bay, where he was drowned.

Of course, the white cow has never been seen again, but more recently, the Table has hosted a few impromptu games of the rumbustious Gaelic brand of hurling or hockey, known as shinty.

The Walk

The 3 mile (4.8km) walk to reach the Table on Quiraing is a serious hill expedition and should only be attempted if you are suitably experienced and equipped. It starts from the small car park at the highest point of the single-track Staffin-Uig road. Crossing the road, an almost Alpine path leads north across the steep grassy slopes to your right. The pinnacled heights of the Prison, in all honesty looking more like the towers of a medieval castle than a gaol, soon appear ahead, but you must carefully cross a rocky stream to reach them.

The path then passes between the Prison and the forbidding cliffs of the reigning summit of Meall na Suiramach, which soar away to your left. The path splits here, with the main one continuing left to eventually reach the grassy, undistinguished summit of Meall na Suiramach.

Ahead on a faint path now you will see an impressive array of Poucher's 'perpendicular buttresses and pinnacles', the highest of which is known as the

Factbox

Location: The Quiraing is situated in Trotternish to the north of Skye. The start of the walk can be from either Staffin or Uig, which are linked by a single-track road. The car park is located at the highest part of the road about 5.5 miles (8.9km) from Uig or 2.5 miles (4km) from Staffin. It is 20 miles (32.2km) from Portree

Postcode: IV51 9JY

Length: The walk is about 3 miles (4.8km) and should take around 1-2 hours

Terrain: Rough, stony and strenuous mountain paths, with an exciting scramble at the end to reach the Table. You should be experienced and equipped for a serious mountain exercise

Map: OS 1:25,000 Explorer OL408, Skye - Trotternish & The Storr

Refreshments: A former Victorian hunting lodge built in 1892, the Flodigarry Hotel, Flodigarry, Portree IV51 9HZ, on the A855 a couple of miles (3-4km) north of the Quiraing claims to be the most northerly hotel on Skye. It boasts on its estate the cottage where the famous Scottish Jacobite heroine Flora MacDonald lived for 20 years

📞 01470 552203
🌐 hotelintheskye.co.uk

The forbidding walls of The Prison

The Prison is a detached outcrop from Meall na Suiramach (note tiny figure in left corner for scale)

Needle, a jagged, overhanging 120 foot (37m)-high pinnacle, which thrusts skywards. To reach the Table, you must go straight ahead behind the Needle and carefully scramble up a narrow, scree-filled gulley between two more bristling rock buttresses.

Once you reach the velvety-grassed meadow, which is bigger than a football field, it's worth taking time to get your breath back and to admire the stupendous views – said to be the finest on Skye – from the clan's magnificent hideaway. The vistas to the east are exceptional, taking in an aerial view of the tiny crofts of the former fishing village of Staffin with the golden sands of its semi-circular bay and sheltering island directly on the coast below, the low-lying islands of Raasay and Rona anchored out in the Sound of Raasay, and beyond them, the higher, often snow-capped hills of Torridon and Wester Ross, including Beinn Eighe and Liathach, on the mainland.

Closer at hand and looking due south across the Quiraing pinnacles, the great stepped escarpment of the Trotternish landslip sweep up to Cleat and Beinn Edra (2,004 feet/611m), finally to reach its highest point of 2,358 feet (719m) at The Storr, north of Portree. Carefully make your return the way you came to re-join the path back to the car park.

If this strenuous route to the Table taking you into the heart of mountains is a bit intimidating, the Quiraing can be circled by car. Take the main A855 road up the east coast of Skye from Portree, passing the Old Man of Storr and Loch Fada and Loch Leathan to the seaside village of Staffin. From there turn left at a sign which indicates Quiraing. The road ascends to the car park on the left of the road, the starting point of our walk. It continues across the plateau to the west, where it meets the A855 again just before Uig. From here follow the sign for Kilmuir to the right, which skirts the Quiraing to the north.

48.

Birds and brides in the broch: Mousa Broch, Mousa, Shetland Islands

Mousa is the finest of Scotland's 500 brochs

Mousa Broch, on the tiny, uninhabited island of Mousa off the east coast of Mainland Shetland, is not only the best preserved and highest standing of Scotland's 500 brochs, but it is also claimed to be among the best-preserved prehistoric buildings in Europe.

Brochs are circular, hollow-walled, drystone structures dating from the Iron Age, around 2,000 years ago. They are exclusively found in Scotland and were built to provide secure accommodation in times of trouble or invasion. The word is thought to be derived from Lowland Scots or English 'brough', meaning a defended place.

Mousa Broch still stands an impressive

44 feet (13m) high on a flat, low rock promontory on the western shore of Mousa, overlooking Mousa Sound, and looks for all the world like an Iron Age cooling tower. Built of flags of the local Old Red Sandstone, it is thought to have been constructed in about 300 BC.

A low hill shelters the broch on the landward side, and archaeologists have discovered that it was originally surrounded by a wall which may have enclosed some beehive-shaped huts. This wall is now only visible from its foundations, which are most obvious on the western side, but the remains show that it was about 7.5 feet (2.3m) thick.

Mousa may have one of the smallest diameters of any broch, but it has some of the thickest walls and smallest interiors. It is its massive construction, in addition to its remote location, which are thought to be the main reasons for its exceptional state of preservation. It is still accessible by an entrance passage on the western side and visitors can climb to the top via the narrow internal staircase built into the walls.

Mousa Broch continued to be used over the centuries and is mentioned in two of the classic Norse sagas as providing

a convenient home for runaway Viking lovers. In Egil's Saga, perhaps the greatest of the Icelandic sagas, it is stated that around the year AD 910 Bjorn Brynjolfsson, the son of a chieftain in the Sogn area of western Norway, eloped with a young woman named Thora Lacecuff, heading for Iceland. According to the saga:

The winds were bad and they were tossed and driven about in the waves for a long time, for they were determined to keep as far away from Norway as they could. Then one day when they were sailing up the east coast of Shetland before a strong gale, they damaged the ship as they tried to put in at Mousa (Moseyjarborg in Old Norse). They carried the cargo ashore and into the broch there, then beached the ship and repaired the damage.

Mousa Broch stands proud on the shores of Mousa Sound

The Mousa ferry prepares to embark from Sandwick Bay

Bjorn and Thora eventually married in Shetland and spent the rest of the winter in Mousa Broch. With the coming of spring and calmer seas, they again set off for Iceland, where their daughter Asgerd was born.

A similarly romantic story is recorded in the late 12th century Orkneyinga Saga, when a young chieftain called Erlend the Young carried off Margaret, the widowed mother of the Orkney Earl Harald Maddadson, from Orkney to Shetland in 1153.

The couple made their home in the broch at Mousa and settled down with their band of followers, where they laid in stores in preparation for a siege. Sure enough, the angry Earl Harald followed them and laid siege to the broch but found it a difficult place to overcome – or 'an unhandy place to get at' as he put it. The episode ended happily with a reconciliation between Erlend and Harald, and Erlend finally married Margaret.

The antiquarian George Low visited Mousa Broch in 1774, and it was he who provided the first descriptions of it. It was also visited by Sir Walter Scott in 1814, who described it as 'a Pictish fortress, the most entire probably in the world'.

The broch was repaired and cleared of debris in 1861 and quantities of animal bones, especially those of otters, who probably used the ruined building for their holt, were found. There were major re-buildings of the broch from 1967 until the 1980s and it is now managed by Historic Environment Scotland as a scheduled ancient monument.

For a short walk around the island, you'll first need to take the 15 minute ferry trip from Sandsayre pier at Sandwick on the eastern mainland of Shetland.

The Walk

Follow the waymarked nature trail to reach the imposing tower, which effectively commands Mousa Sound. The dark, narrow spiral stairway inside the double-skinned stone wall is reached by a doorway in the inner wall. It will take you to the top, and a splendid view south down Mousa Sound to No Ness, and beyond that, to the bold promontory of Sumburgh Head, with its squat Robert Stevenson lighthouse, built in 1821 and the oldest in Shetland.

A hearth and floor tank once existed in the central space on the ground floor of the broch, and there is a low stone bench around the base of the inside wall. It is thought that the broch went through at least two phases of occupation. Originally, it may have contained a wooden roundhouse resting on internal ledges. At a later date the wooden building was demolished and replaced with a small house with three projecting stone piers.

Above the base of the broch six galleries are formed by the space between the two concentric walls of the upper part of the broch and are partly lit by slits. It is possible to walk along most of the galleries and imagine what it must have been like for runaway lovers Bjorn and Thora, or Erlend and Margaret.

Mousa Broch is also famous among birdwatchers for its population of European storm petrels (*Hydrobates pelagicus*), which are best seen after dark on partly or completely overcast summer nights. The broch is home to between

Factbox

Location: The Mousa Boat (Tel: 07901 872339; Web: mousa.co.uk) embarks from Sandwick, which is 14 miles (22.5km) south of Lerwick, signposted off the A970

Postcode: ZE2 9HN

Length: About 1.5 miles (2.4km)

Terrain: Easy walking on level paths

Map: OS 1:25,000 Explorer OL466, Shetland - Mainland South

Refreshments: The nearest restaurants to Sandwick are in Sumburgh, where the Spiggie Hotel, Scousburgh, Shetland ZE2 9JE, is recommended

☎ 01950 460409
🌐 spiggie.co.uk/

Or the Sumburgh Hotel, Sumburgh Virkie, Shetland ZE3 9JN

☎ 01950 460201
🌐 sumburghhotel.com

300 and 400 breeding pairs, which roost in crevices within the walls. The island itself is home to around 12,000 breeding pairs, representing a high proportion of the British and world populations of this tiny, dusky seabird.

The name 'petrel' is a diminutive form of Peter, a reference to Saint Peter, and it was given to these birds because they sometimes appear to walk on water. This

Storm petrel in flight

83,000 pairs in 95 surveyed colonies. Storm petrels are known as 'ala mooties' in Shetland.

Leaving the broch, head inland past a turf-covered burnt mound dating from the Bronze Age to skirt around the tranquil waters of the West Pool, where eider ducks (locally-known as 'dunters') can often be seen loafing. You might also see, as I did, an inquisitive harbour seal popping his head out of the water to check you out. They use this sheltered bay both for pupping and moulting.

is achieved when they occasionally feed by surface pattering, moving their feet across the surface while holding steady above the water. They can also remain stationary by hovering with rapid wing fluttering or by using the wind to anchor themselves in position.

The name 'storm petrel' or 'stormy petrel' is a reference to their habit of apparently hiding in the lee of ships during storms. Early sailors named the petrels 'Mother Carey's Chickens' because they were thought to warn of oncoming storms. The name is based on a corruption of Mater Cara, an alternative name for the Virgin Mary.

European storm petrels are small, dusky-plumaged and white-rumped seabirds that feed far out at sea during the day, and only come ashore to their breeding colonies under the cover of darkness. They breed on rodent-free islands from Iceland and Shetland to the Canary Islands and spend their winters roaming the seas off southern Africa. At the last count, the British Isles held around

Walking on, you may come across the elegant world travellers Arctic terns (locally 'tirricks'), which nest nearby and migrate literally from one end of the Earth to the other, between the Arctic and the Antarctic. There's the possibility of unexpected attacks from a pair of Arctic skuas (locally 'bonxies') here, which will viciously dive-bomb you if you stray too close to their nesting territory. My advice based on personal experience: wear a hat!

The last lap of this delightful, easy 1.5 mile (2.4km) stroll takes you around the hill of Mid Field and back to the ferry.

But if you want a real treat and a truly fantastic experience, take the bookable guided night-time trips with the Mousa Boat from late May to mid-July, which allow you to witness the fantastic spectacle of the bat-like storm petrels swarming around the broch as they enter and leave their nesting chambers. Your ears will be assaulted by the cacophony of their eerie calls – vividly described by one birder as 'like a fairy being sick' – a truly unforgettable ornithological experience.

49.

Catching up with the *Hogwarts Express:*
Glenfinnan Viaduct, Highlands

BELOW The Glenfinnan Monument
RIGHT A steam train chugs across Robert McAlpine's magnificent viaduct, with Loch Shiel in the background

It's one of the best remembered and most thrilling sequences in the blockbuster *Harry Potter* movies, based on JK Rowling's best-selling children's novels. In the 2002 Chris Columbus film, *Harry Potter and the Chamber of Secrets*, Harry (played by Daniel Radcliffe), his schoolmate Ron Weasley (Rupert Grint) and Harry's pet snowy owl Hedwig are desperately trying to catch up with the *Hogwarts Express.*

They had missed it when it left from the fictitious platform nine and three-quarters at London's King's Cross station, bound for their second year at the Hogwarts School of Witchcraft and Wizardry. Piloting Ron's Dad's magically airborne and potentially invisible light blue Ford Anglia, they set off in hot pursuit of the *Hogwarts Express.* (As a mere Muggle, I once owned one of these. It didn't fly but occasionally bits did fly off it.) When they finally catch up with the *Express* as it crosses the magnificent, sweeping Glenfinnan Viaduct at the head of Loch Shiel in the Scottish Highlands, they are violently flung around, swooping above and below the train and between the arches of the viaduct.

In one unforgettable, nail-biting moment, Harry falls out of the car and clings on desperately to a door until Ron valiantly hauls him back in. Eventually Harry and Ron arrive at Hogwarts, crashing the broken-down Anglia into the belligerent Whomping Willow tree in the grounds and eventually facing the wrath of Harry's bête noire, Prof Severus Snape.

The iconic location of the Glenfinnan Viaduct was also later used as a backdrop in three other *Harry Potter* films – and has even featured on a Bank of Scotland £10 note. Although Arthur Weasley's car is identified as a Ford Anglia in JK Rowling's second Harry Potter novel,

Harry Potter and the Chamber of Secrets (1998), the terrifying incident in and around the Glenfinnan Viaduct is purely a figment of Columbus' fertile imagination. As the author explained in a 2002 interview:

'Hogwarts is a very real place to me, and I've always imagined it to be in Scotland... which was never made explicit in the books.

But the British reader will know that because if you do travel for a day from King's Cross Station in London and you go north, you end up in Scotland. So it was always supposed to be here.'

The Glenfinnan Monument lords it over the head of Loch Shiel

Many people believe the West Highland Line, which crosses the Glenfinnan Viaduct, is among the greatest rail journeys in the world. The 164 mile (264km) route between Glasgow and Mallaig was opened by the West Highland Railway Company in 1901. With 11 tunnels and six viaducts, it threads through a breathtaking sequence of mountains, glens, lochs and forests. But it is the Glenfinnan Viaduct which is acknowledged as the major civil engineering feat along the route.

Constructed entirely from mass concrete, at 1,248 feet (380m), the viaduct is the longest concrete railway bridge in Scotland. It was built in 1897 at a cost of £18,900 by Robert McAlpine & Sons, a company headed by Robert McAlpine, who was nicknamed 'Concrete Bob' for his innovative use of concrete. The viaduct crosses the River Finnan at a height of 100 feet (30.5m) and has 21 huge semi-circular spans of 50 feet (15m). But perhaps its most stunning and memorable feature is that it was built on an elegant, sweeping curve of 792 feet (241m).

The Walk

You can experience some of the magic of Glenfinnan and the scene of Harry's aeronautical Anglia in this easy 2.5 mile (4km) walk. It starts at the car park for the Glenfinnan Monument, which was built in 1815 to commemorate where Charles Edward Stuart, Bonnie Prince Charlie, first raised his standard on 19 August 1745, at the start of the abortive Jacobite rebellion. It's worth climbing to the top of the 60 foot (18m)-high monument if only for the superb views down the mountain-hemmed Loch Shiel. The kilted and bonneted statue on top is not Bonnie Prince Charlie as many people assume, but an anonymous Highlander, sculpted by John Greenshields and added in 1835.

Take the path up the glen, eventually crossing a footbridge and continuing beside the river into the glen. The arches of the mighty Glenfinnan Viaduct loom impressively ahead. Approaching the foot of the viaduct, go straight across at a junction with a track.

The path leads quickly up to a fine viewpoint and another great photo opportunity overlooking the monument. Keep right at a junction, passing beneath the arches of the viaduct before continuing to climb on the far side. As more height is gained there are excellent views looking down on the viaduct, with more constructed viewpoints for Muggle photographers, especially when a scheduled steam train

Factbox

Location: The Glenfinnan car park and visitor centre is on the A830 Fort William to Mallaig road, about 16 miles (25.7km) west of Fort William

Postcode: PH37 4LT

Length: 2.5 miles (4km); allow 1-2 hours

Terrain: The path climbing above the viaduct and down to the station is an improved hill path with a stony surface; the rest of the route is on easy tracks

Map: OS 1:25,000 Explorer OL391, Ardgour & Strontian

Refreshments: The Prince's House Hotel, Glenfinnan PH37 4LT, is on the A830 just north-west of the Station Museum

☎ 01397 722246
🌐 glenfinnan.co.uk

The sweeping 792-foot (241m) curve of the Glenfinnan Viaduct

An aerial view of the head of Loch Shiel

crosses the viaduct. It is often the case that there are more people watching the train than actually riding on it.

The clear path climbs a little higher but continues across the hillside. When a path junction is reached, turn left, following downhill towards the railway, passing through a hidden tunnel beneath.

Shortly after the tunnel, go right at a fork, heading across a little bridge and along a section of path constructed out of former railway sleepers. Follow the path as it climbs the steps to Glenfinnan Station, emerging next to the sleeping car (now a hostel). From here you can continue on to the platform to visit the small Glenfinnan Station Museum. Otherwise carry on along the route by turning left from the station and follow the lane down to the main road.

Turn right along the A830 for a short distance, before turning sharp left, shortly before reaching the Glenfinnan House Hotel (currently closed), and down a track past some houses. When the track ends

at the last house, continue ahead on the well-made path, which goes downhill before emerging on a tarmac road at a T-junction. Turn left here and eventually the road emerges on the A830 once more, opposite the start of the walk.

If you would prefer to take the *Hogwarts Express* yourself and experience the stunning views from the viaduct, in summer the steam train, formerly known as the *Jacobite Express*, regularly travels along the route in addition to the scheduled ScotRail trains between Fort William and Mallaig twice a day during the summer months. The *Express* normally stops for a short break at the Glenfinnan Station so you can visit the railway museum.

And you can see the original 1966 105E Ford Anglia used during the filming of *Harry Potter and the Chamber of Secrets* at the National Motor Museum at Beaulieu, on the edge of the New Forest in Hampshire. It was stolen in 2005 but following intense media interest it was later recovered.

50.

To the end of the world: Hermaness, Shetland Islands

BELOW The white radar station on the summit of Saxa Vord is prominent in this view across the waters of Burrafirth
RIGHT A view of Hermaness from the sea, with Muckle Flugga lighthouse prominent to the left

Shetland has always been a place apart. If you look at an atlas of the British Isles, you'll usually find the Shetland Islands tucked away like an afterthought in its own little box in the top right-hand corner, much to the annoyance of its inhabitants. The reason is simple. It's 130 miles (209km) north of mainland Scotland and 110 miles (177km) north of Orkney, and cartographers don't want to waste that much map on an empty sea.

Actually, Shetland is far closer to the Arctic Circle than it is to London and closer to Bergen in Norway than it is to Aberdeen. It lies on about the same northerly latitude as Bergen, Helsinki in Finland, Anchorage in Alaska, and the southernmost tip of Greenland.

Recently receiving prominence on our

small screens by the dramatisation of Ann Cleeves' best-selling novels and spin-off TV dramas featuring the troubled detective Jimmy Perez, Shetland has since found many new devotees to its wild and windswept shores.

The archipelago of Shetland is over 100 miles (161km) long, boasts more than

1,500 miles (2,414km) of coastline, and consists of over 100 islands, 17 of which are uninhabited skerries (small rocky islands). Rather confusingly for non-Shetlanders the largest island is known as Mainland, but this walk takes us to the most remote and northernmost of all the islands – Unst.

A gannet wheels above the lighthouse

The isolated, often mist-shrouded peninsula of Hermaness on Unst is as far as you can go north in Britain – and when you walk out onto the breezy clifftops facing lighthouse-topped Muckle Flugga, it really feels as if you've reached the end of the Earth. I was lucky on my first visit because I had Rory Tallack, the amiable ranger on the Hermaness National Nature Reserve (NNR), as my guide to this walk to the end of the world.

The Walk

Leaving Burrafirth, which is at the head of the Burra Firth, follow waymarked posts west to the shallow dale of the Burn of Winnaswarta and take the plastic board-walked trail across the blanket bog of Sothers Brecks to reach the bleak high point of Hermaness Hill (656 feet/200m).

The crossing of the open moorland is not without its perils. You can be constantly attacked, as we were, by marauding great skuas – those dusky-brown feathered pirates of the sea locally known as 'bonxies' – who will dive-bomb and attack you with their pick-axe bills if you dare to approach too close to their territory. On our visit, they came so close we could hear the whistle of their 5 foot (1.5m)-span wings as they swooshed past our unprotected heads.

Whimbrel, golden plover and dunlin also nest on the heather and sphagnum dominated moorland, and closer to the cliffs, you might be lucky enough to catch a glimpse of the small brown-feathered finch called a twite, and the unique

Birdwatchers enjoy the view from Hermaness, with a 'bonxie' about to attack (top right)

Factbox

Location: As might be expected, Unst is not easy to get to. A 12 hour overnight ferry from Aberdeen, or flights from Glasgow, Edinburgh, Inverness or Aberdeen, will only get you to Lerwick in Mainland Shetland. Then it's two ferries and the 15 mile (24.1km) crossing of Yell before you even reach Unst, and another 12 miles (19.3km) to Burrafirth and Hermaness

Postcode: ZE2 9EQ

Length: It's about 2.5 miles (4km) to Hermaness from Burrafirth, making a round trip of about 5 miles (8km)

Terrain: The worst of the bogs of Sothers Brecks are avoided by sticking to the boardwalk. Some fairly serious moorland and coastal walking

Map: OS 1:25,000 Explorer OL470, Shetland – Unst, Yell and Fetlar

Refreshments: The Balta Light, on the A968 at Baltasound, Unst ZE2 9TW, is the nearest pub to Hermaness

☎ 01957 711545
🌐 facebook.com/BaltaLightBar

Or you could try Victoria's Vintage Tea Rooms, Old Haroldswick Shop, Haroldswick, Shetland ZE2 9DU

☎ 01957 711885
🌐 victoriasvintagetearooms.co.uk

The white-painted NatureScot (formerly Scottish Natural Heritage) visitor centre on the shores of Burrafirth faces across to Saxa Vord

Shetland wren. This tiny bird (*Troglodytes troglodytes zetlandicus*) is a subspecies of the common Eurasian wren and is endemic to Shetland. It is distinguished from the mainland form by its darker and more rufous-brown colouring, with a heavily barred underside and thicker beak.

During the summer, the breck is awash with colour, with heather, crowberry, bilberry and mosses all adding their subtle tones to the palette. On the grasslands closer to the coast, spring squill shows its delicate blue-starred bloom soon to be followed by the arrival of candyfloss-pink thrift, also known as sea pink.

As we reached the summit, Rory related the legend of how the peninsula of 'Herma's headland' got its name. 'It was named after a mythical giant Herma, who was said to live here', he said. 'Herma and a rival giant named Saxa, who lived on nearby Saxa Vord, lobbed rocks at each other across Burra Firth, one of which became Out Stack, which is actually the most northerly point of Britain'.

From this viewpoint you can clearly see Out Stack, beyond the seabird-haunted skerries of Muckle Flugga, which is usually quoted as the northernmost point. The white-painted lighthouse on Muckle Flugga, originally called the North Unst lighthouse, was designed and built by the brothers Thomas and David Stevenson in 1854. It came into use on New Year's Day 1858, and it remains Britain's most northerly lighthouse. The tower stands 64 feet (19.5m) high and has 103 steps to the top. The dazzling white light beam, fully automated in 1995, flashes every 20 seconds and has a range of 22 miles (35.4km).

The 'puffinry' at Hermaness

20,000 to 30,000 pairs of puffins (six per cent of the British population), another 16,000 pairs of guillemots and 10,000 pairs of fulmars.

If you add these to the kittiwakes, shags, great and Arctic skuas and gulls, you have as cosmopolitan a seabird colony as you could find anywhere. Any reasonably flat surface is dotted by the white shapes of breeding birds and the sky is filled with their mournful cries. You could spend a pleasant hour or two watching as this avian cast of thousands swoop and dive in a dizzying aerobatic display at the very northern tip of Britain.

This most gregarious of avian populations even included a long-lived black-browed albatross, nicknamed Albert, who resided here on his own ledge for many years in the 1970s to 1990s. Black-browed albatross are usually found 8,000 miles (12, 875km) away, south of the Equator.

If you have time, and there's usually enough of that in the Shetland 'summer dim' (what passes for the night in summertime in Shetland), you could take in another of Unst's unheralded NNRs – the Keen of Hamar, which is situated off the A968 east of Baltasound.

The barren rocks of the Keen really don't look much at first glance – they were even described as 'a load of old rubble' by a visitor. Seeming to be more in place in somewhere like Iceland rather than Scotland, the 400-million-year-old frost-shattered serpentine scree here is the closest you'll come to what Britain must have looked like at the end of the Ice Age 10,000 years ago.

Thomas' son, the author Robert Louis Stevenson, is known to have visited the lighthouse as a young man in 1869. His visit to Unst is thought to have been the inspiration for his map of Treasure Island in Stevenson's most famous swashbuckling novel of the same name, first published in 1883. There is undoubtedly more than a passing resemblance in the profiles of the two, although neither Long John Silver nor Ben Gunn has yet been spotted on Muckle Flugga.

But if you want to take a closer look at one of Britain's largest seabird colonies, it's now just a gentle descent westward towards the storm-battered west coast, punctuated here by dramatic rock stacks and geos (a wave-carved inlet or deep, narrow cleft in the face of a cliff).

The vertiginous cliffs of Hermaness and the outlying skerries are home to over 100,000 breeding seabirds, including no less than 30,000 pairs of gannets,

This sparsest of soils together with a high concentration of toxic metals gives rise to an extraordinary range of some of Britain's rarest montane and maritime flowers. These include northern rock cress, moss campion, spring squill, stone bramble, mountain everlasting, Norwegian sandwort, and – rarest of all – Edmondston's chickweed.

This insignificant little, white-flowered plant was discovered in 1837 by a very bright 12-year-old doctor's son from nearby Buness named Thomas Edmondston. He published a paper on his discovery in 1843 at the age of 18, after which the rare chickweed was given his name. Thomas's early enthusiasm for botany was soon fulfilled because he went on to publish *A Flora of Shetland* in 1845 and become Professor of Botany at Anderson (now Strathclyde) University in Glasgow at the tender age of 20. Tragically, he died less than a year later in an accident while on an expedition to Peru.

The Keen of Hamar reminded me of a few lines by the great Scottish poet Hugh MacDiarmid, who lived on the island of Whalsay off the east coast of Shetland from 1933 until 1942. As he wrote in his epic poem 'On a Raised Beach' (1934):

These bare stones
bring me straight back to reality.
I grasp one of them and I have in my grip
The beginning and the end of the world...

Looking south along the rugged Hermaness coastline

Further Reading

Alexander, Mike, *Skomer Island*, Y Lolfa Cyf, 2021

Barkham, Patrick, *Coastlines*, Granta Books, 2015

Baxter, Stephen, *Revolutions in the Earth*, Weidenfeld & Nicholson, 2003

Beresford, Maurice & Hurst, John, *English Heritage Book of Wharram Percy Deserted Medieval Village*, BT Batsford/English Heritage, 1990

Bird, Vivian, *Exploring the West Midlands*, BT Batsford, 1977

Blackadder, Jill Slee, *Shetland*, Colin Baxter Photography Ltd, 2007

Boardman, AW, *Towton 1461*, The History Press, 2022

Burl, Aubrey, *The Stone Circles of the British Isles*, Yale, 1976

Burnham, Andy (Ed.), *The Old Stones*, Watkins Publishing, 2018

Comfort, Nicholas, *The Lost City of Dunwich*, Terence Dalton Ltd, 1994

Crowther, Jan, *The People along the Sand: The Spurn Peninsula & Kilnsea*, Phillimore & Co Ltd, 2010

Fiorato, Veronica, Boylston, Anthea & Knüsel, Christopher (Ed.), *Blood Red Roses*, Oxbow Books, 2000

Ford, Trevor D, *The Rocks of Bradgate Park*, The Bradgate Park Trust, 1975

Goodwin, George, *Fatal Colours: The Battle of Towton, 1461*, Weidenfeld & Nicholson, 2011

Gordon, Helen, *Notes from Deep Time*, Profile Books, 2021

Grinsell, Leslie V, *Folklore of Prehistoric Sites in Britain*, David & Charles, 1976

Hawkes, Jacquetta, *A Land*, Collins Nature Library, 2012

Hawkes, Jacquetta, *The Shell Guide to British Archaeology*, Michael Joseph, 1986

Hey, Gill & Frodsham, Paul (Ed.), *New Light on the Neolithic of Northern England*, Oxbow Books, 2021

Hillaby, John, *Journey Through Britain*, Constable, 1968

Hurle, Pamela, *The Malvern Hills*, Phillimore & Co Ltd, 1992

Jarman, Derek, *Derek Jarman's Garden*, Thames & Hudson, 1995

Johnson, David (Ed.), *Encounters with Wainwright*, The Wainwright Society, 2016

Mabey, Richard, *Gilbert White*, Century, 2006

MacArthur, E Mairi, *Iona*, Colin Baxter, 2001

Macfarlane, Robert, *The Old Ways*, Hamish Hamilton, 2012

Matthews, Jane, *Skomer: Portrait of a Welsh Island*, Graffeg, 2011

Poucher, WA, *The Scottish Peaks*, Constable, 1968

Reeve, Tori, *Down House: the Home of Charles Darwin*, English Heritage, 2009

Rollins, Julian, *Land Marks: Impressions of England's National Nature Reserves*, English Nature, 2003

Schei, Liv Kjørsvik, *The Shetland Isles*, Colin Baxter Photography Ltd, 2006

Shrubsole, Guy, *The Lost Rainforests of Britain*, William Collins, 2022

Smith, Roly, *Collins Rambler's Guide: Peak District*, Harper Collins, 2000

Smith, Roly, *Heritage Landscapes*, AA Publishing, 2011

Smith, Roly (Ed.), *Kinder Scout: Portrait of a Mountain*, Derbyshire County Council, 2002

Smith, Roly, *National Parks of Britain*, AA Publishing, 2011

Smith, Roly, *Walking the Great Views*, David & Charles, 1991

Smith, Roly, *Wildest Britain*, David & Charles, 1983

Smith, Roly, *World Heritage Sites of Britain*, AA Publishing, 2010

Smith, Roly & Cornish, Joe, *This Land*, Frances Lincoln, 2015

Stone, Brian (Trans.), *Sir Gawain and the Green Knight*, Penguin Classics, 1979

Tourism Marketing Unit, Winchester City Council, *Keats' Walk*, Winchester City Council, 2003

Turnbull, Ronald, *Sandstone and Sea Stacks*, Frances Lincoln, 2011

Waite, Vincent, *Shropshire Hill Country*, J M Dent, 1970

Wainwright, A, *Pennine Way Companion*, Westmorland Gazette, 1968

Williamson, Richard, *The Great Yew Forest: the Natural History of Kingley Vale*, Macmillan, 1978

Wilson, AN, *Charles Darwin: Victorian Mythmaker*, John Murray, 2017

Photography Credits

(Top = T, Bottom = B)

Marcus Ginns: 8; Terry Marsh: 144, 146B;

ADOBE STOCK: Acceleratorhams: 272, 273T; Alexey Fedorenko: 16-17; Andrew: 32; AngieC: 210; Anita: 279; Annacurnow: 18; Anthony: 168; Barneyboogles: 66; Bernd Brueggemann: 15, 82-3, 89, 136-7, 195, 197, 198, 227, 245, 253; Caroline: 92; Chris Lofty: 73; Cisek Ciesielski: 290; Cliff: 276; Colin: 99; Collins Photography: 70; Coxy58: 222B; Craig: 170; Dave: 118; David EP Dennis: 20; David Matthew Lyons: 50, 125, 203, 204; Dirkseyfried: 56; Drhfoto: 56, 141, 167, 219; Eddie Cloud: 120, 273, 281; Electric Egg Ltd.: 250; Foto-Jagla.de: 289; Fstopphotography: 289; Geoff Sowrey: 270; Harry: 131; Irisphoto1: 28; Ivan Kmit: 295T; Jackie Davies: 57; Jaroslav Moravcik: 274; Jason Wells: 64, 69; Jenny: 184; Jeremyabaxter: 232; Jim: 49; jmh photography: 151; Joe: 160, 166; Joshua Adejumo/Wirestock: 132B; Julian Gazzard: 29, 39; Lars Johansson: 284; Leighton collins: 248B; Lisastrachan: 283; Lukasz: 140; Maciej Olszewski: 292-3; MarkGodden: 264; MuzzyCo: 288; Neil: 119B; Nicholas: 116; Nickos: 77;

Nicola: 110, 113, 135; Pawel Pajor: 291; Petejeff: 149; Phil: 257; Philippe: 277, 295B, 296; Pixs:sell: 2-3; Postywood1: 255; RamblingTog: 185, 188T; Rob: 75; Robin: 138; Salarko: 224-5 Snapvision: 117, 246T; Spumador: 269; Stefan: 19; Stephen Davies: 236; Steve: 108; SuxxesPhoto: 42; Tim Hill: 208, 212; Tonymills: 287; U-JINN Photography: 139, 153; Veneration: 249; Whitcomberd: 243; Wideyes: 12-13 William: 71; Zdenka: 297;

ALAMY: Duncan Vere Green: 46; Iain Sarjeant: 268; Michael Walters 2: 156; Mr. Nut: 209; Nick Hatton: 98; Paul Weston: 102; Peter Noyce GBR: 48; Rob Ford: 172; Rodger Tamblyn: 150; Simon Whaley: 103;

FLICKR: Verity Cridland: 68;

GEOGRAPH: Alan Hughes: 251, 258-9; Alan Murray-Rust: 97; Andrew Curtis: 192; Andrew Hill: 96, 182, 214; Anne Burgess: 262, Basher Eyre: 63; Bill Boaden: 132T; Brian Abbott: 171; Chris: 95; Chris Allen: 207B; Chris Heaton: 79, 161, 163; Colin Park: 178; Colin Smith: 285; Dave Dunford: 88; Dave Pickersgill: 181; Dave Spicer: 81; David Medcalf: 206; David P Howard: 61; David Robinson: 169, 201; Deborah Tilley: 256; DS Pugh: 233; Gareth James: 237B; George Tod: 246B; Gordon Hatton: 238; Graham Hogg: 217; Guy Wareham: 22; Humphrey Bolton: 126; 188-9; I Love Colour: 235; Ian Capper: 107; Ian Cunliffe: 38; Jeff Buck: 100; John Slater: 215; Karl and Ali: 186; M J Richardson: 266, 267; Marathon: 59; Mick Garratt: 130; Mike Green: 280; mrallen: 155; Pauline E: 158B; Philip Barker: 220; Philip Halling: 241, 242; Philip Pankhurst: 105; Richard Croft: 94, 134, 154; Robert Goulden: 93; Robert Walker: 104; Roger Templeman: 200; Russel Wills: 222T; Simon Tomson: 158T; SMJ: 157; Stephen Richards: 123; Stuart Logan: 106; wfmillar: 221;

GETTY IMAGES: Abigail Berry: 67; Adam Makara: 175T; Alanphillips: 91; Ashley Cooper: 207T, 271, 294; Birdsonline: 254; Central Press/Stringer: 114; Chris McLoughlin: 162, 164, 165; Coastalrunner: 65; Darrell Evans/500px: 142; Davemhuntphotography: 6; David_Crosbie: 40; Dukas/Universal Images Group: 45, 53; Duncan_Andison: 190; English Heritage/Heritage Images: 36, 58, 60, 62; FatManPhotoUK: 23; FelixStrummer: 121; Flavio Vallenari: 299; George W Johnson: 84; James Ennis: 87; James Warwick: 298; Julien David: 275, 278; Khrizmo: 193; Lakeland-Photos: 184T; Paul Mansfield Photography: 34, 76, 78; philmacdphotography: 211; Photo by Joel Sharpe: 240; Photos by R A Kearton: 122, 124, 174, 176, 179, 180, 216, 218; Pilesasmiles: 25; ProjectB: 27; Quatrain: 202; Southern Lightscapes-Australia: 43, Steve Brookwell: 80; Tim Grist Photography: 54; Tonywestphoto: 194B; U.Knakis Photography: 173; Wayne Hutchinson/Farm Images/Universal Images: 196; Wellwoods: 191; Westend61: 244, 260-1; William Lowis: 146T; Wirestock: 248T;

WIKIMEDIA COMMONS: Colin: 282; Dave Souza: 265; David Martyn Hunt: 115; DimiTalen: 35; Enchufla Con Clave: 127T, 127B, 129; John Tenniel: 10; Kev747: 111; Llywelyn2000: 226, 228-9; Marcin Floryan: 175B; Mark Rickaby: 183; Marsupium Photography: 263; Michal Louč: 31; Mira66: 143; NotFromUtrecht: 112; Paul Lakin: 159; Saffron Blaze: 119T; Simon Burchell: 44; The Air Base: 145; The Library of Congress @ Flickr Commons: 24; Tony Lockhart: 72; Wikipedia user Swpmre: 205

Index

Acknowledgements

My first and warmest thanks must go to my good friend and fellow countryside campaigner for over 40 years, Dame Fiona Reynolds, who kindly found time in her busy schedule to contribute her generous and very flattering Foreword. I dubbed Fiona the 'Grande Dame of British Conservation' in my last book (*Walking Class Heroes*, 2020), because she has served as Secretary of the Council (now Campaign) for National Parks (CPRE); Director of CPRE, the Countryside Charity; Director-General of the National Trust; Master of Emmanuel College, Cambridge, and is currently Chair of the National Audit Office.

I must also acknowledge Andy Peitrasic, former Travel Editor of *The Guardian*, and Cameron McNeish and Carey Davies, Editors of *The Great Outdoors* (TGO) for commissioning the original versions of some of these walks, and for kindly giving permission for them to be adapted for this book.

Jenny Clark has been my genial Commissioning Editor for Bloomsbury and I'd like to express my sincere thanks for her unwavering enthusiasm for the project. Project Editor Kathryn Beer and Copy Editor Jane Cumberlidge were equally enthusiastic and improved my text with their meticulous editing. Any remaining faults are my own. I'd also like to thank Lee-May Lim and Nick Avery, the designers of the book, for their sensitive and attractive lay-outs. It's been a real team effort, and my thanks go to everyone at Bloomsbury.

Although I prefer to walk alone, many of my family and good friends have accompanied me on these walks and added immeasurably to my enjoyment of them. They include Val, my loving wife and long-suffering partner for over 60 years; our three brilliant children Claire, Neil and Iain; and my good friends and loyal partners in many of these adventures, John Cleare, Mark Richards and Tom Waghorn.

For the inspiration which encouraged me to take poet Robert Frost's 'road less travelled', I would like to pay tribute to the countryside writers and access campaigners I've long admired and respected, many of whom sadly are no longer with us. They include Tom Stephenson, Benny Rothman, Walter Poucher, Kenneth Allsop, John Hillaby, John Wyatt, Rennie McOwan, Roger Redfern, Jim Perrin, Terry Howard and last but by no means least, Kate Ashbrook, Marion Shoard and, of course, Fiona Reynolds.

Finally, I'd like to dedicate this book to my three beautiful granddaughters, Amy, Chloe and Holly, in the fond hope that they'll always be as curious as their grandad.